How to Make a Good Mind Great

Andrew Lynch

**For Toni,
with love**

First published 2007

NLP MindFrame Patterns© is copyright of Andrew Lynch 2006

All rights reserved. No part of this book subject to copyright may be reproduced in any form or by any means without prior permission in writing from the publisher or copyright holder.

ISBN 978-1-905217-64-9

Published by Jeremy Mills Publishing Limited

www.jeremymillspublishing.co.uk

Contents

About the Author iv
Foreword v

Part I: How It Works

Chapter 1	NLP MindFrame Patterns	2
Chapter 2	Models of Excellence	8
Chapter 3	How MindFrame Patterns Work	17

Part II: Insight

Chapter 4	Internal State, Earth	28
Chapter 5	Earth Values	34
Chapter 6	Earth Change Patterns	42
Chapter 7	Earth Storage Patterns	52
Chapter 8	Earth Strategy Patterns	57
Chapter 9	Internal Process, Water	63
Chapter 10	Beliefs, Something Inspirational	70
Chapter 11	Belief Change Patterns	75
Chapter 12	Belief Storage Patterns	81
Chapter 13	Belief Strategy Patterns	87
Chapter 14	Behaviour, Fire	94
Chapter 15	Deep Structure, Air	101
Chapter 16	Internal Understanding	108
Chapter 17	Collective Understanding	112

Part III: Putting It All Together

Chapter 18	MindFrame Contexts	120
Chapter 19	Earth, Environment	127
Chapter 20	Environment, Work	136
Chapter 21	Environment, Rest	143
Chapter 22	Environment, Play	148
Chapter 23	Water, Movement	156
Chapter 24	Movement, Goal Setting	163
Chapter 25	Movement, Goal Getting	173
Chapter 26	Movement, Goal Attaining	179
Chapter 27	Fire, Communications	184
Chapter 28	Communications, Self	191
Chapter 29	Communications, Sex	198
Chapter 30	Communications, Social	205

Part IV: Modelling Excellence

Chapter 31	Modelling Excellence	212
Chapter 32	Final Frame	225

Acknowledgements 229

About the Author

Andrew brings many years experience as a writer and journalist to his Mind Coaching and is currently an Editor within the public sector.

He has adapted and developed the tools and techniques used to coach gold medal winning Olympic athletes and applied these to the business world to improve every area of performance. This has led to the development of NLP MindFrame Patterns©, a trail of techniques designed so people can be in the right frame of mind at the right time to consistently achieve their outcomes in every situation.

Andrew is also the creator of the VALUES Coaching Model© which, where appropriate, assimilates the values, beliefs and behaviours of the individual to their organisation in order to maximise contribution.

Andrew is a Master Coach accredited by the International Neuro-Linguistic Programming Trainers Association.

To find out more about coaching and training with Andrew visit: www.tlsassociates.co.uk

Foreword

It may seem a little strange to begin a foreword in this way - almost like a personality reference. I find it useful, however, to look at personal development skills in terms of the individual author and their view of the world.

I first met with Andrew in the summer of 2006. The outcome of the meeting was unexpected, as for me it is rare to find an immediate convergence of minds and a truly productive and reciprocal relationship. We often talk about achieving a 'win-win' result in the business context and yet either one party (or both) do not quite obtain the 'win' they desire. Refreshingly, my interactions with Andrew have been consistently open, honest, enjoyable and generative.

In business as well as in personal relationships, we have an opportunity to stretch our individual boundaries and learn and apply something new. Andrew is a proven exponent of all the skills he describes within the following pages.

We both believe there is great personal value in learning and developing the skills of NLP. Whether you are looking for 'happiness', 'success' or 'results', these are an invaluable set of techniques for your tool kit.

Currently, there is a movement in the United Kingdom for practical 'coping strategies' for people who are struggling with life and experiencing anxiety and depression. Many of the techniques described here are exactly those people can use to change their view of the world and then change their actual world.

In fact, many of the skills to be discovered within this book are precisely those I wish I had learned 16 years ago (in my final stages of school). This approach of not needing to have a 'pathology' in order to learn such things is healthy – education of oneself is much kinder and easier than rehabilitation.

A moment ago I took a step back and picked up my Ipod, flicked through a few artists and decided upon appropriate tracks. Modern, mellow background music heartens me. Just like choosing the 'mood', you can choose what to do with the skills you will learn from this book.

Simply flick through to the appropriate mix (for instance choosing an emotional state, setting an appropriate frame of mind, loosening your beliefs etc) and you can change your internal world set up and be ready to create the results you want. NLP is like the electricity that powers the Ipod, which in turn sets the scene for you to take action.

So what will you do with these skills? That one is up to you.

I trust you will enjoy the life changing journey Andrew takes you on.

Martin Shervington
Managing Director, John Seymour Associates.
Author of *Don't Think of Purple Spotted Oranges*, *Integral Coaching*, co-author of *Peak Performance Through NLP*, contributory author to *The Successful Manager's Handbook* and *Human* by Lord Robert Winston.

Part I: How It Works

Chapter 1

NLP MindFrame Patterns

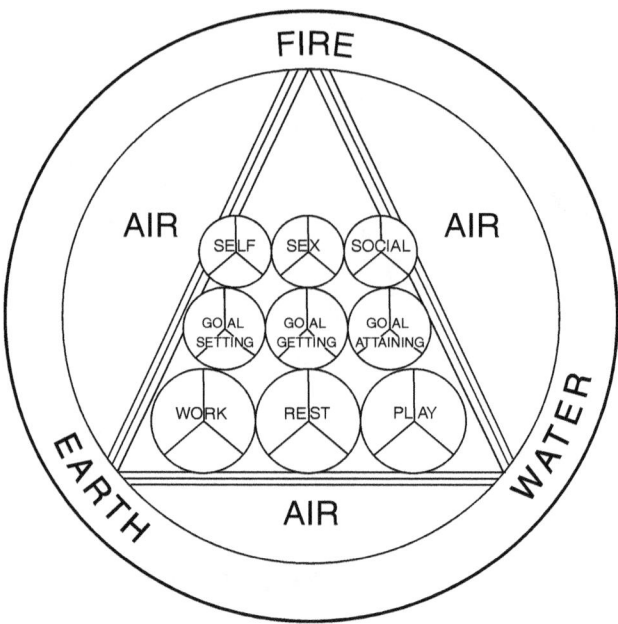

Our frame of mind determines everything: how we are the way we are, and why we get the results we get. Change our mind, change the result. Change our frame of mind, change our lives.

If we are in control of our minds, then we should be able to control our frame of mind and therefore how we act in certain situations. Unfortunately, we often do not. And therein lays the problem. If we could change our frame of mind so we are able to act for our own best purposes, then we are far more likely to get the results we want.

Ever heard the expression, "I'm not in the right frame of mind to do that," or "I have to be in the right frame of mind to do this…"

It is a mantra we use to excuse or justify our actions. However, it goes much further than that, as it strikes at the core of who we are.

We are what we project, that is what we perceive, we project, consciously or unconsciously. If we believe we can not do something, we will invariably prove ourselves correct. If we believe we can do something, we are far more likely to achieve that. Henry Ford once said, 'If you believe you absolutely can or believe you absolutely can't, you're absolutely right'.

Our frame of mind can also be seen in how we are behaving, and is essential in getting what we want. That could be as huge as achieving a lifetime's ambition or as simple as feeling comfortable around friends and family.

> **'What MindFrames can do is give each and every one of us the capacity to do what we want, when we want it, by using all the resources we already have**

Is our frame of mind the state we are in? Yes it is. It is how we are when we are in a particular setting doing a particular thing. States are simple emotional frames that can change moment to moment: from happiness to sadness, from determined to uncaring. However, our frame of mind goes much deeper than that. Our frame of mind can determine whether we succeed or fail, whether we slip from sadness to a deeper depression, or happiness to ecstasy. It underpins everything that we want to be, do or have.

Whilst a frame of mind can be represented by a state, if directed in the right way, it can go much deeper, producing much more profound results.

If a frame of mind can deliver all that we want to be, do or have, why is it that we can not achieve that right now? Quite simply, we can.

Ever felt totally energised to do something straight away, to jump on it whilst the iron's hot, when you feel determined to get it done? That is an achievement frame of mind that has doubtless served you well to realise your goals and inspire you to press on in spite of obstacles that may arise. It is just the sort of frame of mind that many people would welcome, particularly when approaching tasks or workloads that require a single-minded approach and indominatable spirit.

If that frame of mind could be maintained over an extended period of time until we can achieve all that we wish and beyond, then the rewards would be great. Some people can manage that, whilst others can not. Some people can do it for a small task, yet become overawed if the task is broadened or if other issues arise. Even people who have this frame of mind for extended periods can eventually feel pressure or tired through exerting a lot of effort.

What MindFrames can do is give each and every one of us the capacity to do what we want, when we want it, by using all the resources we already have. It is about tapping into our vast potential to unleash everything we need to get everything we want, in every situation in life.

Using Our Resources

Yes, we can have the right frame of mind, right now, to achieve our goals. To prolong that, to ensure we reach our aim, or attain whatever it is we desire, we need to tap into those resources. We may already be aware of tools and techniques that are useful to help us on our way, whether practical guides like personal organisers for time management, or through focusing on our priorities. These are fine and can certainly be effective. To reinforce these and to ensure there are no gaps, we also need to tap into our vast unconscious resource.

Vast because 90 per cent of what we are is beneath the surface. The 10 per cent that is within our awareness, our waking, conscious state, is the tip of the iceberg. To rely on this 10 per cent alone means we are leaving out a large part of ourselves that could be incredibly useful and empowering. We could also exhaust ourselves through working largely with the conscious part.

'A MindFrame is a personal approach or strategy to one aspect of our lives that ensures we get the result we want'

Becoming aware of our unconscious resources, and how to direct these to get the results we want, gives us more control of our minds and therefore the results we get. What we must be aware of is the need to be aligned, between our conscious and unconscious, so that we are congruent in what we want and how to achieve that. If we are aligned we are in balance, everything is working in harmony and we feel stable, or centred. That means we are congruent, functioning properly.

If we are incongruent, or unbalanced, then the conscious and unconscious are not working together, and invariably we will not get what we want. Henry Ford's quote can also be applied to the unconscious: "If you unknowingly believe that you absolutely can or absolutely can't, then you're absolutely right".

Unknowingly, because if we are not achieving what we want and are trying everything consciously, then there is something amiss or we are misaligned at an unconscious level. If we have a problem, any problem, of an emotional sort: anxiety, stress, sadness, guilt, anger… it is because we are out of alignment with our unconscious. We are incongruent.

So to be in the right frame of mind – our MindFrame – we must look towards our conscious and unconscious and work with them both together, in unison.

Changing MindSets

Creating the right MindFrame for you is a subjective and personal experience. What may be the right frame of mind for one person, could be intolerable for another. What works for one person, does not always work for the next.

It is about what works well for each one of us. Who is anybody else to tell you what frame of mind you should be in to get what you want, or be how you wish to be? It is about discovering for yourself what works best for you.

A frame of mind or unresourceful state that is not working for us is a MindSet, as in it is set in its way. It is when we are stuck or keep getting the same results over and over. As the brain is a self-patterning system, we keep repeating the same patterns, or same mistakes, or same habits. We tend to do the same thing that we have done before because that is what the brain recognises and responds to.

Imagine a steep-sided valley with furrows running down its sides. When the rains come the water fills the existing channels and run down the same rivulets and streams. If there is a downpour then the waters can overflow and run everywhere (like when we are overwhelmed). Otherwise the water flows along established routes. That is how our brain works. It follows the same patterns unless something radical causes the water to flow in a different direction and another groove is created for the water to pass through. In terms of how our brain works, it is about creating a new neurological pathway, redirecting the flow.

To move from a MindSet, when we are stuck repeating the same patterns and getting nowhere, to doing what will work for us, we need to jump from an existing MindSet and create that new neurological pathway.

That becomes our MindFrame, the change pattern that opens up new ways of thinking, behaving and being. To ensure continued success all MindFrames should be open-ended so that further progress can be made. There is no full-stop or closure. This means revisiting what is working for us and updating our responses to make sure it continues to work. Otherwise it could lapse and become another MindSet.

What qualifies as a MindSet? Once again, it is only what we in our individual interpretation denote as a stuck state, or one that no longer gives the rewards that we seek. There are two categories therefore. The first is when what we are doing is not working. The second is when what we are doing is not working well enough for us. Both categories will show patterns of behaviours and outcomes that keep repeating themselves.

If the repeat patterns are causing us no problems and doing us no harm, then there may be no wish to change them. One person's problem can be another's success story. On the other hand, through changing one MindSet it may be seen as advantageous to change another. What is most important is to know what you want, to know your outcome, so that every change has a positive purpose. Change for change's sake brings little but a little change. Real change occurs when we know what we want to change and why.

Changing Situations

To bring about the big change that is necessary to attain our aspirations, we need to ensure we have the right MindFrame for the right situation. To have one MindFrame for every aspect of our life would be inflexible and blinkered, and would most likely lead to patterns being established across all areas of our lives.

To have multiple MindFrames bouncing around our heads so that we can pick the right one for the right situation, could lead to confusion and misapplication. It may not be wise to be belligerent, for example, during a romantic anniversary celebration, or overly attentive to the needs of others whilst focusing on a task on a computer screen.

Separate MindFrames have therefore been identified for nine key situations in which we find ourselves in everyday life. These are: work, rest and play, goal setting, goal getting and goal attaining, self, sex and social. These nine areas can split into bands of three, the three broad areas that make up our lives. First, work, rest and play. Second, the directional aspect which each of us follows, goal setting, goal getting and goal attaining. Finally, the three communication modes in which we find ourselves, alone, in a close relationship with another person, and as part of a group.

We can then choose to have the right MindFrame for each situation. That means that if everything is fine with most aspects of our lives, but we are experiencing difficulty with, for example, completing tasks, we could look at our 'goal getting' MindSet. Or if everything is OK at work and at home, but we are encountering difficulties with friends, then the 'social' MindSet may need addressing.

Or there may be a combination which needs changing. For example, we may be encountering problems at work with our employees, which is having a knock-on effect at home. That may require changing the 'work', 'rest' and 'social' MindSets. On the other hand, changing one MindSet may have a knock-on effect and impart the required change on all other aspects of our lives.

Addressing MindFrames under separate situations is necessary as we do behave and respond differently under different conditions. Everything is context specific. We are not the same in every aspect of our lives and can often behave entirely differently. The most important aspect is to establish positive MindFrames that can have a beneficial effect on other areas.

A MindFrame is a personal approach or strategy to one aspect of our lives that ensures we get the result we want. Once the pieces have been explained and put together, it becomes a straightforward approach that will be mentally engrained so we can meet our objectives more easily and effortlessly.

Using our unconscious resources, aligning our conscious and unconscious parts, and finding a pathway that is desirable and congruent gives us the springboard to achieve all we want.

As we control our minds, we control our frame of mind to change our mind and change our results. Change our frame of mind, change our lives.

Chapter 2

Models of Excellence

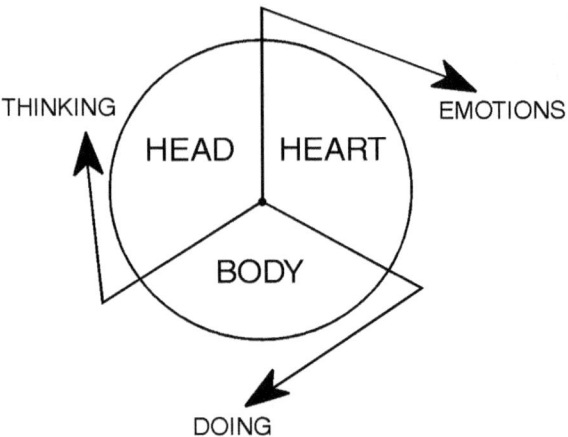

Have you ever wondered why some people can communicate better than others? Or why some people who appear similar to ourselves can apparently achieve so much more? Or have you ever been troubled by your inability to progress beyond a particular point whilst others seem to move effortlessly to the next level?

Questions like these were the inspiration for the founders of Neuro-Linguistic Programming, John Grinder and Richard Bandler. They decided to study how successful people did what they did. They began by observing three skilled communicators: family therapist Virginia Satir, hypnotherapist Milton Erickson and the founder of Gestalt therapy, Fritz Pearls.

Grinder and Bandler scrutinised every detail of how each expert operated and produced a model, or structure, to explain how they did that. The pair would then use these same approaches to perform similar functions. They soon found that they could achieve remarkable results by following the patterns that the experts would do naturally.

From this experience, Grinder and Bandler believed that if one person can do something well then so can another, if they follow the same procedures. NLP was therefore born of a pursuit of excellence, of modelling what works well and using, or installing it, on oneself. It is about following a trail of techniques that leads to a successful outcome.

NLP MindFrame Patterns were developed to further simplify these structures and produce a framework – that is a frame that works – so that everybody can use it.

Many of us may find it appealing to find out how some people can communicate better than others. Or find out how people similar to ourselves can achieve so much more than we ever thought possible. We may like to know how some people can progress easily and effortlessly to the next level. In finding those things out, it may then be really useful to help us move forward more easily.

With this information we can use the power of our minds to achieve the results we want in life and stop denying ourselves the opportunity to progress.

'If one person can, so can another'

What is Neuro-Linguistic Programming?

First of all 'neuro' refers to our nervous system. These are the channels through which all of our life experiences are processed. They come via our five senses: visual, sound, feeling, smell and taste.

'Linguistic' refers to our communication and how we 'encode' what we see, hear, feel, smell and taste. These are the pictures and sounds we have in our head and the feelings we associate with them.

'Programming' is the process by which we communicate to ourselves and others. If we change this language of the mind, we can change the results we get.

The NLP Communication Model helps explain this.

We see, hear, feel, smell and touch external events and process these through our 'filters'. Our filters are made up of things like our values and beliefs, attitudes, decisions, memories, and time.

Each of us deletes, distorts and generalises the events around us, or 'reality', to create our version of the world. Every one of us has a different version of the world, because we all have different filters. This version is called a 'map' as it is a representation, not the real thing.

If we think back to childhood and recall a particular event, such as a holiday, we may find that our recollections of this are different from friends or family. We may remember things that they could not recall. Or we may see an event entirely differently to that of a brother or sister. "Mrs Muggins was a horrible teacher," we might remember, whilst our elder sister may say, "She was so sweet and considerate." It is almost as if at times we experience things in an entirely different way.

This can happen with recent events. What might be a great party or social occasion to one person, can be miserable to another who spent the evening trapped by a terrible bore.

From this we can see that each of us carries our own 'map' of the world. These maps are neither right or wrong, they are just how we see, hear and feel events.

> *'If one person can so can another. What is stopping you from achieving your outcome, right now? If the answer is you then move yourself aside and let your successful self through'*

Maps of the World

The filters which distort, generalise and delete our experience to produce our map of the world are very important. That is because we can only handle between five and nine pieces of information at any one time. If we did not distort, generalise and delete we would be overwhelmed and unable to function.

Imagine trying to complete a really simple activity like crossing the road if we had to process a million bits of information at a time? That is what is happening around us, as there are millions of things that we can see, hear, smell, taste and feel at any one moment. Our minds choose to ignore most of these so we can get on with life. Thank goodness for that!

Distortions, generalisation and deletions therefore play an important role in helping us to get on with doing things. We can quickly categorise people and events so we know what to do and how to act in a given situation. This often works well and gives us the opportunity to progress quickly when doing things with which we are familiar, such as planning journeys.

The brain is a self-patterning system and so it follows repeat patterns, like the streams running down the valley mentioned in the previous chapter. Likewise, it also categorises events and people to give them similar meanings. It is easier for us to handle if we can fit something into a category or box that is comparable to something else.

It is like when we see a person behaving in a particular way, such as being loud and brash, and we recognise those traits in someone else we know. "Oh, they're just like my ex-boss, showy and arrogant". This may be the case, or the person may be mostly unlike the ex-boss to which we are comparing them. Therefore we are doing them a disservice.

This is where these filters become unhelpful. We can over-categorise, label people and events that perhaps deserve wider consideration. This over-simplification can lead to problems and our 'map' or 'model' of the world becomes distorted. We may be leaving out bits of information that may be important and really useful.

Models of Excellence

Do you find that when you see or hear someone who reminds you of someone you do not like, that you then ignore them? Or a particular comment reminds you of an unfavourable meeting that you attended, so you try and get away as soon as possible? This is what can happen all the time with distortions, generalisations and deletions.

You may know people who appear blinkered, or small minded, unable to appreciate other people's points of views. They are often labelled as being in "a world of their own". And they are, as each of us is. The difficulty is when our world becomes isolated or is in collision with other worlds and causes other people and ourselves problems.

As we become more aware of how we distort, generalise and delete, we can make sure we are not becoming too blinkered or dismissing people out of hand, or limiting ourselves in what we can achieve.

So what are distortions, generalisations and deletions?

- Distortions are misrepresentations of what is happening.
- Generalisations are broad conclusions which fit into categories based upon previous experience.
- Deletions are when we pay selective attention to only certain aspects of our experience.

Deletions are most common place as we all need to delete a good proportion of our experience in order to function properly. Distortions should be monitored closely as they can have the biggest effect on our lives, if we are not careful.

Once filtered we then store these events and they become our memories. We tend to pay little attention to how we store these experiences. That is the pictures, sounds and feelings that come to mind when we remember particular events.

What happens is that we store different events in a variety of ways. They are made up of a combination of mental images, sounds and feelings. Some are like movies, with people rushing around, whilst others are like snapshots. Some have music in the background, or people talking, whist others are silent. Similarly, we may see a whole range of colours, such as when remembering a wonderful landscape view, whilst others may be in black and white.

The sizes of these pictures may also change. Some may be really small, whilst others can totally surround us. We may think of some pictures, or representations, as being far off in the distance, whilst others are just in front of us, or down to the side. We store these representations in different areas spatially, so that some can be to our right or left, others right in front, and others above or below us.

Some people do not see clear pictures, but distinct sounds, such as people singing or music playing. Some people see only colours or shades of colours that represent certain memories. A few people only associate feelings, such as butterflies in the stomach or excitement rushing through their chest like flowing water.

Think of a time when you were really happy, maybe on holiday or at a party. What does the scene look like, sound like? Are you looking through your own eyes, or are you in the picture? Where are any feelings located? Is the picture large or small? Does it move, vibrate? Is it light or heavy? Where is the picture located spatially? Is it right in front of you or far away? Above or below? To the left or the right? What sounds are there? Can you hear music or people speaking?

Now do the same with a more mundane recollection, such as a conversation with a neighbour or colleague at work. You will probably find that the picture and feelings and sounds are quite different. This is because we store and encode events in different ways. If we alter these, by shifting the locations, pictures, sounds and feelings, then our attitude towards them can also shift significantly.

However we store these representations is fine. They are how we see, feel and hear the world. It is our 'Map of the World'.

'You have all the resources you need to succeed right now. Taking responsibility for yourself you take responsibility for your success'

Presuppositions of NLP

If we presuppose certain things to be true, it can be very helpful. If we take a puppy to the stream and gently coax it into chasing a stick into the water, we presuppose it will have the ability to swim further out to grasp it between its teeth. If not we may have to buy the puppy inflatable wings and take it for swimming lessons.

Likewise, we presuppose all sorts of things that mean we do not spend hours scrutinising what everybody says. We presuppose a doctor wearing a white coat in hospital is indeed a doctor and knows what they are talking about. We presuppose that a mechanic can fix a car and a teacher can teach children. We presuppose that a plumber can fix a leak. There is already a flaw creeping into these presuppositions.

That is that not all the above necessarily know how to fix a leak or mend our car or teach children. Indeed, not all dogs can swim! Most of the time, they do and most of the time what we presuppose is true.

Models of Excellence

The above demonstrates that believing things to be absolutely true or absolutely false is unhelpful. It is the shades of grey, the gradients mentioned in chapter 1 that are most useful. However, if we believe things to be largely true, or largely false, then we tend to hit the target more often than not. If we check into a hospital and someone is dressed as a nurse, we usually consider it safe to take medicine from them. If we are walking along a dark street and we see a menacing figure swaying towards us, most of us would err on the side of caution and cross over the road.

The following presuppositions are neither true nor false. They are convenient beliefs that can prove very helpful.

1. *The map is not the territory*

    What we experience is not the event itself, but our representation of it. It is our map or model of the world.

2. *Respect other people's map of the world*

    Everyone has a different map of the world and no matter how greatly these can differ from our own, every person deserves to have their view respected.

3. *People have all the resources they need to succeed*

    Everyone is capable of achieving their specific outcomes, if they use the resources they have.

4. *You are responsible for you own mind therefore the results you get*

    We are responsible for our own minds and therefore the results we get.

5. *Everyone is doing the best they can with the resources they have*

    All behaviour comes from a positive intention to do the best we can for ourselves, no matter the outcome of that behaviour.

6. *The meaning of communication is the response you get*

    If we are in control of the communication and take responsibility for that, it is up to us to get the result we seek.

7. *You cannot not communicate*

    It is impossible not to communicate. Even if we are doing nothing, we are sending out a signal and other people can read into it what they will. We are unconsciously communicating all the time. It is better to communicate consciously with positive intent rather than unconsciously with a negative effect.

8. *There is only feedback*

   There is no failure, only feedback. If every setback is seen as a failure, it can be debilitating leading to inaction. If a setback is seen as a learning opportunity, the individual can keep going until success is gained. The word mistake comes from the movie industry. A 'miss-take' was a film clip that did not work and would need to be re-shot. If we view mistakes as that, as opportunities to improve performance next time round, then that is empowering rather than deflating.

9. *All changes should be evaluated in terms of context and ecology*

   Ecology is the study of consequences. If change happens in one area, the effect on other areas should be monitored to ensure there is not a negative impact.

Mercedes Model

The presuppositions of NLP were developed from Grinder and Bandler's research findings. Their work on internal representations and the processes of how we store and encode memories also led to further investigations on how we are constructed.

According to the Mercedes Model (so named because of its resemblance to the car insignia) our internal representation is one third of our make-up. We also have an internal state and external behaviour.

The internal state is our identity, who we are. It is attached to our emotions, our heart. Our values, the things that are most important to us, are situated here.

Our internal representations are concerned with how we do what we do. It is attached to our thinking, or our head. It is concerned with our processes and is associated with our beliefs. Beliefs are the things that we hold to be true about ourselves, the rules that govern our lives.

The external behaviour is what we are. That is our behaviour, our physical actions, the demonstration of what we value and believe.

Internal state, internal representation and external behaviour are brought together in this model because they all inter-act. You cannot change one without it impacting the other. On this basis, every change should be monitored to measure impact elsewhere.

This model includes the major concepts of NLP and is the inspiration for MindFrame Patterns, which draws it together into a useable step-by-step structure for personal growth.

NLP Keys To An Achievable Outcome

The NLP Outcome Model is a useful tool to help you achieve your desired outcome. This can be applied to any goal or aspiration, however big or small, whether personal or business, and is a sure way of measuring progress. As we constantly refer to 'outcomes' it would be beneficial to feature here, although it is addressed in more detail in the Goal Setting chapter.

1. Stated in the positive.

    What specifically do you want?

2. Specify present situation.

    Where are you now?

3. Specify outcome.

    What will you see, hear, feel etc when you have it?

4. Specify evidence procedure.

    How will you know when you have it?

5. Is it congruently desirable?

    What will this outcome get for you or allow you to do?

6. Is it self-initiated and self-maintained?

    Is it only for you?

7. Is it appropriately contextualised?

    Where, when, how and with whom do you want it?

8. What resources are needed?

    What do you have now, and what do you need to get your outcome?

    Have you ever had or done this before?

    Do you know anyone who has?

    Can you act as if you have it?

9. Is it ecological?

    For what purpose do you want this?

    What will you gain or lose if you have it?

We often find ourselves coming up short of our targets despite putting in a huge amount of effort. There can be many reasons for this. A frequent cause is that we do not accurately define what we want.

"I want to be rich this time next year," or "I want to be happy," are vague expectations and it is unsurprising that we so often fall short. The first step to achieving our outcome is to be very clear on what it is we want. If we then define in no uncertain terms what it is we want and ensure that it is possible from the outset, we can achieve anything.

If we can achieve anything, we are already well on the way to getting whatever it is we want. That is hard to deny when it has already been acknowledged at a deeper level.

'You cannot not communicate. Do you want to communicate consciously and ethically or unconsciously and destructively?'

Chapter 3

How MindFrame Patterns Work

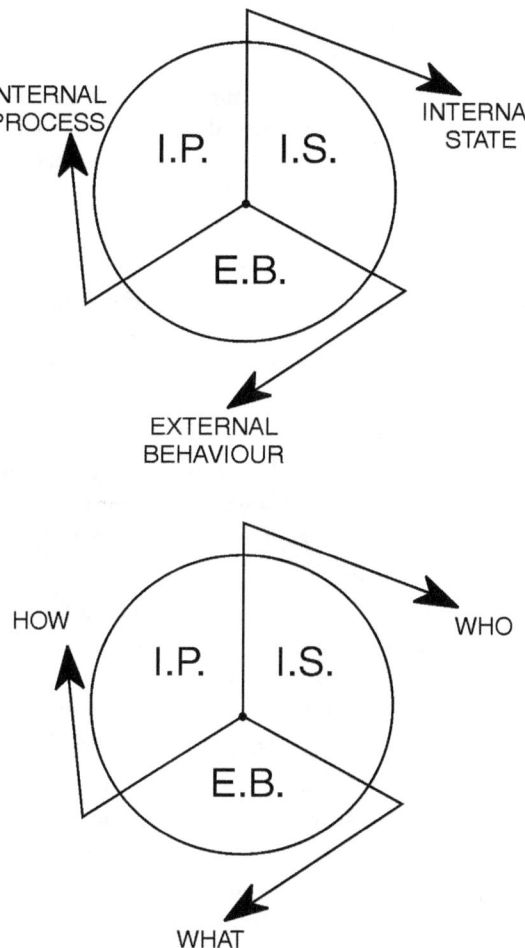

'To be in the right frame of mind to be successful in every area of our lives, we need to have our heart, soul and mind behind what we are doing'

Inspiration is a funny thing. Sometimes we can feel full of energy and enthusiasm to go out and do something right away: mow the lawn, do the paperwork, take the dog for a walk, paint the spare room, buy a new refrigerator. Other times the very thought of rummaging through the shed to dig out the cobweb covered lawnmower, or sit down to wade through a mountain of bills, or take the dog out in the driving rain, fills us with dread. Even something that we began with enthusiasm and commitment can quickly become a drag. Painting the spare room required much more wallpaper stripping than we anticipated, making a decision on which refrigerator is not easy, they all seem so alike...

These changes of state are commonplace and something we take for granted. On larger more important issues, they can hold us back. Would it not be wonderful to be in the right frame of mind from the start to the finish of whatever it is we are doing? In fact, being in the right frame of mind for as much of the time as we want, in whichever situation, would be very desirable.

To do that we must ensure that our state of mind does not get derailed by everyday distractions, or obstacles that get in our way. How often do we find ourselves distracted by a phone call, or conversation, or something on the television or in a newspaper when we want to get a task completed? When we come back to start again we can find ourselves in a different mood, unwilling to continue.

Obstructions can derail us altogether. Why bother continuing if things just keep landing in our way? Almost as if it was not meant to happen. How can we mow the lawn if the blade keeps getting clogged up with grass? Or paint the spare room if we run out of paint?

We may be compelled to do something. Like going to work when we do not feel too well. Or completing a job for our employers because they have demanded it is completed by a particular date. The incentive in this case may be pay and job security. If we did not do that then sooner or later we would find ourselves out of work. That is not to say our heart and soul is behind it.

To be in the right frame of mind to be successful in every area of our lives, we need to have our heart, soul and mind behind what we are doing. We also need to ensure that we have the right frame of mind for the right function.

The following is an introduction to NLP MindFrame Patterns intended as a general overview. A detailed explanation of each pattern is provided in later chapters.

Strength Athletes

We have everything we need to succeed. We have mowed the lawn before. We have painted the spare room, bought a refrigerator, done a whole variety of things, large and small. We have moved jobs, been promoted, moved school, made new friends. We have boyfriends, girlfriends, wives, husbands, mothers, aunts, uncles, children, pets and friends and enemies and multitudes of experiences to call upon, each and every one of us. That is all on a conscious level. On an unconscious level, that 90 per cent beneath the surface mentioned in Chapter 1, we have so much more, more than we realise.

How MindFrame Patterns Work 19

If we are only aware of the 10 per cent, if that is what we have used to get this far in life, then we are truly remarkable people, every one of us. It is amazing to think that we expended all that energy and effort when 90 per cent of what we are was away doing something else. We are like strongmen pulling those huge trucks with a rope. Would it not be so much easier to take off the harness, jump in the cab and drive away? What we have achieved so far in life is truly amazing. The question now is, what more can we achieve if we tap into that deep, largely unused well?

There is no point in driving the truck if we don't know where we're going. What would be the point? The journey might be pleasant but ultimately we may end up anywhere. We can make a conscious decision to get to a particular point. Maybe a friend's house, or that of a relative. Once we know where we are going we can get in the car, or board the train, or get on the bike, and drive or ride straight there.

How often have you arrived somewhere and not remembered much or any of the journey? It happens all the time. Who do you think is looking after us? Who stops at the red light? Who ensures there is a safe distance between ourselves and the car in front? Who makes sure we get off at the right stop? It is our self, me, myself and I. It is that part of ourselves that looks after our self all the time. We set the course consciously and our unconscious part takes over. It happens all the time.

This is how MindFrame Patterns work. We set the course consciously and we ensure that our unconscious is giving us all the resources we need to get there. Using conscious effort, or willpower alone, is lunacy: like pulling the truck when we could be driving it. If we combine the unconscious and conscious, set them in the right direction, fully aligned, then we can achieve anything.

> ***'We set the course consciously and we ensure that our unconscious is giving us all the resources we need to get there'***

Categories

If we take the internal state, internal process and external behaviour of the last chapter, we can begin to see how the patterns are laid out.

The internal state is our heart, our emotions, who we are. The internal process is our thinking, our head, how we are. The external behaviour is our actions, our physicality, what we are.

These essential components, or elements, are what define us, are what make us what we are, how we operate and who we are. The thinking, feeling and doing. If we can find out a little bit more about each part of ourselves then we can work out how best to motivate and inspire ourselves to do what we want. However, we must also remember to tap into the unconscious part to ensure we are giving ourselves all the resources we need. And we really do have all the resources we need.

As human beings we are incredibly complex. We are made up of an infinite variety of components that make us the unique individuals we are. We all have similar elements, however we combine them in different ways. It is these elements that make us what we are. What we can sometimes forget is just how complex we are.

We are also incredibly versatile. We do not always respond in one way. We tend to respond differently in different circumstances. We can be a hard worker at work, a caring parent or sibling at home, a fun-loving party animal with friends, a scholar in the evenings, a whole host of different people in different situations. We can have different behaviours, different beliefs and different values in various contexts.

At work we may believe it good to 'be cruel to be kind'. That patience is not a virtue when something needs doing 'right now'. At home we may believe the opposite as we spend hours helping a three year old learn to read.

Because of how different we are under different contexts, MindFrames splits into different categories to ensure we can be at our best in each. These are the contexts and are split into three categories of three. That is work, rest and play. Goal setting, goal getting and goal attaining. And self, sex and social. These cover every situation in life.

Within each context we have the three main elements: the heart, the head and the physical. The emotion, the thinking and the doing. These different parts of ourselves can also be categorised as elements.

The heart, our internal state, is represented by earth, our grounding, the very essence of who we are.

The head, our internal process, is represented by water, the movement, the process of how we are.

The physical, our external behaviour, is represented by fire, the doing, the demonstration of what we are.

There is of course one more element, air. Air represents the deep unconscious, or the deep structure, the load the truck is carrying. We will return to this later, but for now will refer in the main to the three elements: Earth, Water and Fire.

Here we have the three practical elements of who, how and what we are. To make sure we know as much about ourselves as possible, we should also look at the unconscious parts of each. So we can break down the patterns further into earth, conscious and unconscious, water, conscious and unconscious, and fire, conscious and unconscious.

There is naturally much overlap between conscious and unconscious. Unconscious is basically anything we are not aware of. It is out of our conscious understanding. Once we begin to find out more about ourselves and how we operate then we will have a conscious understanding and so it is no longer unconscious. However, even if we understand how and why we are doing what we are doing, we are still largely doing those things unconsciously.

Although these patterns categorise conscious and unconscious as being largely distinct, it is not black and white, on or off, right or wrong. These thought processes, views and opinions can be placed, for ease of recognition, in one segment or the other. They will be largely conscious, or largely unconscious.

Given this, it also follows that the more practised we become in using the patterns, the less the distinctions will matter. Like most categories and labels, they serve a purpose and are a good starting point. We can then decide for ourselves if it is useful to continue referring to them as such. The purpose, it must be remembered, is to align the conscious and unconscious, so integrating them should not be a problem if the understanding is there.

'If we combine the unconscious and conscious, set them in the right direction, fully aligned, then we can achieve anything'

Elements

Conscious Elements:
- Earth – Values
- Water – Beliefs
- Fire – Behaviour.

Values, earth, are the things that we spend most of our time, money and energy moving towards or away from.

If we apply it to a category, or context, one at a time, then we can find out what are our highest values. For example in the Work category, we could look at what our values are by thinking about what is most important to us about work. For example, people, achieving tasks, getting satisfaction from what we do, hitting a target, and so forth. To work out accurately what our highest values are, as opposed to what we think they are, we can break up the working week and work out the percentages for the amount of time we are living that value, the amount of resources we put into it, and the amount of energy expended.

Beliefs, water, are the guiding rules by which we live our lives. They are neither true nor false but we tend to hold them as such. "I can't get that promotion," "I am good at my job," "I'm a terrible father," "I'm a good mother," are all examples of beliefs that we hold true, because we have set ourselves those expectations. Beliefs always reinforce our values.

Behaviour, fire, is the most obviously recognisable character trait. It is what we do, how we behave, our actions. This is most obvious to people around us, if not always ourselves. We can not hide who we are and our behaviour demonstrates that.

By altering any of the above, by moving values around, changing our beliefs and getting rid of limiting ones, or adjusting our actions, huge change can happen. Just having an awareness of these things can begin to shift our model or map of the world. However, before adjusting anything it is important to be aware of our unconscious patterns.

Unconscious Patterns:

- Change Patterns
- Storage Patterns
- Strategy Patterns

The unconscious patterns are less straightforward but only because we may not be used to the definitions. All can be easily understood once practised.

Change Patterns

Change Patterns, otherwise know as Meta (meaning over) Programs, are the patterns that indicate how we do what we do. As always they are context specific, although we will carry over many programs into different parts of our lives. There are nine* main patterns to which we refer. These are: Change, Primary Interest, Information, Evaluation, Decision, Motivation, Motive, Activity, and Organisation.

Change, for example, is how we view the world. Do we recognise sameness or appreciate difference? Some people have a tendency to spot differences, whilst others will notice how things resemble each other. There is also an inbetween, where we notice some differences but most things are the same, or we notice mostly differences and some similarities.

To experience if you recognise sameness or appreciate difference, randomly place three coins on a surface in front of you. Now tell yourself what you see, describe what is in front of you. If the first thing you say to yourself is that you see two heads and a tail, then that would imply sameness. If you say to yourself that there is one tail and two heads, then that would imply difference.

How MindFrame Patterns Work 23

Each of these programs indicates how we are in different situations. If we begin to adjust these reactions then there can be greatly varied results to what we do. For example, the Motivation Pattern determines whether we are a 'towards' or 'away from' person, depending on the context. In the Work category, it may be that we are motivated to produce results so that we do not lose our job. That indicates an 'away from' motivation. If we are motivated to produce results to receive a pay rise, that suggests a 'towards' motivation. If we apply this to the various aspects of work, such as pay, working conditions, inter-action with colleagues, we can work out if we are a largely 'towards' or 'away from' person in this context.

Once we have discovered that, and we are not getting the results we want, then it may be beneficial to begin to make efforts to move in the other direction. Having the ability to move between extremes or find a balance is the goal.

> *'A MindFrame is a series of conscious and unconscious patterns applied to a specific event to ensure we consistently achieve our specific and desired outcome'*

Storage Patterns

Storage Patterns, otherwise know as Sub Modalities, are how we encode and store every event. Our Modalities refer to our senses: seeing, hearing, feeling, tasting and smelling.

Sub Modalities are broken down further into the component pieces of how we store every memory. They are how we store recollections, the visual, auditory and emotional representations referred to in the last chapter. It is how we see events, what colours they are constructed of, whether it is a movie or still, framed or panoramic and so forth. They are also made up of noises and sounds, as well as feelings we attach to them. Of crucial importance is where we locate these pictures and sounds and feelings.

By moving these representations around we can make a huge difference to our unconscious patterns and transform our approach. For example if something is working really well for us and we have a clear picture of that, we can move the representation of something that is not working so well and place it where the clear picture is, transferring the positive qualities across.

Strategy Patterns

A Strategy Pattern is the process we go through every time we do something.

Every strategy is made up of a sequence of seeing, hearing, feeling, tasting or smelling steps we go through. For example, in buying something from a shop we may see an item, compare it to a visual representation of what we want to buy, check with our auditory digital (logical) side that the price is right, hear ourselves say that it is alright, touch the item to make sure it has the right feel, once again compare the item to the visual representation so that it matches our expectations, and get the feeling we want to buy it.

It sounds complicated, but it is the sort of process every one of us goes through when doing something as simple as purchasing a new coat or deciding what to order from a restaurant.

This process can be defined every time we undertake a task. It always concludes with a 'synaesthesia', that is a combination of two senses to confirm that is what we will do. This normally consists of seeing and feeling, or hearing and feeling. It is what happens every time we do not want to do something and feel bad about it, or when we are very excited about doing something. We see or hear something and it makes us feel a particular way.

This connects us to our internal state, earth, how we feel emotionally, what state we are in from moment to moment.

To use strategies in a productive way, we need to first elicit the process that is not working so well for us and then install a process that would work better, by changing certain steps. For instance a shopaholic will quite often have a two step strategy: see it, compare it to a visual recollection of a similar item that had been bought previously and feel an overriding urge to buy. The second step is the synesthesia.

If we introduce another couple of steps this can make all the difference. For example: see it, hear yourself advising caution, see yourself with all the things you already have, and finally, feel good about that. That extended process may then hinder the person from going out and buying items they do not really need.

It is not so easy to know your own strategy for doing something. This is because eye patterns give an indication of what the person is thinking as well as saying. If we look up and to the left, for example, that means we are accessing the visual recall part of our brain, so we can remember what things look like. We will look at eye patterns in more detail in the Strategy Pattern Chapter.

Direct questions also prove useful, for example in working out our motivation strategy.

Start by asking, what is the very first thing that happened that made me know that it was time to… was it something I saw, heard or felt? The follow-up question would be, what was the very next thing that happened so that I knew it was totally right to… was it something I saw, heard or felt etc? This question repeats until each step of our strategy is revealed. For example, we could apply it to the Rest context, and knowing when it is time to relax. Even then we go through a process to decide that it is time to sit or lie down. Human beings really are complex!

Contexts

This is the basic approach to each MindFrame. What we need to ensure is that for every change we make, it is context specific. In fact every series of changes, earth, water and fire, conscious and unconscious, needs to be for a set context, or MindFrame. In a nutshell, that is a MindFrame: a series of conscious and unconscious patterns applied to a specific event to ensure we consistently achieve our specific and desired outcome.

The events cover the whole gamut of human existence.

These can also be categorised as earth, water and fire.

Earth covers all the practical situations we find ourselves in: work, rest and play.

Water includes every movement we make: goal setting, goal getting and goal attaining. Goals in this context do not have to be big objectives. They can be as simple as planning a journey, followed by experiencing the journey and how we are once we get there. That is, what state are we in when we achieve our outcome? Are we in the best shape possible to achieve our next goal? There are different stages and states and it is important to be aware of each.

Fire covers all aspects of interaction and communication: self, sex and social. Self is when we are alone. Sex is when we are 'one-to-one', in a close relationship with another person, although it does not have to be a sexual relationship. Social is when we are with more than one person.

These contexts cover every situation we will ever find ourselves in. Now all we need to do is ensure we are in the right MindFrame to prosper in each.

NLP MindFrames Patterns in brief:

Each pattern consists of:
- Earth Conscious: Values
- Water Conscious: Beliefs
- Fire Conscious: Behaviours

Unconscious patterns consist of:
- Change Patterns
- Storage Patterns
- Strategy Patterns

Air: Deep Structure

Patterns are applied to contexts of:
- Earth: Work, Rest & Play
- Water: Goal Setting, Goal Getting, Goal Attaining
- Fire: Self, Sex & Social

* In his book People Pattern Power, Dr Wyatt Woodsmall picks nine change patterns that are most crucial to business change. Because NLP MindFrame Patterns is based upon Models of Excellence, we refer to this as a best practice model, although our terminology differs slightly.

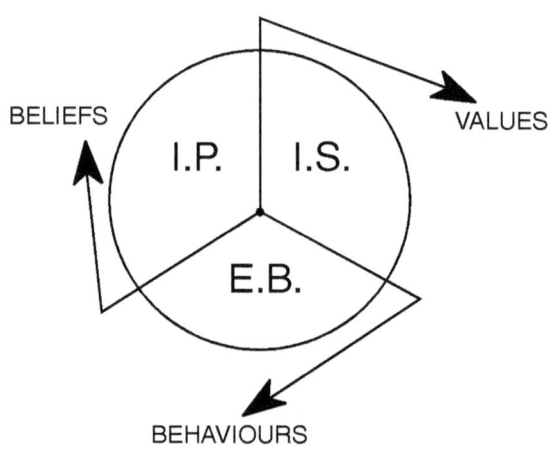

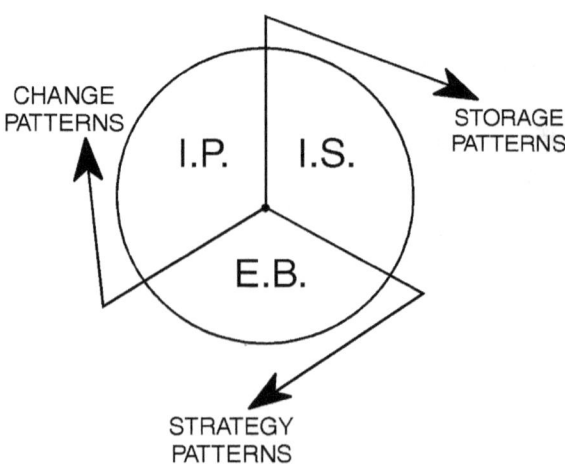

Part II: Insight

Chapter 4

Internal State, Earth

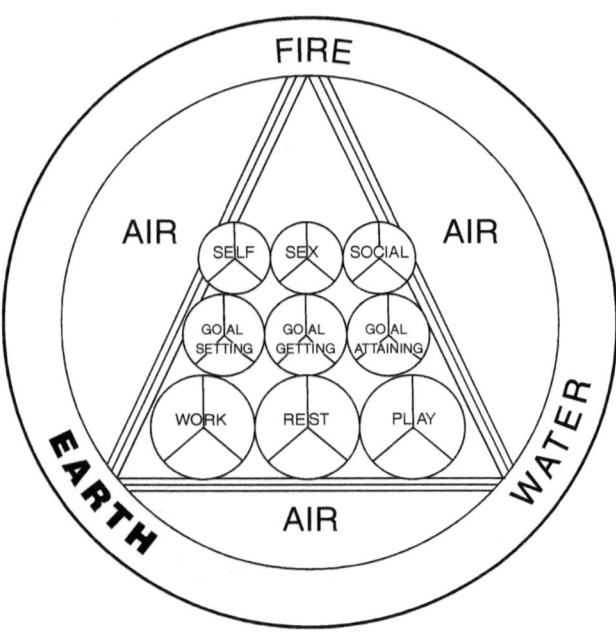

'Just because someone says we are an idiot, does not make us an idiot. We have to put more of an effort into being an idiot. Being an idiot should not be taken lightly'

Life's a rollercoaster, some people are fond of saying. One minute you're up, next you're down. Sometimes we're hurtling along at full pelt, going hell for leather to reach our destination, other times we're nose to tail in traffic, honking our horn and cursing congestion.

There are days when the roads are clear, the sky is bright, and the highways and byways feel like our own. There are other days when the rain lashes down so hard and fast we can not see further than three feet in front of us.

Does our mood always depend upon the weather, the congestion, the pace of life, slow or fast? Yes it is. Only in that it is down to each of us to respond in the way want.

We see the rain, recall a miserable soaking we received last time it poured down, and associate that with our current experience. Misery. Or we feel the sun's warm rays and recall a golden beach, palm trees and a rich blue sea. Ecstasy.

A white-faced night owl strolling the streets of a metropolis the morning after an all night party might recoil at the merest hint of the sun's glare, whilst a farmer whistles merrily as the crops awaken to a refreshing torrent. What's good for the goose is not always good for the gander.

What the chirpy farmer and the night owl have in common is conditioning. They are conditioned, through habit, through repeat patterns, to respond the way they do. So are we when we curse at traffic or revel in the sunlight (the latter may be an entirely British phenomenon!). We are so used to what happens when the rain falls, or the sun shines, or night falls, that our mind and body repeats the reaction from last time. The weary sigh, slumped shoulders and sinking feeling of gloom. Or the heart lifting warmth of bright light, heat and contentment. Every time that happens we experience a synaesthesia. That is the coming together of two of our senses, one of which is always emotion, feeling. See it, feel it. Hear it, feel it. Smell it, feel it. Taste it, feel it. Touch it, feel it.

The emotional part, the feeling, is the direct link to our internal state. A friend says, "It's raining out," we say, "doh!". A friend says, "It's going to be a scorcher," we say, "great" (if we're British).

"So, your Honour, the witness before us is presenting evidence that is 'twice removed from reality'. I move that the case be dismissed. The witness is obviously an idiot..."

An Idiot's Guide to Self-Control

Isn't this blindingly obvious? Of course it is. Except we tend not to pay any notice to it. If we are feeling down we spend hours telling friends or family, or go the other way and store it all up. We dwell on it, analyse it, and if it becomes extreme, seek help or write to an agony aunt.

At the end of the day we do anything but seek the simplest solution. That is to look at how we respond the way we do to put ourselves in the state that we do.

After all, we are responsible for our minds, therefore the results we get. No-one else puts us in a mood, makes us feel down. We do that ourselves.

"Yes but what about when he looks at me like that, in that really hurtful way, or says those nasty things. That's him saying that, looking at me like that, not me. I'm not shouting at myself." Yes, of course we are not shouting at ourselves, but we might as well be. Just after he has called us an idiot, we may as well call ourselves an idiot too, for all the good our previous responses have done.

Just because someone says we are an idiot, does not make us an idiot. We have to put more of an effort into being an idiot. Being an idiot should not be taken lightly. We can not qualify as an idiot just because someone decides to label us as such. We do not become a genius because a friend compliments us after we come up with a suggestion to help them find their car keys.

It is an offence to idiots everywhere if any old person can qualify. It reduces the meaning. Real idiots could get really offended. As could real geniuses.

If we are not idiots then what are we? We are left feeling like an idiot (once again this is conjecture as we dare not speculate on what a real idiot feels like). We have idiot-ised ourselves. "I feel like an idiot for having been spoken to like an idiot. That guy's a jerk." That he may be, but let us not reduce the world of jerks to a single put-down either.

So where is all this leading? Hopefully, on a little detour around Idiotsville. It's a tiny village just outside of our control where we let everybody else decide what mood we are going to be in. If it rains there, everybody feels down. If the sun shines, everybody's singing. If it's a grey day that might brighten up later then the elder decides how everyone should be. Some days it can be alright, other days, fair to middling, and others, over the moon, especially on Wednesdays. It depends how he's feeling.

What this all comes down to is that it is not up to the 'jerk' boyfriend or temperamental village elder as to how we feel. It is entirely down to us. How we choose to respond, how we choose to react to every event.

It is a simple concept, yet incredibly complex to overcome. That is because we have spent a lifetime rehearsing limiting behaviours. We learn from each other. We look at how other people respond and repeat their patterns, even if we do not realise it. We learn from society, from the media, from schools and institutions, even from governments.

They all contribute to fashioning what we are. And we mould this emotional baggage into our very being. We get angry, annoyed, frustrated, elated, deflated, apoplectic, insouciant, vehement, chilled, enraged, apathetic, demonstrative… we practice and rehearse these routines so often, that we and certainly our friends, family and loved ones can predict exactly how we are going to behave given a certain event.

"If she'd have said that to you, you would've hit the roof…"

"I wouldn't have been as laid back as you…"

"I could just see you exploding at that…"

There is nothing wrong with any one response, unless it causes us or people around us a problem. What we have largely forgotten is that we can control how we respond and determine what state we are in.

It is not at all difficult. Once we begin to understand how our Change Patterns work, how we can use our Storage Patterns and Strategies to alter the way we feel about things, that control can be ours.

It is only 'incredibly complex' if we choose to do nothing to change how we are.

We are in charge of our minds, therefore the results we get. Just by switching our internal representations, or rearranging our strategies, we can begin to see, hear and feel things entirely differently.

How good would it feel not to feel like an idiot when someone mistakenly says we are one? Instead we could feel relaxed, happy, glad, apathetic… anything we want to feel instead. Controlling our own minds is the first step towards acquiring a purposeful MindFrame.

Without it, we would be left floundering. How can we realise our outcomes, plan and control our pathway, if we can not control our mind? The tools are laid down throughout the following chapters. All we have to do is pick them up, use what works, engage the unconscious and switch to cruise control…

Content or Crud?

Our internal state is the seat of all our ambitions, all our introspection, all of our understanding about who we are. It is where our content resides. That is the whys and wherefores of where we are currently in life.

There is nothing wrong with content. Some people seem to delight in regaling friends, colleagues and passers-by with every tiny detail about themselves. Other people never seem to give anything away, as if they believe their background is of little importance. Our content *can* be important. However, it can be misleading to believe that is all we are. The process and patterns to which we refer, more about the how and what than the why, can provoke the biggest change.

Content is not wrong. It can be deceptive. We can spend hours mulling over why we are the way we are, wrapping ourselves in information and recollections that are often misleading, even to ourselves.

If we consider the implications of Chapter 2 on distortions, generalisations and deletions. So much of our memories have been filtered and distorted, generalised and deleted that our map of the world is twice removed from 'reality'. That is our experiences have gone through the first set of filters of how we perceive events at the time and then the secondary filters of how we store these memories.

To refer to this matter as a reliable source of evidence for reviewing our life and potential problems would not appear wise.

"So, your Honour, the witness before us is presenting evidence that is *'twice removed from reality'*. I move that the case be dismissed. The witness is obviously an idiot…"

We may be thrown out of court but the content should not be dismissed entirely. It is neither right nor wrong. It just is. And it just is the first thing that most of us dive into when trying to resolve an issue or problem.

No wonder we find ourselves going round in circles, confiding in one friend after another, and still finding no satisfactory answer. The reason is because there is not an answer in there. All there is down there is content and more content. The processes and patterns of how we are on an unconscious level is where the answer lies and it is difficult to acquire that knowledge through chatting to a friend.

"Have you noticed my unconscious thought processes? If you could just point out to me what my frame of reference is please… and pass the crystal ball, I want to figure out the meaning of life…"

It will not happen. What can happen is that if we hold a mirror up to ourselves, we can begin to notice how we are and begin to do something about it.

When we talk about our internal state, our earth, we are therefore not going down those blind alleys of talking about irrelevancies. It is difficult because we have become so used to explaining ourselves in analytical terms.

It is how we label ourselves and others. He is "shy" or she is "outgoing". It happens from earliest childhood and is reinforced over and over again by friends, family, teachers and guardians. We soon become to embody those characteristics because that is how we see ourselves as being.

"Yes I am shy." That one comment made to our self when we are eight years old can remain with us for decades, without our consciously being aware of it. Suddenly we find we cannot speak at a meeting without feeling and sounding nervous. Or we can not enter a room without blushing, or make a presentation without stuttering…

These labels and boundaries are reinforced by society and societal expectations. We are expected to behave in a particular way when we are in certain organisations, or groupings. We can find ourselves categorised and stereotyped without ever subscribing to the beliefs or values of that group or organisation. Or we can go along with things until we begin to embody those beliefs.

Boundaries and labels can restrict us to such an extent that we can lose our identity. And we can so easily go along with being categorised until we believe it ourselves.

Internal State, Earth 33

This is where the unconscious takes over. The unconscious always acts on our best behalf. If it thinks this is for our benefit, it will continue to reinforce it. Until we become aware of how we are acting we will continue to believe, on a deep unconscious level, things that can be very limiting and self-defeating. This self sabotage must be overcome.

This is where we get to the crucial part. What is really important. That is values. These are the deepest part of the content. Broadly speaking, everything else can be nudged aside as we go straight to the source.

Values we can use. Values can inspire us, propel us forward, take us to the next level. If we are going to employ labels, because even a value is a label, let us label ourselves in the best possible way. Bold, bright and brilliant is better than shy, retiring and reluctant... which truism do we prefer?

'Bold, bright and brilliant is better than shy, retiring and reluctant... which truism do we prefer?'

Chapter 5

Earth Values

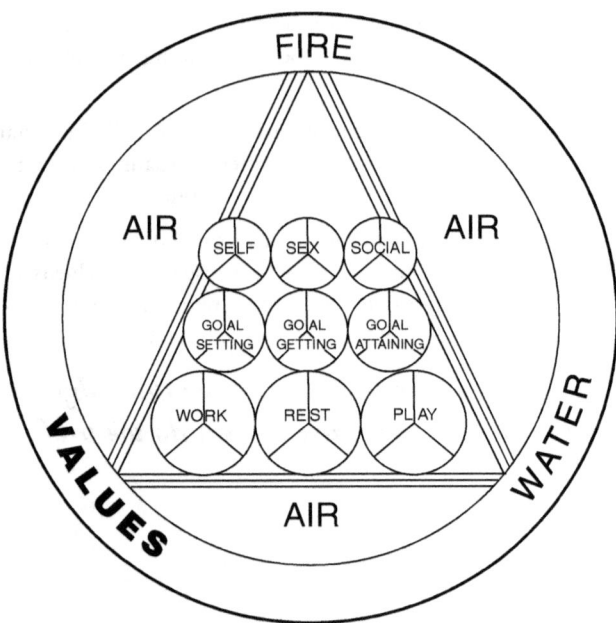

'To truly value ourselves we must have values that truly work'

When things go array, when the sea gets choppy and the waves start to rise, we can find ourselves caught off balance, out of kilter. Amidst the general mayhem and upheaval there is a moment when everything becomes too much, we breathe a deep sigh, sit down and reflect upon the disarray.

It is then that we ask ourselves, what we are doing, why are we going round in circles or failing to make progress? We challenge why we are doing what we are doing. What is the point in moving house, or starting a new job, or falling out with a school friend, or splitting up with a boyfriend? What are we all about? What do I want out of life? What are my priorities? What are my goals, ambitions? What makes me happy, fulfilled, content? What inspires me, lifts me up and sets me free? What am I really here for?

The answer to these questions comes down to our identity, who we are, who we think we are. What is most important to us. What drives us.

These are our values, what makes us unique, what define us to ourselves. Our values can cover a whole range of issues and yet be captured in one word.

'Love' for example, can mean strong affection, unselfish concern for another, holding dear and cherished. Whatever defines it for you is just right. 'Achievement' can mean hitting goals, that sense of accomplishment/success, getting the results you want and need. To another person who may have physical difficulties to overcome, it could mean simply getting out of bed, or walking across the room. We all have different models of the world.

Most value words tend to be nominalisations, which are vague terms that can cover a range of subjects and can have many different meanings for people. Nominalisations are nouns that are frozen in time. The benefit of having a nominalisation as a value is that we put our own meaning onto that word. After all, words are just labels and can have many different meanings, depending on the individual's perspective.

Our internal state is a highly subjective way of being. No-one can experience exactly what we are experiencing. We can recognise specific conditions such as happiness, sadness, excitement or boredom, but we all experience these things differently. It is those unique combinations of factors that make us who we are.

When considering our values, we must always follow our instinct, our own true self. Just because another person's values may seem righteous and compelling, that does not mean we should adopt them for ourselves. We must work with what we are and adjust or add to that where appropriate. There is no point in making up a fictitious self that sounds or feels good. That would be artificial and we would be fooling no-one but ourselves.

We have all the resources we need to succeed. Every one of us is a remarkable feat of biological engineering. Do not underestimate the power, resilience and brilliance of the self. We have all we need, so we may as well work with what we have got.

'When we have all the resources we need it is up to each of us individually to rummage inside and find what it is we need to enrich our lives'

Some Values

What is a value? A value is something that is important to us, something that drives, motivates, compels us forward. They are the most important things which we spend our time, money and energy moving towards or away from. Why towards or away? We may think that all of our values are towards. These are the things I want: health, happiness, comfort, for example.

Take health. Yes it is wonderful to be fit and well, full of energy and vitality. We may aspire to be slim, to fit into that dress or those trousers once again. Or to be able to run a mile without stopping, or cycle to work everyday, or swim five lengths. And how good would that feel once we have achieved that? Great perhaps.

What is really inspiring us though? Is it really just that sense of achievement? Or is it the thought of being over-weight, falling short of breath, being laid up in bed, ill and infirm? It may be a combination, desiring to be stronger and fitter, whilst dreading looking overweight and feeling miserable.

This is quite common. Our values tend to be a mixture of towards and away from motivations. So is it better to be towards or away from? That depends upon your model of the world, what motivates you to act and achieve. If a strong away from motivation means we acquire what we set out to achieve, then good for us.

Too much of an emphasis on away from motivation can have a negative impact. Away from energy, that is negative energy, is more likely to drain us. Towards energy, that is positive energy, is much less likely to hold us back. There is a strong link between negative energy and ill health. If our main values all have strong away from motivations then we may wish to redress the balance.

Some examples of values follow. This is by no means exhaustive, nor should we feel obliged to fit into one category or another. The definitions can also be changed. It does serve as an indicator of some of the areas that we may feel are our priorities in life. The following are a selection of categories defined by NLP Master Coach Bob King, bob.king@bestyearyet.com, in his 'What's Important To You' card set.

Health

Physical and mental well-being

Fit and active

In good shape – weight, heart rate etc

Resilience

Ability to bounce back into shape quickly

Can take the knocks which come

Carry on despite the setbacks

Economic Security

Steady, reliable income

Adequate money to get by modestly

Earth Values

A roof over our heads

Friendship

Relationship with others

Having rapport with a group of people

Sharing interests and fun

Family

Partner

Children

Wider family relationships

Commitment

Obligated to a cause or causes

Pledging to support

Sticking with it, come what may

Competitiveness

Striving to win

Wanting to be the best

Even in situations that are not important

Self Esteem

Confidence and satisfaction in oneself

Valued for who you are

Feeling of worth

Tolerance

Willing to put up with things

Capacity to endure pain or hardship

Sympathy for others' shortcomings

Spirituality

Belief in greater, positive force

Faith

Importance of our soul – not just worldly things

Sport

In general, or one or two in particular

Favourite team

Participant, player

Hobbies

One or more interests

Of special importance to you

Activity, club, society, pastime

Harmony

Internal calm and tranquillity

At peace with self and others

Pleasing arrangements (art, flowers, music)

Honesty

Truthful

Free from deceit

Genuine and sincere

Respect

Has regard for self and others

Belief in own and others abilities

Places importance on self-esteem

Wisdom

Knowledge and experiences

Insight

Enlightenment

Wealth

Lots of money

Material abundance

Affluent, well off

Optimistic

Looking on the bright side

Seeing the best possible outcome

The glass is 'half-full' not half empty

Integrity

Earth Values

Authentic and sincere

Standing up for own beliefs

Honest and direct

Power

Influence and control

Position of importance

Status

Trust

Able to place confidence in

Accurate and truthful

Capable of keeping things in care and intact

Reliability

Dependable

Consistent

Acts and delivers in the same way

Diversity

Welcoming variety

Appreciating differences

Likes a range of qualities

Caring

Attentive to the needs of others

Showing concern, compassion

Making sure all are included

Freedom

Independence

Autonomy

Liberty

Loyalty

Remaining committed to a person or cause

Dependable

Dedicated and supportive

Humour

Fun, enjoyment, laughter

Ability to see the funny side

Pleasure – having a good time

Determination

Strong resolve

Not prepared to give up

Endeavour and 'grit'

Personal Development

Education, learning, qualifications

Developing own knowledge and skills

Ongoing learning

Creativity

Desire to invent

Artistic flair

Imaginative and original

Resource Rich and Revelling in it

These are just some of the values that may resemble our own. Placing the values in order, that is which of these is most important, is no easy task. To pick our top ten, or even top five values can be difficult. Also, what we choose may not reflect what is actually happening.

If we take each value in turn and work out the percentage of time during an average week that we are actually engaged with that value, it may not tally. We can then do the same thing for the percentage of money we spend on that value and the same again for energy. Quite often it transpires that we are not living our values. That is, our external behaviour does not reflect who we think we are.

It is like when somebody describes us in a particular way that we disagree with. It can be the opposite of how we see ourselves. That can be because our actions, our body language, voice tone and every behavioural indication is at odds with what we value. This is when we need to seek alignment between what we are and how we act. Or change the value altogether.

Health can be a good example of this. Health is regular placed as a high value for many people. However, lots of people do little or no exercise, eat the wrong things and generally live unhealthily, yet claim health to be a high value! To know how much time, money and energy we are giving to our high values can therefore be a revelation.

If one value is not working for us, in fact is holding us back, then we can always realign, and place another value closer to the top. It may be useful to have 'determination' higher up our list for example to complete an arduous project, or 'resilience' if many things are happening at once. Chapter 7 goes into further detail on how to re-align values to get the results we want.

Values apply to different areas of our lives and can change at different times of life. It is important to relate the value to the context.

So what do those higher values mean to us? In a word, everything. We find our highest value and we are looking through a window into our soul. It is the essence of who we are. Our DNA. If these values and other high values are useful, if they can help us move forward, just by having awareness of what they are, helps focus and provide some of the momentum we need.

If there is a value that seems attractive to us, that would be useful, that would bring added 'value' to our make-up, why not integrate that, make us stronger, more balanced and able to call upon more resources? While it is necessary to acknowledge where we are now and be honest on what our values are, there is nothing to stop us from drawing on a whole host of values, should they be of use.

Scanning the list above, there is not one of us who can not relate to every one of those values, who could not take any one of those and add it to our armoury, should it be necessary. When we have all the resources we need it is up to each of us individually to rummage inside and find what it is we need to enrich our lives.

Thinking about it now, what would be the very best value or values to take on board, to absorb and integrate? To truly value ourselves we must have values that truly work. So when things do go array, when the seas get choppy, we can respond in the way in which we want, resource rich and revelling in it!

'If there is a value that seems attractive to us, that would be useful, that would bring added 'value' to our make-up, why not integrate that, make us stronger, more balanced and able to call upon more resources?'

Chapter 6

Earth Change Patterns

'In many ways, each of us is our very own alien. We are complex, mechanical creatures consisting of millions of variable features'

Planet earth has some strange inhabitants. Although we were all born here, it appears that many of us come from a galaxy far, far away. Some of us continue to orbit the earth at around 3,000 miles, whilst others are apparently visiting from another dimension on a foreign exchange programme.

In many ways, each of us is our very own alien. We are complex, mechanical creatures consisting of millions of variable features.

What connects all these features together, built into the mainframe, is a series of patterns that take us in the same, or quite often different, directions. They are the patterns that guide our lives, that recur in similar circumstances and repeat themselves. They are such strong drivers that they determine the results we get and the people we are. They shape our destiny and guide us, underlying everything we do.

They are the deepest, unconscious processes of how we do what we do, how we act in every situation and explain why we get the outcome we get repeatedly. They are our Change Patterns and fortunately, they are easy to discover. Once unfurled, the world is our pistachio, for each and every nut crunching alien one of us.

How do we discover these Change Patterns?

Simply answer these questions, this time in the context of work. They are on a sliding scale. We do not have to be one or the other, however, we all tend to lean in one direction for each of the nine Change Patterns categories.*

1) Change. Do I like change?

2) Primary Interest. What do I prefer to talk about most?

3) Information. Do I pay attention to the big picture first or the detail/specifics?

4) Evaluation. Do I need to be told I'm doing well or do I tell myself?

5) Decision. Do I do something because it looks right, sounds right, feels right or makes sense?

6) Motivation. Do I move away from negatives or towards positives?

7) Motive. Am I power, achievement or affiliation oriented?

8) Activity. Do I live in the moment or plan for the future?

9) Organisation. Do I need to do this or do I want to?

Change

Do I like change?

Walking hand in hand along Brighton beach after invading planet earth, Zulog the Zulog sees two pebbles that are almost perfectly rounded and an old tin can. Gologon the Nogolog spots the tin can and the two, almost perfectly rounded pebbles. Zulug the Zulug has had trouble settling down since moving from Alpha Major Nine and has been longing for home and the symmetrical pineapple fields. Gologon the Nogolog has loved every minute of the trip and is bored stupid with endless symmetry, pineapples and mindless repetition.

Gologon the Nogolog loves change. Zulog the Zulog hates change. Gologon is a difference alien. Zulog is a sameness alien. They are extremes, as most aliens are. However we all tend to move in one direction over another.

How am I at work? Do I notice differences first, or similarities? How long have I been in this role, in this department, in this job? Do I find comfort in keeping things the way they are or do I like to mix things up, change the scenery, do something else?

The scale goes from sameness to difference. Between that is sameness with a little difference and difference with a little sameness. Do I see the two pebbles first, ie the similarity, or notice the lone tin can? Where am I on the scale?

Is it working for me?

Primary Interest

What do I prefer to talk about most?

On returning from planet Earth, Zulog the Zulog is weighed down with seaside rock and a crate of South African pineapples. She can not stop talking about where she has been, how interesting the Tower of London was, with all those tourists wearing funny costumes, and how much she loved the seaside, despite it being so uncomfortable to sleep on land. Gologon the Nogolog soon bored of strange tourists and headed for the hills, skiing, paragliding, pineapple hurling... and regaled his twelve headed audience with tales of daring-do and how nifty the quad bikes were.

Zulog is primarily a Places alien, with a secondary interest in People. Gologon is an Activities alien, with a secondary interest in Things. Every one of us has a preferred interest and our conversation will betray our preference. If Gologon or Zulog had given their audience a detailed description of everything they did, down to the tiniest detail, their primary interest would be Information.

What do I talk about mainly? Do I prefer talking about people or places, objects or activities? Or do I drill down to the details? Which is my preference?

Is it working for me?

Information

Do I pay attention to the big picture first or the detail/specifics?

Around the same time Zulog and Gologon were visiting the Museum of Inter Galactic Artefacts, the curate had convinced the head of security not to throw out the two characters wearing alien costumes. The curate believed that throwing people out because they looked different would soon lead to mass ejections and a fall in revenue. The head of security said the pair did not conform to the dress code and should be evicted come what may. The pair often argued. The curate was frustrated that the head of security would always jump on the tiniest details whilst the head of security could never understand why the curate always talked about things happening in the future which seemed to have no relevance to the present.

The head of security is specific. The curate is big picture. The curate is always looking ahead, concerned with how things will develop further down the line. The head of security cares about the here and now, the small stuff, what is happening in the present.

How do I approach my work? Do I think big? Do I plan for the future? Or do I get right on with what is happening here and now? Do I get my head down and burrow into the specifics or do I try and foresee the consequences of everything I do? Where am I on the scale? Am I global first and then specific or the other way round?

Whichever way I am, is it working for me?

Evaluation

Do I need to be told I'm doing well or do I tell myself?

The pineapple grower on the Transvaal plantation, who had recently sold 3,000 of his prize produce to a strange looking creature from a faraway continent, knew when he had a good fruit. He would feel them, squeeze them, drop them and squash them, push them to their limits. He knew when he had a good yield.

He also knew when he'd performed well, done the best he could with the volatile weather conditions in the valley. He never needed to be told he was the best farmer he could be, he just knew it.

The security guard at the Museum for Inter Galactic Artefacts could not tell a ripe pineapple from a total dud. He could however spot a troublemaker from a mile away and was on the two louts dressed up as aliens like a dog on a bone. The head of security, a real stickler, was most grateful for the speedy discovery of the troublemakers and praised Harry to the hilt. Harry liked that. In fact he liked it a lot. Whenever the head of security thanked him, or gave him credit for anything, he positively beamed. If he did something that he thought was positive, but the head of security paid no notice, Harry would quickly sink into a mood, wondering if he had done the right thing in the first place, worried he had screwed up.

Harry needs praise. The South African plantation owner needs none. Harry has a strong external frame of reference. That is, he needs approval and feedback from others. Pineapple man has a strong internal frame of reference. That is, he needs little or no encouragement from outside. He knows when he's doing well.

How do I know when I'm doing a good job? Do I need to be told by others, or do I know it inside, without being told? Do I work better on my own, or as part of a team? What inspires me, motivates me to do more? Is it a feeling inside, that I'm doing well, or when others applaud my work? Where am I on the scale? Closer to external approval, or nearer to internal knowledge?

Wherever I am placed, is it working for me?

Decision

Do I do something because it looks right, sounds right, feels right or makes sense?

Harry liked the Museum of Inter Galactic Artefacts. It was safer than some of the haunts he had tried to secure, despite the occasional troublemaker in fancy dress.

The last place he had guarded was the halls of residence of a city hospital. One night a doctor had gone on a drunken rampage, ransacking the nurses' dormitory and raising hell in the geriatrics' ward. Harry had been stuck on the reception desk giggling as he listened to the frantic efforts of his colleagues as they tried to capture the wayward healer. He could imagine the doctor running through the wards, picking up bed sheets and throwing them over his shoulders as elderly matrons pursued him vigorously and patients screamed at the sudden exposure. Harry could always see things clearly, visualise events described to him in some detail.

When it came to buying his house, he had decided to buy it on first viewing, because it looked right to him. When he bought new clothes, he would always purchase what looked right to him, and rarely concerned himself with the feel of the clothing. Harry is a visual person, a 'looks right' man. His decision making strategy always finishes with a picture. It might include consideration of cost (sense, or logic), he may listen to what others have to say, but ultimately he always makes a decision based upon it looking right.

How do I make the decision to do something? Does it always have to feel right, or look right? Or does it have to make sense to me? Do I have to weigh up all the options and decide once I have evaluated all the alternatives? Or do I get a 'gut feeling' that it is right and go with that? We tend to use a combination of these decision making strategies, depending on the context. Ultimately, we all favour one of those sensory stimuli over the other. Does that sound right, look right, feel right, or make sense?

Does my decision making preference work best for me at work?

Motivation

Do I move away from negatives or towards positives?

The curate's wife had soon tired of her husband's obsession with bits of space rock and moon dust, resorting instead to indulgence and a life of luxury. She had been born into a life of abject poverty, the daughter of a Romanian miner and elder sister of six rowdy siblings. Ever since moving to England she had pursued riches, anything to ensure she never returned to the squalor of her youth. First she educated herself to the highest degree. Next she captured the highest paid job with the greatest promotional potential, and finally she retired, at the age of 33, with an investment portfolio to rival Romania's GDP. To keep her beloved hubby occupied, she acquired 3,000 square metres of central London real estate so he could pursue his hobby.

The curate, who loved his wife as much as his vast inter-planetary collection of space rock, pursued his work with a passion. He had always loved space, the planets, the stars and astronomy. His life's work had been devoted to finding out more about what happens out there and why, and sharing those findings with the rest of mankind. His was the eternal search for answers to the big questions on the big bang and black holes and space/time continuum. The curate is a 'towards' person. The Romanian miner's daughter is an 'away from' person.

Do I move away from failure or towards success? Am I driven by fear or inspired by achievement? Where am I on the scale? Am I primarily moving away from a negative or towards a positive? Although we can be successful using powerful 'away from' motivations, such as with the curate's wife, these can be draining. 'Towards' motivations inspire and propel us forward, giving us momentum, whilst 'away from' motivations can debilitate and lead, in some cases, to ill health.

Earth Change Patterns

Where am I on the scale? Am I more towards or away from? Which would be better for me?

Motive

Am I power, achievement or affiliation oriented?

There are three types of people in the world, thought Gologon, in a moment of rare reflection whilst overcoming space lag. From what he had seen on earth, he reckoned upon three distinct species. There were those with a predilection for 'power'. They were the sort who would thrive on domination, winning at all costs and coming first, no matter what.

There were those who seemed to thrive on 'achievement', upon bettering themselves, on attaining a goal and accomplishing something.

Finally there were those who liked nothing better than the company of others and helping them get along, the 'affiliation' types. They loved to help others and work for the team.

Gologon, who had eaten several species during his time in the Galaxy, knew introverted and extroverted aliens inside out and liked nothing better than to categorise conquered races. He noticed earthlings, separate to other planetary inhabitants, had a further motivation. They were either 'towards' or 'away' from. So aggressive 'power' humanoids either lived in fear of being dominated or bullied, or delighted in dominating or bullying. Same for 'achievement' sorts. They either worried about not accomplishing enough or were driven to achieve more in light of further gains. The 'affiliation' types either dreaded being on their own or delighted in the company of others.

If he were to be a human, Gologon mused, he wondered which he would be. Despite being as gregarious and likeable an inter galactic traveller as one would hope to meet, Gologon tended to conquer, mutilate and dance upon the corpses of his decapitated foes. A complex soul. He decides he is something of a 'power' type. Being that he would be forced to have each of his 27 ears shredded through the thrashing mill of his own lethal teeth if he failed to deliver a head from every summer holiday, he determines that he must be 'power, away'.

Do I like to eat my colleagues or befriend them? Am I scared of being eaten or thrive to be liked? What inspires me? Accomplishment or winning? Being part of a team or succeeding on my own?

Is it working for me?

Activity

Do I live in the moment or plan for the future?

The space time continuum processing plant on Delta 9 had 3,600 employees. Harry knew them all by name. He had a simple method for remembering each one. He numbered them. Number 636, Zulog the Zulog, is in charge of Sector 10, the forced repatriation detention centre. Number 2,345, Gologon the Nogolog, is the trans-universal over-ruler in general. Or the top dog, as Harry likes to refer to him.

Harry had loved models since early childhood, having spent hundreds of hours fashioning shapes from clay and plasticine and shown infinite patience painting each one to his own level of perfection. He had carried this pastime into adulthood and continues to spend as much free time as possible adding to his impressive collection of figurines. Since working at the Museum of Inter Galactic Artefacts he had begun to fashion alien miniatures and created another dimension. Such was his immersion in the other world of modelling that he could not recall if Zulog the Zulog and Gologon the Nogolog had been created first and resembled the fancy dress wearing intruders at the museum, or visa versa.

The only downside was that Harry would often be late for work, or appointments, or meetings with friends. In fact Harry would normally be late. Friends and colleagues would be so used to Harry's irregular timekeeping that they would expect him to be late. What infuriated them more was that Harry never seemed to mind. He gave a half-hearted apology and continued on, apparently blissfully unaware of the disruption his lateness often caused. The head of security, whilst being a keen admirer of Harry's skilled manufacturer of tiny sculptures, had given him several warnings for poor time-keeping. The head of security had become so exasperated that he had spoken to the curate about cancelling Harry's special exhibition at the museum.

The curate, who knew a thing or two about living in the moment, waved the complaint away. The quality of the exhibition was what mattered. And Harry had produced a wonderful alien display, formed entirely of meteor rock.

Do I live in the moment? Do I become so involved in what I am doing that time seems to slip away? Am I constantly late for meetings, work, appointments? Or do I plan ahead, make sure everything is according to schedule? Am I 'in time', that is living in the moment, or 'through time', that is planning ahead? Which end of the scale do I slide towards, in the context of work?

Is it working for me?

Organisation

Do I need to do this or do I want to?

The Miniature Alien Exhibition at the Museum of Inter Galactic Artefacts was almost a sell-out. The head of security overcame his frustration at Harry turning up late to his own exhibition by sharing his annoyance with the curate's wife, who did not want to be there in the first place. She felt she had to come to support her husband. The head of security confided that he had to attend otherwise her husband would sack him.

The curate had been looking forward to the exhibition for weeks and was particularly excited about how life-like, or alien-like, Harry had made the models look. Especially as they had been sculpted from space rock that could have come from a galaxy far, far away.

Gologon the Nogolog really had not wanted to come along at all and resented having to stand still like a piece of space blob whilst a bunch of freakish aliens gawped over his shrunken appearance. He had wanted to go skinny dipping in the Volta Veta Volcano but Zugon the Zugon had been so excited about returning to earth and observing the funny people that he had relented. Especially when she informed him that he could pretend to be the trans-universal over-ruler in general. Or "top dog" as Zugon had put it. Now that he was here, he had an over-riding urge to return home for his Friday night skinny dipping spree. Zugon told him to hush up and stand still. "I can't move, I'm a pile of clay," he hissed back angrily.

'If this is earth, I'm off', he thought. Zugon stepped inside his mind and told him to stop moaning and pretend he is back home. Gologon accepted the advice and switched dimensions using simultaneous thought processing transposition. 'Thanks', he transmitted from three million light years away.

'Fine, just remember to put the rubbish out would you?'

'It never stops,' he thought.

'What doesn't?' she enquired.

'Oh nothing…'

Harry awoke later that night with a start, heart racing and drenched in sweat. His latest falling dream was into a volcano…

Do I want to do what I do or do I have to do it? Do I feel compelled to act or desire to do something? Do I do things from compulsion or enjoyment?

Is it working?

Back on Earth

It can be invigorating to take a tiny detour around the contours of our mind. What are we if we are not capable of simultaneous thought processing transposition?

So what does it all mean? Nothing in isolation. Everything in context.

Take a situation at work. It could be a project that is proving tiresome. A colleague that is hard to get along with. A client who always says "no". A boss who bullies or an employee who harasses. Whatever it is, large or small, take a close look at how we are in that situation. Take a look at ourselves as if we were an alien trying to understand how we do what we do.

What is our top value in that context? What is most relevant?

Take the value and put it into that situation. When we are living that value, in that context, what are we doing?

In that particular situation are we 'towards' or 'away'? Are we 'sameness' or 'difference'? Are we 'power', 'achievement' or 'affiliation'? Are we 'through time' or 'in time'? Are we 'global' or 'specific'? Go through the list.

Now, which two or three jump out at us? Which would the alien perceive as being the most relevant? Which seem to be most extreme?

If each of these patterns is a sliding scale, figuratively speaking, slide a finger from one end of the scale towards the opposite. If we are 'away from', go 'towards'. If we are 'global', go towards 'specific'. If we are 'internal' frame of reference go towards 'external'.

We can then go into the workplace, wherever that may be, and apply the differences.

Watch, listen, feel and record what happens.

The strange inhabitants of earth may begin to appear different, yet strangely familiar.

If this all sounds a little far-fetched then here is a practical guide to changing Change Patterns!

Changing Change Patterns

1. Identify the Change Pattern that needs changing in which context and for what reason.
2. Identify the preferred Change Pattern in whichever context and detail exactly how it needs to run.

Earth Change Patterns

3. Associate into the new Change Pattern. Imagine using that Change Pattern in a specific context. From Chapter 7, use the appropriate Storage Patterns to re-enforce that change. Notice how it feels, sounds and looks.

4. Check that it works. Look at the changes made from another perspective, looking through the eyes of a colleague, friend or family member. Make sure that these changes fit with values and beliefs. Check the ecology. How does it impact other areas of life, the people around? Ensure that any changes are congruently desirable. If there are any problems, go back and begin the process again, ensuring that every change is desirable.

5. Practice running through the new Change Pattern in your imagination in the context in which it will be used. Re-run this change until it becomes familiar. Install the new Change Pattern for a specific period, perhaps a day or two. Check how it runs, on how it impacts every area of life. If it works well continue to run the Change Pattern in the appropriate context.

'What are we if we are not capable of simultaneous thought processing transposition?'

*The nine change patterns described here are taken from the book 'People Pattern Power' by Marilyne Woodsmall and Wyatt Woodsmall, published by Next Step Press. Visit: www.inlpta.com

Chapter 7

Earth Storage Patterns

'There is no reason why these slide shows, home movies or full-length feature films can not be edited, re-crafted and re-shot to create our very own masterpiece'

The warehouse is vast. It is inconceivably large. Row upon row upon row of pallets stretching for as far as the eye can see, stacked as high as sky scrapers, split by aisles as wide as highways, each running for miles and miles. Each of the millions upon millions of pallets is stacked high with boxes, and each box has a different label, and each label has a sub-heading.

The nearest box on the nearest pallet is labelled, 'the last thing you said'. The sub-heading reads, 'to yourself'. The label on the box on top of the next pallet along reads, 'the last thing you saw', with a sub-heading which reads, 'with your glasses on'. A few pallets along there is a box with a label reach reads, 'the last thing you did', with a sub-heading, 'to your best friend'.

A golf buggy sits nearby. We take the golf buggy and drive down one of the aisles. The boxes and pallets become a blur as the golf buggy zooms along. Twenty minutes later we stop and read the label on one of the boxes. It reads, 'yesterday'. The sub-heading reads, 'last thought before sleep'.

Welcome to the memory bank of our brain.

It is interesting that the boxes and pallets and rows are perfectly symmetrical. It seems the architect of our brain also designed the street layout for New York City. Fortunately there is less traffic. Strangely though, a yellow cab pulls up and we hop in the back. Two hours of erratic driving and excuses about getting lost "somewhere during your surprise birthday party" we arrive at a four-way junction. A street sign reads 'values central square', with others pointing in different directions. 'Values avenue', 'core values plaza', 'values high street' and 'values way' denote the contents of each row. A forklift truck is parked along 'core values plaza' and is depositing a pallet in the aisle.

We walk over and observe the label on the box. 'Value # 1', with the sub-heading 'play'. As with most of the other boxes we have seen, it appears to be well wrapped and previously unopened. As we touch the box it opens of its own accord. As soon as we do so, symmetry and order disappear to be replaced by a swirling vortex of sound, pictures and feelings and we are instantly sucked in.

Welcome to the storage pattern of our play value.

Show Time

As we think of play, of enjoying activities, whether social, sporting, whatever we do for recreation, there is a value pertinent to that. It may be 'hobbies',

Earth Storage Patterns 53

or 'harmony', or 'friends', or something less obvious such as 'wealth' even, or 'power'. Who knows? Whatever it is for each of us, that is perfectly fine. The representation of that value can be an event, perhaps from childhood, or it can be a feeling connected with a holiday, or doing something enjoyable. Perhaps a recent recollection of participating in a game that had everything associated with that value.

As we imagine whatever that representation is, begin to pay attention to the detail. What does it look like? Who is in the picture? What are they doing? Are you in the picture? Are you associated, looking through your own eyes at what is happening, or dissociated, seeing yourself in the picture? Is it moving or is it still like a photograph? What are the colours? Is there any contrast? Is the picture or movie three dimensional? Is it bright or dim, near or far? Is it in focus or is it hazy? What angle are you viewing it from? Is it large or small? Where is it located in your spatial awareness, to your left or right, up or down?

Begin to notice if there are any sounds associated with the picture or movie. Where are they located? From which direction are they coming? Are they inside your head or outside? Is it the sound of voices or music? Are the sounds loud or soft? Notice the variations. What is the tone, the duration, the pitch?

Are there any smells associated with the picture? Are there any tastes?

What are the feelings associated with the image? Where are the feelings located? In your head, chest, stomach, arms etc? What is the size of these feelings? What is the shape, the intensity? Are they heavy or light? Do they move around your body? Are they warm or hot? Do they vibrate?

Having noted all these things, we have described how we store our memories, our associations with particular values. The subtle differences make all the difference. Otherwise each box would contain the same things and be of little consequence. Because there are subtle differences contained within each box, we can differentiate our subjective interpretation of life. Otherwise we would be automatons, robots. These subtle variations make us who we are and how we are.

Up Close and Personal

Put the associations with that value away in the box again for a moment. Pick up the box and step outside the warehouse. Now place the box in front of the huge cinema screen that has suddenly appeared in front of us. The box opens itself up and we see the value right in front of us, played out on the screen.

Here is where the process has a similarity for each and every one of us, and these are the key elements. We will either be in the picture, part of it, that is dissociated, or watching through our own eyes, that is associated. If we are associated, we tend to be living in the moment, in touch with our feelings. If we are dissociated, that tends to mean we are slightly more detached and less emotional. That is because we are watching ourselves, therefore not in our own bodies. If we are in our own bodies we can be emotionally involved. As we watch the movie or picture on screen, if we are associated then we are probably feeling more emotionally attached to the proceedings.

Now notice where the picture is on the cinema screen. Location, our spatial awareness, is very important. It is essential to where we store things. Are we looking up at the screen, or down? Is the image in the top left, or bottom right? Is it far away or right in front of us?

How we store this event is key to how we are. If it is an unpleasant event and we are associated, it may be helpful to dissociate and watch ourselves in the picture. If it is a pleasant event and we were previously dissociated, it will help attach ourselves to the emotion of the occasion by being associated.

In the context of 'play' this value may not be working for us. At present being 'caring' for example does not seem to be having the desired effect that it used to. We could do one of two things. Change the value for something that could work, or alter how we store the 'caring' value to replicate how we store a value that works in another context.

For example, 'honesty' may work for us when we are at 'rest'. Pop over to the warehouse, jump into the yellow cab, or maybe drive the golf buggy, to pick up the box that is labelled 'honesty' with a sub-heading, 'play'. (We never have to search hard to find these boxes, they always seem to be right in front of us as soon as we hop out of whatever mode of transport we use).

Take the box and place it in front of the cinema screen and let the events play out. Notice the distinctions from the previous 'caring' value, especially the distinctions on being either dissociated or associated, and also pay close attention to the angle, and the size and location of the picture or movie. Notice anything else that is particularly different. Once we have run through the event, picking up all the pictures, sounds and feelings that are important, we can pop it back into the box, drop it back into the warehouse, pick up the 'caring' box and bring it back to the cinema.

We open the 'caring' box again, but this time, we shift those distinctions to how they were for the 'honesty' picture or movie. So if it was near for 'honesty' but far away for 'caring', we can bring it up close. If it was associated for 'honesty', but dissociated for 'caring', we can switch.

In essence, we are transferring the distinctions of what works for one value over to what is not working for another value. Alternatively, we can replace one value that works in one context, and use it in another context where we are not being successful.

Earth Storage Patterns   55

Why is all this important? It is how we operate. How we store things, the subtle distinctions underlie how we approach things in life.

How can adjusting the distinctions of what I see, hear and feel make such a difference? That is too simplistic, surely.

Yes. Take away the vast storage system of the brain and the infinite complexity and variation that each of us places on every single event and we can reduce it to the simple world of our senses. We see, hear, feel, touch, and smell everything. That is how we construct how we are and the subtle variations of how we store and utilise these sensory experiences is how we shape our lives. If we want to re-shape our lives, we reshape the sensory storage system. As simple as that.

Pump Up the Volume

The cinema screen has a use. Now that we have elicited what works for us, we can improve the distinctions further. So if something works well, why not make it work better? Can we do that? Is it not artificial?

As stated in Chapter 2, our version of our events is twice removed from reality. That is, the first time we experience something, we see it entirely differently from other people. The events are distorted, generalised and deleted by our experiences, language, change patterns, plus time, space and energy. We then put the boxes away in the storage warehouse of our brains. When we open the boxes again they are further distorted, generalised and deleted by our subsequent experiences which serve to change our language etc. So our models or maps of the world are twice removed from reality.

The memories and recollections that we currently have are no more 'real' than a Disney cartoon – they are our versions of reality. Therefore, there is no reason why these slide shows, home movies or full-length feature films can not be edited, re-crafted and re-shot to create our very own masterpiece. Or more simply, we can turn up the volume and make the representation as satisfyingly compelling as we require.

So if we take a value that is known to work for us and is already proving positive in the context of 'play' for example, we can add to the distinctions to provide a truly compelling image.

Look at the visual aspects. The colours, the angles, the focus and so forth. Now we can turn these up, increase the brightness, bring out the positive aspects. We can increase the size until it is huge and bright and powerful. Likewise, any sounds that are important can be amplified. If there is any background music that could be inspirational, we can turn that up until it is booming, pulsing through our bodies. Any laughter, any encouraging sounds can be amplified until it resonates powerfully. Finally, we can increase any feelings that are associated.

Pump up the feelings until they are as large, or fluid, or as hot as we prefer. Really associate in the moment, feel the feelings of being totally empowered and inspired and see and hear everything that compels us towards that destination and hold that moment, clearly in our minds.

When the feelings and sounds and images are at their most powerful, place them in the box and place the box in the warehouse of our mind, right near the entrance, so we can reach out and touch them at any moment. In fact, in that context it can be automatically accessed every time we enter the situation.

Try this. Place the common picture that comes up every time we enter a particular situation. For 'play' it may be a picture of friends in a café. At the bottom left hand corner of the screen place the new, powerful value as a tiny dot, bursting with energy. This time, dissociate and see ourself in the picture.

In a moment the dot will explode big and bright across the common picture in a trajectory of bottom left to top right of the screen, obliterating the common picture and covering the screen with the big, bright, visually compelling value.

Do it quickly and clear the screen after each explosion, bringing the common picture back and pushing the big, bright compelling value back into the dot. Repeat over and over again and see how compelling that future becomes.

Back in the vast warehouse, near the entrance, workers are busy constructing a new gantry and piles of boxes are scattered ready to be loaded onto the pallets. These boxes are without labels and sub-headings. A marker pen lies on the ground. A yellow cab pulls up.

"Going anywhere?" the cabby asks.

"Yeah. First, can you pick up a box for me?"

"Sure. Which one?"

"Mmm. So many to choose from…"

"Can I make a suggestion."

"Sure… What's that? I didn't quite catch what you said."

"I said, you already know what you need to know. I'll help you find what you need to remember…"

'We already know what we need to know. We only need to know how to remember what we need to remember'

Chapter 8

Earth Strategy Patterns

'If you go down to the woods today...'

Lying there sleeping. Dreaming of the fairies. Deeply unaware of the dawning day. A world away from waking matters and morning freshness. Down there, laying low and hiding out, hibernating the night away. Grumpy little grizzlies, every one of us.

When the light grows brighter and the alarm starts shouting, we lean over, hit the 'sleep' button and enter that light sleep mode, gently preparing ourselves for full re-entry into everyday existence.

The descent is gradual as we acclimatise our senses to the harsh reality of consciousness. "Would passengers please fasten their seat belts as we begin our initial descent for landing."

We are drowsy, barely aware that the alarm is yelling again, and as we have turned away to hide from the nasty tempered device we have to flip back over, shooting out a lazy arm to wallop it silent again. "Could you please fasten your seat belt," a caring steward demands, wincing from the side swipe.

An even shorter time later the irrepressible irritant hollers again, like a spoilt brat needing attention, and we thump it into submission. "Crew cross check and take positions for landing."

By now we have begun to realise that the electronic shock therapy has well and truly broken our resistance and we raise our weary bodies to face the washing/awakening ritual marking our official arrival to the day. "Business or pleasure?" the passport control officer enquires. "Bit of both, with any luck," we remark before flossing.

Such a process is typical for most of us (apart from passport control). There are those who will, when they feel the first streams of sunlight touch their exposed skin, leap to attention like a doe sensing a lion, and rush head-long into the day. All they hear is, 'thank you for flying 'rapid arrival airlines', have a safe onward journey'. They do not stop at customs and are out of the house, wrestling with their jacket, toast crust between their teeth, whilst we are still placing our seat into the upright position.

There are others who are at 35,000 feet, windows up, seat reclined, blindfold in place, snoring and dribbling to their heart's content long after everyone else has disembarked. They heard the captain, were prodded awake by the stewardess, had even been shouted at by the screeching brat of an alarm clock, yet still could not muster enough energy to rise. These are the hardened grizzlies.

Naïve tourists are walking around national parks with dismembered limbs tucked in their rucksacks having approached these cuddly looking creatures. Do not be fooled. They can be extremely vicious. Especially at high altitude and strapped into economy class seats.

Waking Patterns

John hears the alarm clock. He says to himself that he must get up, in a few minutes. He sees the breakfast he is going to have, the butter and toast and marmalade and begins to feel a warm, pleasant sensation.

Jo hears the alarm clock. She hears a high, shrill siren. It is the only sound, she has found, that wakes her up. She has an instant picture of the clock face and can hear voices telling her to get up. The voices sound like her boss, or is it her mother? She feels dog tired and worries that she has not had enough sleep.

Malcolm wakes just before the alarm goes off. (This is a very big bed by the way). He sees the audience at today's performance, happy, smiling faces peering up at him. He hears their applause and cheers. He feels the excitement of a child and, checking that it is not too early, flings the bed sheets aside and rises.

Jo, dreaming that she is being mauled by a bear, goes to thump him.

John's pattern is auditory external, auditory internal, visual external and kinaesthetic internal. That is he hears a sound, speaks to himself, sees a picture and feels good about it.

Jo's pattern is auditory external, visual external, auditory internal tonal and kinaesthetic. A similar pattern but with drastically different results.

Malcolm is visual internal (that is he is creating the picture not recalling it as the others had), auditory internal and kinaesthetic.

As described in Chapter 3, we have strategies for virtually everything we do. However, there are five broad strategies that tend to cover most things. These are:

Memory – this comes from our Decision pattern in our Change Patterns, that is our primary representation system. Looking right, sounding right, feeling right, or making sense.

Convincer – this is our reality strategy, how we know or believe things to be true.

Decision – this is the criteria we follow for deciding to do what we do.

Motivation – this is the impetus we need to act. It always comes from a synesthesia. That is connecting two sensory pieces of information together, usually seeing and feeling, or hearing and feeling.

Earth Strategy Patterns

Learning – here the above strategies often come together so we can undertake a particular function.

The model of our strategy is known as a TOTE. That is test, operate, test, exit.

The first 'test' activates the strategy. It is the start point that lets us know when we should make the decision, or motivate ourselves. It is also the criteria, that is the evidence we need to let us know we can achieve our outcome. Without this we can keep on looping and never exit.

The 'operate' part is the things we do to achieve our outcome. That is, make a picture, hear a sound, feel a certain way etc. The more operational sequences, the more flexible we are and the more likely we are to achieve the results we want. Unsatisfactory strategies tend to be short ones.

The second 'test' lets us know if we are nearer to achieving our outcome. It is the evaluation of where we are and uses the criteria presented by the first test.

'Exit' occurs just before external action takes place. That is the last step that gives us the go-ahead to make the decision, or be motivated, or whatever else it is we are wanting to do. It basically lets us know if the 'test' has been satisfactory. If not, if the criteria set by the original 'test' did not match up, we will loop around again.

A part of the criteria for people who tend to sleep in a lot will be that they have not had enough sleep, they feel tired. Re-tuning the internal voice and logical/auditory digital messaging service and the sleeper may be able to 'exit' much easier. Otherwise they will keep looping and keep sleeping.

Ecology Check

The following strategy relates to the context of 'rest'. What we will do now as an example is apply a value that works in one area, elicit the distinctions, or sub modalities, using earlier Storage Pattern techniques (Chapter 7), and apply to a strategy that does not work in the context of 'rest'.

Jo's unsuccessful waking strategy is doing her no favours at all. This might be fine if she does not have any problems. She may enjoy sleeping in and can accommodate this around the rest of her life. On the other hand, it may be causing her no end of problems. She may wish to change it.

Right away, there are more alarm bells ringing, of a different kind. What if she has a medical condition? OK, she goes to the doctor. The doctor can see that nothing is medically wrong with her. The doctor prescribes sleeping tablets. Jo takes these for a number of years. The sleeping tablets have a side effect.

She is drowsy at work. She returns to another doctor. The doctor says there is nothing intrinsically 'wrong' with her. It is her body clock. He recommends therapy... and so on.

Checking the ecology, that is looking at what will happen elsewhere if we change one small thing, is a necessity. MindFrame Patterns calls for an ecology check on every change, however small.

Apart from the medical aspect, there also needs to be consideration of what will happen if Jo can begin to awaken more 'normally', that is not sleep in beyond her designated wake-up call. Would she become more industrious, thus going against a value that contrasts with one she holds highly, such as 'relaxation' for example.

Or is there a secondary gain that arises from having the problem continue? That is, some form of benefit that occurs unconsciously which necessitates the continuation of the condition. This could be sleeping in means she does not have to travel through rush hour traffic. It may not be as obvious as that, but secondary gain is commonplace because we may try every conscious way we know to stop doing something, or do something different, but can not overcome it. This is because there is great benefit occurring out of our conscious awareness. Becoming aware of that secondary gain may cause the problem to disappear altogether.

Given that Jo does not have any secondary gain and has checked thoroughly (see Chapter 2, Keys to an Achievable Outcome) that she will only prosper from waking when she wants, she can install another strategy.

Running A Strategy Pattern

So Jo hears the alarm clock. She hears a high, shrill siren. It is the only sound, she has found, that wakes her up. She has an instant picture of the clock face and can hear voices telling her to get up. The voices sound like her boss, or is it her mother? She feels dog tired and worries that she has not had enough sleep.

To recap, Jo's pattern is auditory external, visual external, auditory internal tonal and kinaesthetic.

When Jo is wide awake and 'buzzing', on the top of her form, she sings a lot. She also paints and sees lots of bright colours. However, in the process of waking Jo tends to see only greys and dull colours and all she hears is the nagging voice of her mother, a hangover from childhood when she would be moaned at to get out of bed for school.

Instead of hearing the alarm and picturing the clock face and hearing that nagging voice, Jo can replace parts of the sequence. As soon as she hears the

Earth Strategy Patterns 61

bleeping, it can activate a cacophony of pleasant sounds that she associates with her favourite music. In turn that can activate a mixture of primary colours that can create a rainbow effect. The internal voice can then be re-tuned. Perhaps she can recite to herself over and over again reassuring words which can inspire her, or she can even hear them as a song. "It's gonna be a lovely day, a lovely day, a lovely, lovely, lovely day…" or something heavier if she prefers. A bit of Mahler or Wagner. Or Black Sabbath. Whatever tickles her fancy.

The strategy is more likely to be effective if the distinctions or the sub modalities of the Storage Pattern value are used. That is the colours, textures, feelings, sounds are intensified and applied to the waking strategy.

How does it work in practice?

Jo will run through the strategy repeatedly until all the steps are drilled in. That may take ten, twenty or even thirty rehearsals, but in real time, will only take a few minutes. Once the drill is in place a new pattern has been established. The brain will accept that as real. It will follow that pattern the next time the alarm sounds. How? Because Jo has re-programmed her mind to respond the way she wants. Remember, the brain is a self-patterning system. It can not differentiate between what is real and what is highly imagined. What is real anyway, we might ask?

In addition, Jo may wish to move her eyes in the direction which corresponds with each part of the strategy. That is because when we move our eyes in a particular direction, we are accessing the part of the brain that deals with that function. So looking down to our right accesses our emotional feelings. Up to the left accesses visual recall, that is pictures we remember. Up and to the right is visual construct, or pictures we create. Middle right is sounds we construct and middle left is sounds we remember. Finally, bottom left is auditory digital, that is lists, logic and sense.

As Jo pictures the colours of the rainbow, she can look to the top left, which would place them in the visual remembered part of her brain.

Using Storage Patterns in combination with Strategy Patterns makes them more powerful. So Jo may wish to use the cinema screen from Chapter 7, and repeatedly switch the picture of the alarm with a desirable picture of herself, in full flow, 'buzzing'.

Our Strategy Patterns are not easy to self-decipher. What we can do is look at particular contexts where we are not doing something to our satisfaction. For example, we could be slow in reaching a decision under the 'social' context.

We can then analyse the steps we take to reach that decision. Further, useful steps can be added, using the distinctions or sub modalities from a strong value Storage Pattern.

Go through the upgraded steps repeatedly, until it becomes natural. Remember, if any part of the sequence does not feel bright enough, or loud enough, or inspiring enough, enter into that Storage Pattern and re-tune. We are each our own internal Grand Designer, or Great Director. If we don't like the rushes, we can ditch them until we create the masterpiece we desire.

If this sounds, or feels, or looks complicated, re-wind a moment. It is merely a sequence of looking, sounding, sensing and feeling, not necessarily in that order. Within those looks, sounds and feelings there are distinctions. These are the shades, the gradients we apply to what we see, hear and feel. Simple as that.

If a strategy or sequence is not working, we can adapt it to make sure it does. Using core values that work, eliciting the distinctions within the Storage Patterns, and applying these to a Strategy Pattern, is remarkably effective.

Reading this book in sequence will ensure we have all the steps we need to get the outcome we desire. If we can see, hear and feel, we've pretty much got it nailed.

"Ladies and gentlemen, for those of you seated on the right hand side of the plane, if you look out of your window you will be able to see the Great Wall of China. Please do not move if you are on the left hand side of the plane, as you will be able to see it in a few short moments. Mrs Delecoat, I believe you would like to get up for work in a few moments.

"If you'd just like to sit back and relax we'll play the music from Gone with the Wind. I know it's a favourite of yours. Also, if you don't mind, Clark Gable will take over from here.

Clark: "Ladies and gentlemen, we will be preparing to land in a few moments..." [the score to *Gone With The Wind* sounds loudly over the speaker] "... and Mrs Delecoat, by God I do give a damn... I give a damn about you... [music builds to a crescendo] and now I'm going to hand over to the Four Tops..."

> *'If we can see, hear and feel, we've pretty much got it nailed'*

Chapter 9

Internal Process, Water

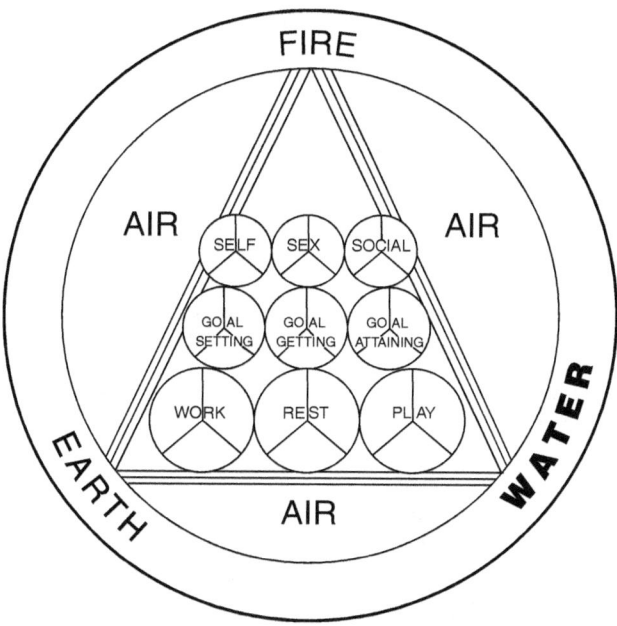

'Whether you believe you absolutely can or you absolutely can't, you're absolutely right...'

And then the rains came. The skies opened up. The clouds collided and the water came gushing down. A seamless torrent of pelting drops bouncing off the hardened soil until it cracked and opened. And the rains kept coming.

The water spread its searching fingers into every hole and divot, squirmed its way into the ground and when there was nowhere else to plummet, it ran along the earth, pooling its resources like an army massing for attack. The liquid platoons scavenged and plundered every socket of earth, running down hillsides into valleys and rivers, filling lakes and meres. And finally, when the skies cleared and the rains stopped, the earth lay swollen and molested, beaten by the avenging elements. Bloated and bedraggled the earth began to freshen as the waters lapsed and the soils dried. The new landscape brought fresh fruits, bright flowers and buzzing insects and birds. The land had been born anew.

Memories of sweeping floods and drowned earth were soon replaced by famished plants and scorched soil. How quickly land forgets. And all too soon the skies darken again, the winds harden and the clouds swell with their heavy load. And the rains return...

The fresh floods search out their old stomping ground and fill every crack and gap they can, filing along old channels and gullets. And every time the rains come anew, they search for more, always prying and fishing for new ground, new lands to conquer. And sometimes they succeed. Cutting through fresh earth, finding easier, more convenient paths, hurtling down slicker channels. Old routes are continuously re-established and up-graded, whilst new avenues are explored and acquired. Such is the water cycle.

The farmer with the thirsty crops believes rain is a good thing.

The Philippine villagers, vulnerable to landslides, believe sudden downpours are a bad thing.

Sudanese refugees believe sustained rainfall is their lifeline. It's a good thing.

Mississippi delta inhabitants believe sustained rain threatens their livelihood. Heavy rain is bad.

Trisha believes rain is bad because it always ruins her hair.

Alan has no hair and quite likes the feeling of raindrops bouncing off his head.

None of those people are wrong. In their environment it is perfectly understandable to believe one thing or the other. In a different environment such a belief may be inappropriate. If Alan had Trisha's hair he would probably never go out in the rain. Or any other time, come to that.

What each have in common is that their experience of their environment has shaped their belief about water.

Water is movement, process, change. It sculpts us and shapes us, guides us in the direction we take. It is not definitive. It is ever-changing. It can not be defined, stacked in a pile and made to stay in place. Like us, it constantly moves, shifts, spreads, changes shape and if left unchecked, can run amok.

What else is water?

'In our own internal vista we can go dancing naked in the rain anytime we want'

Lifeblood

It is our life blood. We need it to survive. We imbue it and it fuels our bodies, provides us with energy. We do not become it because we imbibe it. Just like we do not become wine if we like to drink wine. We do become wine if we like to drink too much wine. Then it really does become us.

Because, as human beings, we are fluid, flexible creatures, just because we take one thing, do one thing, act in one way, that does not define us. Unless we choose to let it. If we clam up during a school concert at four years of age, that does not make us shy, or embarrassed or nervous. Yet it can if we take hold of that mantle and allow it to settle around us.

"Ah, look at her, isn't she shy?"

"Aren't you shy?"

"Isn't she just?"

"A little shy thing, she is."

"Aw, cutesy little shy thing."

"Aren't you just?"

"Isn't she just?"

"Aren't I just?"

"Sure I am. Cutesy, shy little thing."

There we have it. Shaped for life. If we let it.

"He's harsh."

"Isn't he just?"

"Just like his father."

"Just like his father. Harsh."

"Harsh like his father."

"Harsh in a good way, mum?"

"Harsh in a harsh way. Just like your father."

"Harsh you say? Harsh it is then. Just like my father."

"You're too soft."

"Oh, I know, a real teddy bear."

"I wish you'd harden up."

"You should have seen me when I was younger."

"You weren't always soft?"

"Hell no. I used to be harsh. Just like my father."

"I'd like to see that."

"I can do it if you want."

"I can't imagine it."

"You can't imagine me being soft and harsh?"

"Nah."

Of course, she could imagine it. If she tried. Saying that she could not imagine it, does not mean it could not be true. It means that at that moment in time, she believes that she can not do something. Just because we say we can do something, does not mean we immediately can. Likewise, just because we say we can't do something, doesn't necessarily mean we can never do it. However, these sayings become our beliefs, and our beliefs become steadfast and we create our belief system based upon, well, based upon bits of information that we mould together to form what we think is right at the time. Later on, it may need upgrading, or disbanding altogether.

So what has this got to do with water?

If we keep travelling along the same tributaries, streams and rivers we will eventually get to the same sea along the same route, doing the same things.

If we take a different route, start another tributary, we can journey in a thousand different directions and end up in a thousand different destinations. We may even end up in the same sea, but at least the scenery is different.

Our beliefs are the tributaries and streams and rivers that channel us to get to where we want to go. They guide us, provide the momentum to get us where we want. And the beautiful thing is, they are neither true nor false. Not any of them. Not a single one.

If we have a limiting belief, that is a belief that holds us back, or is no longer useful, we can change it. In fact, seeing as it is almost impossible not to have beliefs, we might as well make the beliefs we have as empowering as possible.

Within the confines of reality that is. "I am superman," is not a very empowering belief to have if we think we have x-ray eyes. It could be empowering if we are about to jump out of an aeroplane and strike a pose for the cameras (so long as all the safety arrangements are in place). Being superman is neither true nor false. It is the interpretation we bring to it. The literal comic-book character is not false. He's a cartoon character. Very real in that respect. The skills that he has are not necessarily false either. We can all fly (with the aid of technology). We can all see through walls (with the aid of technology). And we can all wear our underpants on the outside (with the aid of super-human daring-do).

In short, we can believe in whatever we want, as long as it does not do ourselves or any other person any harm. "I believe I can fly" is the sanest thing in the world to say, in this age of aviation. Believing I can fly without the aid of transport is dangerous. Or is it? If we were to let our imaginations free and fly high above ourselves, looking down, and then move around, high above the house where we live and float out across the country, we are flying, are we not?

Almost every belief we hold can be put under such scrutiny and we can come away holding that it is neither true nor false. It can become true if we plot, plan and detail the journey we need to take to ensure it comes true. We control the possibility of a belief becoming true. 'If you believe you absolutely can, or if you believe you absolutely can't, you're absolutely right'.

Think about the language we use all the time.

"I couldn't do that."

"That's not me."

"If only I could…"

"I don't like 'x'"

"It's not my sort of thing…"

"If I were ten years younger…"

"I'm too old to learn new tricks."

"I'm too young to be doing that…"

The list goes on.

Because we drink the wine does not mean to say we are the wine. We can taste the wine, appreciate the wine. Notice the delicate flavours. Educate our palette to enjoy the sensations of a high quality vintage. We can add to our knowledge. Furnish our understanding.

We can begin to believe that we can learn more about subjects we are interested in. The first time a learner picks up a guitar he might not believe that he will be as good as Eric Clapton, but a couple of years later, after many lessons and hundreds of hours practice, he may believe he is capable of something special. Our beliefs change like the changing seasons. Some we choose to discard as being no longer relevant. Some we choose to carry with us throughout our lives, taken from our earliest remembrances.

"It's good to work."

"Family comes first."

"All you need is love."

"All you need is good health."

"I'm incomplete without a man."

"I don't need a man to make me happy."

"Only the love of a good woman can make me happy."

"Fish. All I need is fish."

And so on.

If fish works then fish is fine. The fish at the bottom of the fish tank thinks a lot about how he would live his life again, if he could live it over again. He likes the shipwreck. And the different species which keep appearing and he keeps eating. He likes the abundance of food. He even likes the huge creature with the massive eyes which drops the food into the water. There is not much to dislike. The view's fairly repetitive and there is not too many places to visit. Procreation is tough at times. Overall though, if he had to change one thing, fresh water would be nice.

The difference between us and the fish is that we can change the water any time we want.

What do I believe now? What could I believe differently to improve my life? What could I drop altogether? What would be of use to believe, that could be of use, right now? Even if it is not true now, what could I begin to believe is true, so that in the process of believing it is true, it could become true, for me?

Rain Dance

Once the rains have stopped and the waters have drained away, we can look at the lie of the land. Our version of reality. Our map of the world.

What does it look like. Which direction does the dried up river bed take? Where are the streams and tributaries that feed the river? How many branches are there? Does the river meander, or change direction, or is it in a straight line? Does it run into a lake or directly into the sea? Of all those beliefs, are any more useful than others? Which ones no longer help us? What is the point in keeping them going?

And then the rains come again. The skies open up. The clouds collide and the water comes gushing down. A seamless torrent of pelting drops bounce off the hardened soil until it cracks and opens. And the rains keep coming. The rains keep coming as we keep thinking...

Rain drops are individual thoughts and decisions. They are governed entirely by our own internal guidance director. The clouds are sectors of our lives: home, work, relationships... and as they clash together we allow our downpour to rain upon us.

Internal Process, Water

In the past it has happened unconsciously, thoughtlessly. It is the way it is. It has always been that way. Yes, we may have changed as we move through life, but what we say, what we think, is us. And more.

We can now govern each thought, guide each decision to point us in the direction we want to go. We can remould those channels, create new pathways to reach our goals. By thinking consciously we open up the unconscious resources to help us get to where we want to go.

The rains will keep coming. The floods will always be there. It is not an external occurrence. It is internal. We own the rains and the land and the streams and the rivers.

It is our map of the world and we can redraw it any time we choose.

In our own internal vista we can go dancing naked in the rain anytime we want. We can create our own spell, our own chants, our own world. We are the artists, the painters, the sculptors. We are the masters of our world. The world we create. The masters of all we survey.

We have that on the fish at least.

'If one person can, so can another'

Chapter 10

Beliefs, Something Inspirational

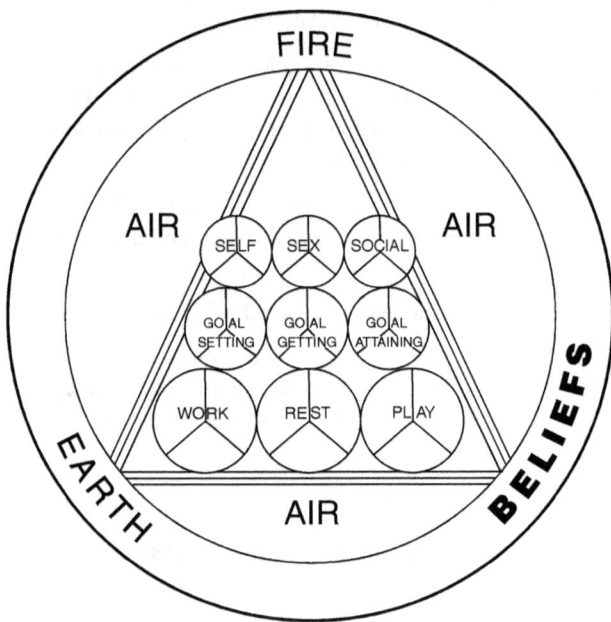

'Beliefs are neither true nor false. They are the rules which guide our lives'

True or False

Beliefs are neither true nor false. They are the rules which guide our lives. We carry them with us like the strength athlete dragging the truck. Some of them can help us. Many hold us back.

There is a health storage depot somewhere in the back of our mind. All sorts of treasures are stored there. Once in a while we take the forklift truck and enter the depot. We choose a few of our favourite things. Inspirational things. We pick up these pallets and load them onto the back of our lorry.

There is anything and everything that can help. Motivation, strength, past honours, honesty, integrity, decency, desire, love, affection, vitality, credibility, conviction, patience, understanding, dreams, concern, charity, magnificence, achievement, winning, succeeding, every positive experience imaginable, every empowering belief we have ever held and some more we have yet to indulge in.

Beliefs, Something Inspirational

Once we load the lorry, we get down from the forklift truck and get in the cab. Somehow, we know how to drive the lorry, which gear to find, and we drive away. The traffic is light because the roads are littered with strength athletes pulling their own trucks. We overtake them and drive into the distance, honking our horns in a friendly, encouraging way as the strength atheletes' biceps threaten to explode.

'The Game of Life it seems is something of a blast, considerably easier than we thought at the start and seriously fun, especially when we take control'

The Game of Life

In the back of the trailer at the bottom of one of the pallets labelled 'priceless goods' is a variety of items. One of the goodies is marked 'games' and, placing the drive mechanism on 'automatic', we drift inside to play a fascinating looking board game called the 'Game of Life'.

Like most games, it is remarkably simple. The object of the game is to win, to get around the rectangle first. The player roles the die, and counts the spaces until they reach the number on the die.

Our players are a ghostly collection of ourselves at various stages in our lives. Although they are quite clearly other-worldly they are non-threatening and the game is played in a spirit of camaraderie, especially towards our six-year-old self who keeps miscounting the squares.

The figurine used to plot our way around the board is a sculpture of our own head, as we are now.

We roll a six. The space is marked 'first set back'. We pick a card from the 'set back' pile. It reads, 'Stay where you are, and miss a go'. The other players land on charitable squares, such as 'have another go', 'give yourself £500' and 'pick a bonus card'. The 'bonus' card pile have all sorts of treats, such as, 'this number ## is the meaning of life'*.

Finally, we roll again and land on the first corner. This states, 'Review where you are now, in words and pictures. Pick up a 'belief' card'. We take stock. The other ghostly players watch us closely, scouring for lies (an untruth leads to a prolonged spell in the dungeon making victory especially hard). Our six-year-old self tries to tickle us to put us off track but mercifully his hand goes straight through our ribcage.

The words and pictures that illustrate our lives have to be accurate. Where am I now? What do I look like? What do I feel like? Where are these feelings located? What does a snapshot of my life, as it is right now, look like?

The 'belief' card instructs, 'What three things do you think you know to be true about yourself that compels you forward? What three things do you think you know to be true about yourself that hold you back?'

The other players roll on and meet similar stumbling blocks. We take our turn and land on an enchanting square. It reads, 'If you could have anything that you wanted to help you get where you want to go, what would it be and what would you have to believe about yourself? Roll again.'

We roll again, a four, which takes us near to the next corner. We land on a square which states, 'What belief is holding you back from getting what you want? If you were to change that belief it would make all the difference. Pick a 'divinity' card.' In turn the 'divinity' card reads, 'Describe what it feels like to be at your best. What do you know to be true about yourself now? What does it look like, sound like, feel like? Where are those pictures, sounds and feelings located?'

On a role, literally, our enthusiasm for the game begins to build. We look at the other players, who seemed to be fading into the background. Competitive ghouls who have lost their edge. We can smell victory. One of our former selves lands on a 'straight to the dungeon' square and, as it is our teenage version, it sighs and begins to sulk. Nevertheless we feel our pulses quicken. It is our turn again.

We roll a two and land on the second corner square. It reads, 'Give yourself everything you want. Pick up a belief card'. The belief card states, 'Now that you have all that you ever wanted or needed, looking back, list the beliefs that helped you get here, in order of importance. What former beliefs proved to be of little value? What beliefs did you have to drop altogether? Which beliefs aligned with your values? What was the most empowering belief?'

With a sense of elation, we play on. We are winning at our own game, as well we should. The shadowy competitors are almost illegible. The game is becoming easier and easier. Every roll of the die seems to add something to our understanding of the game. Even when we pick a 'set back' card it only interrupts our journey rather than stalling it as it had done at first. The momentum is picking up. Those sounds and feelings and pictures are a powerful concoction, something we can not easily put aside. In fact, our senses are peaked. Our awareness is heightened.

We roll again. A three. The square reads, 'Review you life, pick up a 'limiting belief' card'. We pick from the 'limiting belief' pile. The card unravels to reveal a sheet of paper. It states, 'Take all of your empowering beliefs one by one and notice the Storage Patterns for each. Now, take each of your limiting beliefs and switch the Storage Patterns to those of the empowering beliefs. Do it for similar pursuits. A limiting belief may be, 'I can not get a promotion'.

Beliefs, Something Inspirational

An empowering belief may be, 'I am a talented artist capable of high quality work'. Use the Storage Patterns of the talented artist representation and switch the promotion representation to that. [See Chapter 7 – Earth Storage Patterns for information].

'If the limiting belief is one you have carried with you for a while, introduce more steps. Elicit the Storage Patterns for what you no longer want and change them for something that you believe to be no longer true, such as 'I am 14', if you are much older of course. Now elicit the Storage Patterns for something you really want, 'to achieve X'. Now elicit the Storage Patterns you have for something that is definitely true, such as, 'the sun will come up tomorrow'. Change the representations of the thing you really want for the thing that you know is definitely true. Pick up an 'ecology' card.'

The 'ecology' card states, 'Every change must be evaluated in consideration of the system as a whole. Believing something to be true does not make it true, it gives you the impetus to pursue it. Is it worth pursuing for you? What will you get when you have it? What will you not have when you get it? What will you have if you don't get it? What will you not have if you don't get it? Consider every belief in terms of context. Is it realistic? How will it impact the whole?'

Having gone through the procedure and bored the other players into submission, the board is ours. We do not miss our other selves because we know we can use their input whenever we need it in future.

We take the die and roll again. It lands two squares from the end. The square states, 'What am I doing when I'm not doing what I need to be doing to get the result I want?' 'Pardon', we say to ourselves. We read again, 'What am I doing when I'm not doing what I need to be doing to get the result I want?' Phew. We ponder for a while until we know we have digested the question long enough to understand that the answer can arise if we need it in any of the MindFrame contexts.

Underneath, it reads, 'pick a resources card'. The 'resources' card states, 'What one statement of belief sums up everything that I will need to have to achieve what I want to achieve in this context?' Another tough one. Our eyes scan the board and we see the 'help' cards. We rifle through until we find, 'resource statements – examples'.

The first one states, 'I have the strength, drive and determination, combined with a compassion and understanding of colleagues, to eventually achieve my specific and desired outcome of…'

The next reads, 'I have all the energy, commitment, enthusiasm and focus to ensure the house is finished on time. I will ensure this is the case by reviewing my project plan on a daily basis…'

Another states, 'I have the flexibility of behaviour to ensure I achieve 'x' one way or another.'

At this point in the game we can begin to realise how important beliefs can be. Not only for supporting our values, our heart's desires, but also for providing a compelling vision. They are the support structure, the building blocks for getting what we want. Whilst the 'ecology' card should be taken into account with each belief, it is also becoming clearer how useful it is to employ empowering beliefs and drop the limiting ones. If those empowering beliefs are then amplified, adjusted, fine-tuned to display the compelling sounds, pictures and feelings that drive us forward, then we almost have all we need to succeed. The Game of Life it seems is something of a blast, considerably easier than we thought at the start and seriously fun, especially when we take control.

We roll the die again and see the two which puts us on the final square. It reads, 'You win. Pick a 'winners' card. The winner's card states, 'Congratulations, you have done brilliantly so far. You win this game. Move to the next level and start by picking a 'mind expanding belief card', sub category, 'never in my wildest…'

True Lives

We arrive at the hypermarket sooner than we thought and switch from 'automatic' back to 'manual' as if we were going from 'unconscious' to 'conscious'. We reverse up to the loading bay and let the helpers unload the cargo. We get down from the cab and enter the hypermarket.

It is as vast as our storage depot, except every item is on display, twinkling, glistening in the limitless aisles. Every variety of product known to humanity is on the shelves, endlessly attractive and all at a price we can afford. We forego the games aisle which is piled high with a brand new board game called, 'Raising the Stakes' that looks expensive and of very high quality.

The beauty of this shop is that we can reach out and grab any item whenever we want. An announcement is made over the loud speaker in a voice that is instantly recognisable, because it is our own. 'Go for it,' it encourages. And because we own the store, we do not have to pay a penny. Very affordable.

Without thinking we reach out and grasp Something Inspirational and hold it to be true.

> *'Without thinking we reach out and grasp Something Inspirational and hold it to be true'*

* This number has been withheld to protect the innocent.

Chapter 11

Belief Change Patterns

'The five minutes raced by in a second and with soaking wet palms, shaking legs and blurred vision he walked on stage and opened his mouth to speak...'

The audience hushed in keen anticipation. Row upon row of expectant faces peered towards the stage, their bodies crammed together to provide one swaying mass of excitement. Around 120 spectators looked up to the brightly festooned stage, whilst 50 or so more looked down from the balcony circling the auditorium.

The rumblings of delight upon entry, which had reached a crescendo of chattering and occasional laughter, had reduced to a salutary whisper from a mother to an errant child by the time the announcer introduced the first act.

Backstage the players had spread their enthusiasm a little thicker as performance neared and had to be hushed by the assistant director. As the seconds ticked down to the curtain raiser several of the ensemble continued to chatter in nervous staccato, whilst others found themselves a private space and drummed fingers, bit lower lips and mouthed the words they were soon to utter in front of the baying crowd.

One soul, a leading light, took himself a part and sat on a piece of scenery, stared at his shoes and rehearsed his opening line over and over. Once he was content it was down pat he began to run through the previous night's rehearsal, when everything had gone reasonably well, at least from his perspective. The band had missed a few bars and the changeovers had been frantic at best, but nothing drastic, the director had maintained. "Better now than first night," he had repeated so often it became a mantra which the cast began to imitate with glee.

Now, moments before show time he wished he were back then, in the safety of rehearsal and expectation of mistakes and miscues. Everything that went well disappeared in a swirling vortex of self-doubt so that all he could hear was himself stuttering through the first line, even though he had never stuttered in his life. All he could see was the audience shaking their head as one disapproving monster. And all he felt was a mass of nerves, settling deep in his stomach and gradually rising up through his chest, and as it did so, squeezing until he felt unable to breathe properly.

The more he tried to calm down, to breathe deeply, the more images of a baying mob came into his mind. The first line seemed to slip from his memory in an instant. He strained to recollect the first word and as he finally grasped it, he could no longer speak it, even to himself, beyond repeating the first letter.

"Five minutes" the stage hand had announced and his pulse raced, his chest tightened further and a blur of shaking heads overwhelmed his vision.

The five minutes raced by in a second and with soaking wet palms, shaking legs and blurred vision he walked on stage and opened his mouth to speak…

The Best of Times

Thirty years later the auditorium was full. This auditorium was five times larger than the converted chapel used to house the school concert all those years earlier. As the MC introduced him, he sprung to his feet and strode confidently to the lectern, slightly lowering his head in appreciation at the thundering applause. Once in place he raised both palms in plea for calm and as the acclaim gradually subsided, he took a sip of water to compose himself. A consummate performer. Looking out to the hundreds in attendance in the theatre and glancing at the camera with the millions watching around the country, he broke into an easy smile. "Well I never," he began, voice booming. "This is something I'd never dreamed of doing," he professed, "lecturing on the art of performance. To me it's all about belief…"

[Michael had chosen to forget the performance from 30 years previous]. Although he had been nervous back then, as he excitedly informed friends and family gathered around him moments after the performance, he knew he would get through it.

"You couldn't tell dear," his mother had kindly lied to him. He knew different, but he also knew that he had soon found his feet and moved into gear, singing well and timing the jokes to near-perfection. "You're a natural," his father had assured, hiding his terror at how slowly his son had responded to the spotlight.

Like everybody else in the auditorium he had wondered if Michael would finish his first sentence. People were squirming next to him, as if unable to look. He himself had felt like he was watching a car crash in slow motion, except his son was the one driving into a head on collision with an articulated lorry loaded with explosives. After what seemed like minutes, not seconds, Michael had found his way to the end of the sentence and burst into song.

Fortunately, the band drowned out the first few lines, by which time Michael had begun to get his bearings and lose himself in the music, just as he always had. By the end of the night, all those years ago, he had truly stolen the show and had done everybody proud, especially himself.

He would still have nightmares later that night as he recalled the ice running through his veins as the spotlight hit him.

Uplifting Performance

So Michael had chosen to forget that first event before his latest, career-crowning performance, but not before learning everything he could from it. Through the years he had adjusted to a life in show business but the range of experiences had thrown up hurdles every time: TV, radio, press conferences, public speeches. Rather than face one with a fresh terror, only to be overcome through effort and experience, as he had done during his first performance, he preferred to hit the ground running. He wanted every experience to be successful, enjoyable even.

He took his cue from his parents. After arriving home from the first event, his mother had handed him a congratulatory glass of champagne, and as they toasted his success, she declared, "I knew you could do it."

His father confirmed, "I always had faith in you son. Always believed you had it in you."

The next day, after the cold sweat of the nightmare had dried on his forehead, he reviewed his performance, just as the director had advised he do. Although much of it was a great success, he could not get out of his mind that horrific start. As his mind dwelt on the stifling climate of fear which had enveloped him as soon as the curtain rose, he knew he had to overcome those nerves if he were to get any further.

His mind flitted to the congratulatory aftermath, to the toasts and what his parents had said. "I knew you could do it…", "I always had faith in you…", "I always believed you had it in you…" If they had such belief, what was stopping him from having the same? 'But I do believe I can do it, I know I can do it', he told himself. 'What I don't believe is that I can do it without being nervous. Or can I?'

Having begun to look at what beliefs he had about his performance, he began to scrutinise them further, break them down. Although not aware at the time, Michael had begun to look at his unconscious thought processes. A short time later he would acquire the knowledge to work out what his Meta Programs or Change Patterns were. Although this was not entirely what had led to his meteoric rise, it had certainly helped, along with his highly developed skill at controlling his state. Other performers were soon to envy and enquire after how he could become a darling of the chat show format, as well as perform and speak so well in front of crowds of thousands. Michael always shrugged and said, "I know what I'm doing is all," which although accurate seldom left his interviewer satisfied.

To consistently perform at that high level Michael had gone through each of his Change Patterns from the first event.

As described in Chapter 6 these are:

10) Change. *Do I like change?*
11) Primary Interest. *What do I prefer to talk about most?*
12) Information. *Do I pay attention to the big picture first or the detail/specifics?*
13) Evaluation. *Do I need to be told I'm doing well or do I tell myself?*
14) Decision. *Do I do something because it looks right, sounds right, feels right or makes sense?*
15) Motivation. *Do I move away from negatives or toward positives?*
16) Motive. *Am I power, achievement or affiliation oriented?*
17) Activity. *Do I live in the moment or plan for the future?*
18) Organisation. *Do I need to do this or do I want to?*

Change Work

Michael worked out that his three main Change Patterns in this context were: Information, Evaluation and Organisation.

His Information Change Pattern was 'specific'. He was chewing over the small bits of information, rather than looking at the 'bigger picture'. Rather than breaking his part down into the minutiae, he would have been better served by reflecting on how his part developed, how he would get the opportunity to hit the high notes, to produce a scintillating performance that he always had in him. For other people in these circumstances it may have been that focusing on the specific would serve them better, but for Michael, that was counter-productive.

From then on, every time Michael went on stage, or performed in any context, he would always reinforce how capable he is, what a voice he has, and how good he is at what he does.

The next significant Change Pattern was Evaluation. Michael had spent the moments leading up to the performance in nervous contemplation of what the audience would think of him. His frame of reference in this context was highly external, dependent upon what other people were supposedly thinking. To change his performance from the outset, Michael needed to develop a strong internal frame of reference. He needed to build up belief in himself, and not rely upon others to tell him that he was doing well. For many people a strong internal frame of reference would not serve them well in this Context. However, for Michael, it would be the reverse.

Belief Change Patterns

Having worked this out, Michael would spend time evaluating his own performance, reviewing what he had done well, and what he could do better next time. Therefore, every time he went out to perform he knew he would be doing the best that he could. Crucially, he also knew that he would be better. If the last time was great, he knew this time would be greater. He did not need to be told that, he just knew it.

There are other factors that come into evaluating performance, and Michael would also refer to expert advisors to receive their feedback. However in that moment of performance, it is crucial for Michael that he has that strong internal evaluation.

The remaining Change Pattern that Michael realised had to alter was very much concerned with the moment of performance. It is the Organisation Change Pattern, the pattern that indicates whether we are living in the moment, in time, or living for the future, through time. In this context Michael was very much through time, predicting what would happen in future and deliberating over things that he could not control. It is telling that when Michael got into his stride, found his bearings, he performed brilliantly. This was because he was 'lost' in the moment. That is, fully associated, totally committed to the here and now and dedicated to his performance. At first he had remained dissociated, worrying ahead about what the audience was thinking and whether or not he could remember his lines. For Michael to perform at his best he had to enter into that fully associated, in time mode, enjoying the present, living the moment.

In performance terms, this is a very typical state to be in and when done particularly well, it appears to the performer that time has slowed down. Previously to the performance time had been rushing by for Michael. Once in full flow, or in 'the zone', as artists and athletes often call it, time slows or stands still. That is truly living in the moment.

Putting that altogether, Michael realised that to be at the top of his game he needed to focus on the overall performance, to lose himself in the moment and be totally involved in what he is doing, not concerned with the thoughts of others.

Michael realised that he had to be context specific when adjusting his Change Patterns. Whilst having a strong internal frame of reference for his Evaluation Change Pattern served him well on stage, he realised that it did not work well for him with friends and family. As soon as Michael walked off stage he would automatically revert to the Change Patterns that worked well for him in other contexts.

People often remark in surprise just how "down to earth" and "pleasant" Michael is, as if they believe that performers should carry on the act at all times.

Encore!

Before rising to receive his award and conduct the annual lecture at the Performing Arts Lifetime Achievement Awards Michael had visually rehearsed, over and over again, the successful delivery of his address. He had done it so often and to such a high standard that he did not have to worry about the details. He knew it all.

Now, standing there, lost in the moment and thinking only of delivering the finale, the closing message, he launched into his speech with abandon…

The audience rose as one in applause. At that moment Michael sensed that they believed as much as he that his central message were true, that the art of performance can be mastered by knowing yourself. Moments later his friends and family appeared and Michael changed again, from great performer to a gentle and concerned listener as a fan approached, pen in hand, keen anticipation written all over her face.

'Once in full flow, or in 'the zone', as artists and athletes often call it, time slows or stands still. That is truly living in the moment'

Chapter 12

Belief Storage Patterns

'All the logic and reason and calculations in the world do not change the irrefutable fact that we do the vast majority of things that we do purely because it looks right, sounds right, feels right, or makes sense...'

We seldom do anything unless we are invigorated to act. We do things for four different reasons. It looks right, it sounds right, it feels right, or it makes sense.

All the logic and reason and calculations in the world do not change the irrefutable fact that we do the vast majority of things that we do purely because it looks right, sounds right, feels right, or makes sense.

Each of us has a primary representation system as described in the Decision Change Pattern (see Chapter 6). We are primarily visual, auditory, kinaesthetic or auditory digital; sights, sounds, feelings and logic. Being that is so, how we store those visual, auditory and kinaesthetic representations is crucial in the choices we make in life. If the combinations are stored in different ways, we can get different results. The breakdown of those components, the sub modalities are elemental to our personality and why we make the decisions we make. Consequently, these Storage Patterns have a huge impact on our lives, mostly out of our awareness. The Storage Patterns of our beliefs are one of the most significant and widely overlooked parts of NLP.

If we believe something to be true and that belief is steadfast and unerring it will often lead to a definite conclusion. It may not be the one we want and it may not conclude as we would imagine, but it does propel us forward. In fact the belief can be so compelling that it blinkers us to other avenues and opportunities.

How these beliefs are constructed as Storage Patterns dictates how compelling these beliefs are to us. They can drive us forward, motivate, enthuse, inspire and propel us towards or away from a variety of destinies. In some cases the Storage Patterns are so clear, strong and forceful that they can cause all sorts of problems, such as anxiety, fear and depression. In other cases those same Storage Patterns can propel us towards great riches, accomplishments and rewards.

The Power of Love

If we have a compelling Storage Pattern that is working for a belief in one part of our life then we can transfer that to a belief in another part of our life that is not enjoying much success. For example, Pat has a strong belief in the power and strength gained from being in a close relationship and enjoys the fruits of that relationship in the 'Sex' Context. However, a similar belief is not doing Pat any good at work. Having been as flexible as possible with the approach to this belief in the workplace, Pat is still having little success. Time for a belief change. A more empowering belief in the workplace turns out to be being single minded in pursuit of her objectives, as she currently spends a lot of the time asking what other people think. However, although Pat knows this work-based belief would serve her better, she can find little enthusiasm for it and it begins to take its toll, leaving her feeling exhausted at work and cranky at home. It begins to have a negative effect on her relationship.

Taking the powerful Storage Pattern sub modalities from her relationship and applying those to the single minded pursuit of objectives has a startling effect. The tasks seem infinitely easier and achievable. There is clarity of purpose and sense of achievement in accomplishing tasks. She still has time for team members yet her primary focus is achievement (Pat is wise enough to incorporate Change Patterns also).

The difference? There will be a stronger, more compelling urge to succeed in this Context. Pat has harnessed the representations she already has to ensure they are shaped and configured in another area of her life to get the results she wants. Once the internal representations have been shifted consciously, the unconscious connection has been made and she can continue without having to consciously strive to succeed. As we found earlier, that is where all the effort, tension, anxiety, worry and doubt are expended, in consciously striving to succeed, often against all the odds.

In this example, Pat had all the resources she needed from another area of her life. Most of the time, this will suffice for all of us, as we all have a depth of resources that is immense. The belief resource may seem completely disassociated yet still be of use.

Power of Positive Belief

A person with a huge number of problems in the various areas of their life may find it difficult to think of any belief that is inspiring, motivating or even pleasant. They may feel only disdain and despair for themselves, where they are in life and what they are doing. Ask them for a positive belief and they would struggle to find one. However, if we begin to tap into our imagination, there are many beliefs we have that bubble along just beneath our conscious understanding. Even in the blackest pit of despair, few of us would be unable to draw some comfort from a tropical beach, blue skies, palm trees, cocktails, sunny days etc. It might not light everyone's fire but something similar must hit the mark sooner or later.

Belief Storage Patterns

We all have our favourite retreats, special places, ideal scenarios somewhere in mind. With a spiralling mood and worsening circumstances it can seem that these places are billions of miles away and totally unattainable. That is what we can lead our self to believe.

We can just as easily bring our self to believe something totally different. Such as that our ideal scenario, sun scorched beach or moonlit sonata in Venice, whatever is our fancy, is equally obtainable as despair. Which is more preferable?

Being that the mind can not distinguish between the highly imagined and the 'real', that moonlit sonata or scorched beach are indeed readily accessible. All we have to do is tap into our own imagination and transport our self there.

The disassociated belief is therefore just as real as the associated. What we believe now, in this context, with all the evidence laid out in front of us, is no truer than lying on a beach six thousand miles away. If we believe it to be true, it does not mean it is true, it just means we believe.

'Being that the mind can not distinguish between the highly imagined and the 'real', that moonlit sonata or scorched beach are indeed readily accessible'

Swimming with Dolphins

To use disassociated beliefs to empower associated beliefs, swapping the disappointment of now for the empowerment of then or whenever, can have a magical effect. Swap into the disassociated belief for the former associated belief and we can associate happiness immediately. Knowing this we can instantly change our state.

This is something we have known from the start. We can control our state whenever we want, by associating into a time when we did something that we enjoyed. We can then plug into the inspiration and whatever other positive emotions we need at this moment, and we can become that way again by reliving it.

The difference here is that if we do it with our beliefs, the very things that inspire us in the first place, then the effect can be more powerful and lasting. If we can engrain the Storage Patterns of an uplifting/inspiring belief, however dissociated at present, into a belief that would benefit us in a specific Context, then the difference could be enormous. Not only would it change the way we regard a particular aspect of our lives, we would have the unconscious support and drive to see us through. We would not have to keep thinking about how to do something well, or how to keep finding the enthusiasm to do it well. The knowledge would be with us always, at a deep level. And when it comes to doing the deed or task, we would somehow find the impetus to do it without thinking. It would come easily and effortlessly.

How can it be done so easily?

If we take three beliefs that are not working so well for us in a particular Context, say Goal Setting, and then extract a really empowering belief from another, entirely different and inappropriate area, such as knowing that dolphins are great swimmers, we can apply the Storage Patterns of the latter belief and apply it to the former.

It is more powerful to apply a belief about our self, such as believing we are a great swimmer or some such truth we can apply, but failing that an 'unassailable truth', if there is such a thing, can work as well.

The belief that dolphins are great swimmers, which I am sure many of us share, is represented in a particular way. We have a picture of the dolphins, perhaps swimming underwater, or maybe breaching a calm sea. We may have a view of the ocean, of the sky. We may hear their clicking calls, or feel the coolness of the water as we picture those dolphins. It may be simpler than that. It may be the head, the eyes that we see up close. The feelings may be of warmth towards the creature or excitement as we imagine them in motion. We may recall actually seeing a dolphin, perhaps in an aquarium or out at sea. Whatever sights, sounds and feelings we see, hear and feel, are just fine.

Most important, as described in Chapter 7, is how these are broken down and represented. Are we associated or dissociated, looking through our own eyes or seeing our self in the picture? Is the picture moving or still? Is it three dimensional? Is it a movie or is it framed? What colours are there? What is the contrast like? Are there any shadows? Notice every tiny distinction. Is the picture near or far away? Is it up or down, left or right? Is it large or small?

Are there any sounds that are important? Are they high pitched or low? Is the sound constant or periodic? What is the tempo? What is the timbre? Is there any music? Is it loud or soft? Is the sound coming from inside our head or outside?

Are there any feelings that are important? Where are they located? Are they large or small? Is there any movement? Is there any vibration? Is there any pressure? Is there any heat?

These distinctions are crucial to give the fine detail for our Storage Patterns.

We can take the Goal Setting beliefs and elicit the Storage Patterns using the same process. They could be beliefs such as, 'I can get a promotion', or 'I can get on with everybody really well at work', or 'I'm good at what I do'. We may

Belief Storage Patterns

believe all these to be true, but they might not be working quite as effectively as we would like. The beliefs are not providing much momentum as they are currently represented.

Once we have elicited the Storage Patterns for these beliefs we can simply transfer the Storage Pattern from the empowering belief and replace that with the existing belief.

To do this we simply get the picture back of the existing belief, such as 'I'm good at what I do' and take the Storage Patterns from the dolphin picture and impose them over the top. So if the dolphin image was near and to the right, that is how we re-shoot the existing belief picture. We run down the list and do it for each 'sub modality'.

If swimming dolphins do not provide a stirring enough stimulus for us then we can use something that is more inspirational and unique. We have many more resources than we realise and we can prosper greatly by using what we already know.

If the belief is a limiting belief then we must use the process ascribed in Chapter 11 to get the results we want. This version is simpler as we can take existing beliefs and upgrade them. In the Goal Setting Context it is most likely that all we need to do is upgrade our existing resources. If we have a significant problem then it is more than likely due to a limiting belief.

We often take it for granted that it is entirely environmental if we are not enjoying doing something or feeling 'down'. Or we blame other people for our moods. 'So and so gets me down' and so on. What we can do now is take existing beliefs, no matter how seemingly trivial or superficial, such as, 'I'm not bad at doing x' and upgrade it. All we have to do is to re-word the belief to, 'I'm good at doing x', and apply the Storage Pattern of the empowering belief. Note here that we re-word to change the belief into a positive. This is because the mind does not process negatives and so will therefore aim towards doing what we do not want to be doing. It is the principle of not thinking of a pink elephant. In the process of not thinking about it, we automatically envisage the pink elephant. That is how our mind works. If we do not want to do something, we automatically think about the thing we do not want to do and aim towards that. That is why we make the same mistakes over and over again. We get well practiced in doing them.

By the same token, once we have done something well, we can rehearse that over and over again and apply that to a different part of our lives that is not working so well. That is the basis of this book. Simple but effective.

Any number of beliefs can now be upgraded in any number of areas to get the results we want, simply by dipping into what we already know and use that.

Whilst beliefs are neither true nor false, they are also incredibly useful and should be carefully addressed to ensure we are getting the best out of them.

If, at any time, we have trouble accessing empowering beliefs, all we have to do is dip into our imagination, take our positive learning and apply to existing beliefs.

That is when real invigoration takes place.

'Once we have done something well, we can rehearse that over and over again and apply that to a different part of our life that is not working so well'

Chapter 13

Belief Strategy Patterns

'Bearing in mind that we are twice removed from reality, it makes perfect sense to re-assemble that reality to create the most ideal representation'

It looks right, sounds right, feels right, or it makes sense. Almost everything we do does not come down to reason, or logic, or critical insight, it comes down to how we see, hear, feel and deduce.

If life is that simple then why is it that there is a seemingly infinite variety of responses to any given situation?

It is because the combination of these sensory experiences is virtually infinite. As defined in Chapter 8 our Strategy Patterns are usually out of our conscious awareness, yet usually conclude in similar fashion, depending upon our primary representation system. We are primarily visual, auditory, emotional or logical. How we respond in a wide variety of situations tends to be the same. The five broad categories are: memory, convincer, decision, motivation and learning. We will go through the same pattern for each of these strategies.

The convincer, or belief strategy, is most pertinent here. This is how we test between our version of 'reality' and the constructed representations of memory. As we begin to change our beliefs to better serve our outcomes it could be necessary to alter our convincer strategy to create a more compelling and useful 'reality'.

Bearing in mind that we are twice removed from reality, it makes perfect sense to re-assemble that reality to create the most ideal representation. Key to that is our convincer strategy.

Belief Re-Patterning

Gillian has a belief that she cannot make friends easily. Further, she believes that she is uninteresting and dislikeable. At social occasions, she finds it difficult to communicate with people she does not know and is concerned about being perceived as shy or boring. Gillian has had this belief for as long as she can remember.

In other aspects of her life, Gillian is doing very well. She has a career she enjoys and a home life that she loves. However, in the Social Context, Gillian is far from happy and can not seem to get over the 'block' of feeling socially inadequate.

Gillian is articulate, intelligent and perceptive and enjoys a host of hobbies. Although she believes that other people often see her as 'boring' her friends find her company stimulating and enjoyable. Her husband has told her many times how well she appears in company, but she seems unable to be convinced no matter how hard he remonstrates and no matter how much evidence he provides to support his protestations.

Gillian's social discomfort led to her avoiding parties and social occasions where she would come into contact with strangers. During her twenties, this caused little upset as she devoted her time to bringing up a young family and socialising with friends from her school and university days. As the children grew older and her career in advertising drew her into wider social gatherings, her discomfort also grew. In fact it got a lot worse. Gillian became so worried at the thought of social interaction that she would do all she could to avoid contact with strangers.

At work she would implore colleagues to attend meetings with people outside the company or make up excuses as to why she could not attend. Her anxiety over meeting people became so extreme that it interfered with her work performance and she had to take time off sick. It came to a head. If she could not resolve this problem she faced losing her job and further isolating her husband who had become exasperated with her reluctance to meet new people.

Finally, Gillian sought the help of a friend who knew how Strategy Patterns worked.

Gillian, it turned out, had a very straight forward convincer pattern, one well outside of her conscious awareness.

She would look at or imagine a strange face, hear an internal voice which would say things like, 'don't make a fool of yourself', or 'say something interesting, don't be boring'. She would then construct an image of the face looking at her with contempt, and would then hear herself giggle nervously in 'girlish' fashion and instantaneously feel nausea in the pit of her stomach. That would be the moment she would decide not to go out to the party, or turn on her heels on entering a busy room.

Gillian's friend had deciphered that her strategy was entirely structured in the negative. The first thing she would do is imagine or see a strange face and then would hear an internal voice. The internal voice would always frame questions in a derogatory way. 'You're going to show yourself up again…' or 'Don't be boring…' or 'You've got nothing interesting to say…' Listening closely to the internal voice, Gillian worked out that, strangely enough, it was not even her voice. It was much deeper and gravely. In fact, it was the voice of a man.

Belief Strategy Patterns

The voice turns out to be that of one of her first boyfriends who she had known from university. Although the relationship had been brief and had ended friendly enough, she remembered how derogatory and dismissive he could be. He had been going through a 'stage', Gillian recalled, of looking down on other people, always commenting on their clothes, or mannerisms and usually he was contemptuous or mocking. Whilst none of this criticism had been levelled at Gillian, some of the things he used to say would make her recall how she felt when she was much younger and classmates said cruel things to her.

Although Gillian was never bullied at school, she was a 'sensitive child', as her father described her, and used to be upset easily by hurtful comments. Looking back now, Gillian realised that the 'nagging', sardonic voice in her head was identical in tone and timbre to that of her ex-boyfriend. Instead of those comments being levelled at strangers, these comments were being levelled internally, and destructively, at herself.

Our internal dialogue is an incredibly powerful and important component of who we are. It is something we take little or no notice of, yet shapes how we respond in virtually every circumstance. Only when we become aware of what that inner voice is saying, and most importantly, how it is saying it, can we use it to our advantage.

How often do we find our self in a mood, or annoyed, or impatient, because our friend or partner has said something or done something to infuriate us? These are often triggers, or 'buttons', that the other person can press, often consciously. However, what we do not realise is that our response to these triggers can be controlled.

> *'The principle here is that the mind and body are connected. Control the mind and control the body'*

Controlling States

Primarily we can control our state, put our self at cause and respond in just the way we want, to be in the state we desire. We do this by anchoring empowering states, such as happiness or excitement or relaxation, and firing/activating these anchors when a trying situation is upon us.

This is simply achieved through accessing a time when we were in that state of happiness, for example. This could be on holiday, or with friends at a party, any time when we are enjoying our self and are in a 'great' state.

We elicit the Storage Patterns of this state and as we re-live the experience, compress the back of a knuckle or some such area of our body that is within easy reach but is seldom touched. We can then go into several other similar states and 'stack' these on that knuckle. We should compress the knuckle only when the emotion is at its peak, when all the sub modalities are brightest, loudest and clearest, and release before it begins to subside.

Next time a cutting comment, or even a drop of rain touches our head, which would have previously stimulated a negative emotion, we can touch the flesh, or fire the anchor and instantly change the state to one we find desirable. The principle here is that the mind and body are connected. Control the mind and control the body.

Triggers are very powerful.

'He knows which buttons to press…', 'She really knows how to wind me up…', 'As soon as he walks in the door with that look on his face…', 'Every time he opens his mouth I just want to shove a brick…'

These are just a few of the triggers that we encounter almost every day and are aware of. There are so many more triggers that are out of our awareness. They impact our lives in a massive way, putting us in negative states and draining our energy; whether it is the boss at work who causes anxiety by raising his voice, or the sight of a line of traffic in front of us, or the grey, overcast weather causing our spirits to instantly flag. That is why it is important to collapse those triggers or anchors.

We do that by eliciting the sub modalities of the negative trigger. It could be the look on a friend's face, or the sound of someone's voice, or walking into a room. Once again we press a knuckle to anchor that state, making sure it is a different knuckle to the positive, resource anchor.

Having stacked the more positive resource states on the other knuckle we fire them simultaneously whilst imagining that face, or voice or room. The feelings should begin to change immediately. Press the anchors simultaneously for five seconds or so and then release the negative anchor and keep the resource anchor compressed for another five seconds or so, at least until all negative emotions have drained away.

If we go through this process for every trigger that was previously negative, we will soon find that very little puts us in a negative frame of mind. We control our mind, therefore the results we get. We cause how we are, not the weather or someone else who happens to be in a grumpy mood.

Having controlled our state we now need to ensure we maintain our position and ensure we do not enter a negative state. As states change fairly rapidly (we could not go around in one state all the time or we would be incredibly one dimensional and a little dull!), this may seem hard to achieve. Surely we can not walk around all day firing one anchor after the other? We only have ten knuckles…

Belief Strategy Patterns

And even if we have collapsed our negative anchor and stacked a resource anchor to fire at will, we can easily surrender our upbeat disposition by taking heed of our internal dialogue. Once again, this may be out of our awareness, but it is incredibly powerful and coercive. 'Oh, he's saying that on purpose…', 'Here we go again…', 'I hate it when she tuts like that…', 'I'm not in the mood for this…'

Pointedly, this internal dialogue is not in place to support us. Although it can support us up when we need to perform, 'C'mon I can do this…', we seldom use it in a positive way. When we consciously change our internal dialogue that is when we tend to get the results we want. 'I know I'm going to do this well…', 'I will win at this…'.

However, most of the time this dialogue grumbles away out of our conscious awareness. It serves us poorly by coercing us into feeling miserable. We can tell that it is doing ill by the tone it takes.

By listening carefully to the tone of the voice we can work out whether it is for or against us. If it is at a high pitch and fast, it is almost certainly being supportive and that tends to be before we are about to do something that we feel we must gee our self up for, such as giving a speech or taking part in a sporting event. If it is sombre, dour and slow, very low in tone, it is almost certainly dragging us down.

'You can't do that…', 'This evening's going to be dreadful…', 'Oh no, not her again, I can't bare to spend another minute in her company…'

The voice might not always be wrong, which is why it is worth listening to. That is the key; tune into the voice, pay attention to it, and we can begin to make a difference.

The good news is that the internal voice, because it is on our payroll, can be made to work entirely for us. By listening intently to it, working out firstly who it is (it may actually be our mother or father's voice, or in Gilllian's case her ex-boyfriend's voice in the Social context). Secondly, we need to pay attention to what the tone is. If it is low and sombre, it will be serving us little good most of the time.

However, if there is a potentially dangerous situation arising such as walking down a dark alley on our own, it may be serving us well. Once again, this is why it is worth paying close attention to it, rather than dismissing it out of hand. And it is why we should focus on the content.

So thirdly, we should pay attention to exactly what it is saying. Once we have gone through this process we can then begin to change the dialogue. The more radical the better. Why should our guiding voice be a sombre miserabilist or a dour impersonation of a nagging relative? Change it to a high-pitched squall of excitement. Or Mickey Mouse cheerleading. It does not matter what we choose as long as it is encouraging and works. We can then work on what that internal voice is saying.

It can repeat what we want to hear over and over until it is drilled in and becomes an unconscious driver. Such as, 'I will succeed at this…' or 'I'm doing well… I'm on the ball… I'm in control…' Whatever works, works best.

'Have a word with yourself'

Turn Yourself On

Now Gillian can alter that internal dialogue and deal once and for all with the miserable ex-boyfriend. To reiterate, she visually constructs what the stranger would look like and hears the nagging internal voice of her ex-boyfriend. She would then create another construction of the stranger's face showing utter contempt and her response would be a childish giggle. This is an auditory recollection. On hearing that she would then feel sick and would flee. So the exit point is an auditory kinaesthetic synesthesia. That is hearing and feeling simultaneously to cause her to feel awful.

Gillian's Social Context Strategy Pattern is therefore visual construct, auditory internal digital, visual construct, and finally auditory internal tonal and kinaesthetic synesthesia.

Several of these steps can be re-adjusted. The visual constructs can be deconstructed and reassembled using Storage Patterns with compelling visual images. For example, this could be from Gillian's graduation ceremony when there was nothing but encouraging faces and remarks, or from a family birthday or celebration when everybody was warm and encouraging.

The internal dialogue can be altered radically. The ex-boyfriend can be ditched for good and Johnny Depp introduced, if it would do any good. Perhaps Gillian would prefer to hear her own encouraging voice. In the Social Context it is evident that Gillian has a strong external frame of reference, so it may be wise to use an outside voice. However, Gillian would be wiser still to align her Change Patterns, Storage Patterns and Strategy Patterns in the Social Context. That could well mean adjusting to a stronger internal frame of reference and adjusting her Decision Pattern from auditory to visual or auditory digital.

We can also work with Gillian's nausea. This would most likely melt away by adjusting the Strategy Pattern she currently has. She could swap negative visual and auditory representations for positives. Once again, eliciting Storage Patterns for each step would prove most useful.

Belief Strategy Patterns

Because this belief Strategy Pattern has been so well rehearsed, it may be possible to slip back into bad habits. So Gillian would also benefit from introducing other representations, from re-adjusting the order and re-assembling the Strategy Pattern to one that works. Crucially, it should be trialled and installed repeatedly. Twenty or thirty mental rehearsals should be enough to ingrain the new Strategy Pattern.

For example, the first visual construct for Gillian could be a kind, warm face, smiling encouragement and appearing welcoming. The internal voice could be re-tuned and re-scripted to sound like her favourite lecturer at college who always supported and believed in her. 'Do your thing Gillian, you're amazing…' in encouraging tones. Another element could then be introduced. Gillian seeing herself at her best, possibly on stage, or mixing with family and friends when everybody is laughing with her. She may then want to hear the encouraging sounds of family and friends, with perhaps a favourite piece of music in the background. The feeling now would be one of excitement and anticipation experienced by a warm feeling in her chest and lightness in her head. The exit point could be hearing the sound of herself laughing, but this time heartily like when hearing a comedian she likes telling a very funny joke.

The transformation is dramatic. Not only has Gillian's belief Strategy Pattern for the Social context changed incredibly, so has her state and physiology. Now when walking into a room for a social gathering, Gillian is on fire.

If we take a belief we currently have that is not working too well and elicit the Strategy Pattern for that, it may quickly become apparent that a key part of that is the internal dialogue, and more specifically, the tone in which discouraging comments are being made.

We can all adjust our Strategy Patterns simply and effectively by triggering a resource anchor and firing off an uplifting piece of music or bathing our minds in our favourite colour, or even feeling light headed by adjusting our breathing.

The most effective way to enrich our experience of life and create long-lasting empowering beliefs is to talk to our self in the right way. That dialogue is crucial. Listen to it. Turn the tone up. Switch the script. Turn yourself on.

In short, have a word with yourself.

'The most effective way to enrich our experience of life and create long-lasting empowering beliefs is to talk to our self in the right way'

Chapter 14

Behaviour, Fire

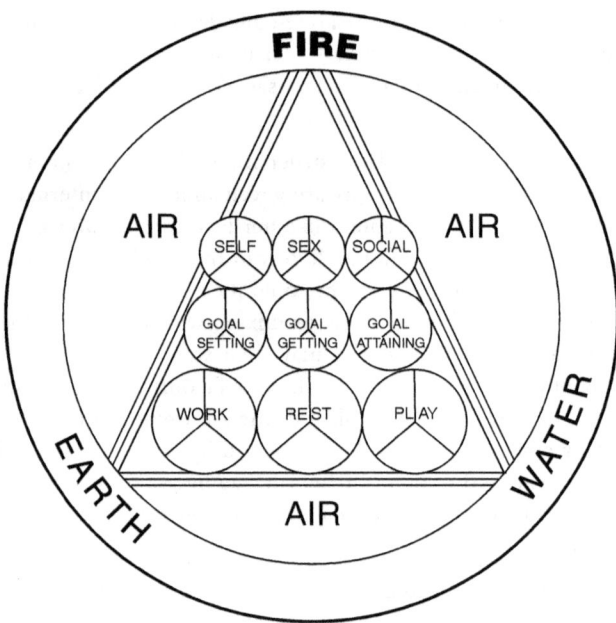

'Unconsciously, we are spreading our emotions like a water sprinkler dousing a lawn'

We cannot not communicate.

It is impossible not to communicate. The very act of not communicating signals the intention of not wanting to communicate. Arms crossed, eyes down, shoulders hunched. The withdrawn, uncommitted posture sends a powerful message. Do not approach. Do not enter into conversation. Do not touch.

Even the tiniest of movements can infer a huge range of emotions. In fact, the slightest gesture can pack the most powerful of punches.

A sorrowful sigh can puncture the pride of the sternest of critics.

A sideways glance arouses a fit of paranoia.

A carefree shrug infuriates the most patient of parents.

A casual smile sends a jealous mate into a rage.

A wink across the room sends a shiver down the spine of a curious voyeur.

Of all the millions of combinations our muscles can make to signal thousands of different intents, it is indeed impossible not to relate to every person, all the time.

The above are some of the conscious actions we take to indicate a preference or dismiss a suggestion. What about the thousands of little things we do that are out of our awareness?

The tut that sends our spouse wild.

The frown every time a disliked name is uttered.

The lowered tone when we speak of our in-law.

The involuntary whistle as we listen to stories of risk taking.

Every one of us makes thousands of involuntary gestures every day. Our behaviour is incredibly hard to control. In fact it is almost impossible to control every muscle movement. What we must ensure is that our behaviour, these gestures and idiosyncrasies, do not betray a negative disposition. If we are feeling a certain way, perhaps bedraggled and dreary, or filled with resentment and disappointment, it is almost impossible to hide.

Yes we can put on a brave face and smile away at the world. We may be beaming broadly whilst we drown inside, thinking we have fooled everyone. Often people will appear too busy to monitor our activity. 'Fooled them again,' we may think to our self. 'If only they knew what I was thinking...', or we may believe, 'they have no idea what's going on with me.'

The wide smile or forced laughter is a cunning guise, we intuit, aided by our years of practiced deceit and spirited refusal to wear our hearts on our sleeve. We become past masters at hiding our emotions, at storing up resentment, or disappointment, or heartache, or even grief.

When we return home from the office, or the pub, or the allotment, or the pot welders' club, we slump in our favourite armchair and regale our mothers, or sons, or lovers with the 'real' story. How we hate our job, or our life, or that idiot at the bingo, and we confide in them how brilliantly we cover our deceit.

'Why don't you just leave then?' our concerned ally enquires.

'Why should I?' is the oft-touted response. If we can carry on our deceit, why should we leave?

Consciously, we may indeed be pulling the wool over some peoples' eyes. We may be misdirecting our boss, who thinks we are a little reticent in her company, but puts that down to shyness, not disdain. We may join in with the hugs and kisses at family reunions, holding back our annoyance at the inclusion of obnoxious Uncle Ivan.

This is where we believe our control over our behaviour is dangerously misinformed.

It is also mind reading on a grand scale.

> *'There are a whole host of indicators that, if we take the time to notice, conspire to make heeding the difference, or calibrating, easy'*

Mind Games

We are basically pretending to know what people think. Just because the boss, or the friend of a friend, or a colleague has not commented upon our reluctance to share their company does not mean they have not noticed. Just because they do not highlight our deceptions, does not mean they have not become apparent.

A lot of things go unsaid.

As we do our best to bury and hide and mask our feelings, so our friends and colleagues and enemies do their best to bury their comments and thoughts. As they do so, we feel the need to fill in the blanks. 'Ah, so and so didn't come to the party. That's because they were intimidated last time...'

If there is a silence in our minds and a lack of instant gratification, we go to enormous lengths to join the dots. 'If he is doing that, it means she must be...'

With no real, practical explanation for what is happening, without the evidence laid out in front of us, we suppose and presuppose that something must have happened or is going to happen. If we take what we know and strip away what we do not really know but presume to know, we often find our self with very little information and not a lot of knowledge.

Being bereft of knowledge and understanding is not a nice place to be, and that is where our imaginations jump to the rescue. 'This means that...' and 'that means this...'

Of course, some of the time we are perfectly right. We are not wrong to infer. Where we can go wrong is conjecturing all the time and replacing evidence, prima face fact, with speculation. If the speculation overrides the evidence that is when things can begin to break down. And that is often where we find our self with behaviour. We think we are covering everything up when we are not.

When people do have time to monitor, when they do have time to sit down and assess what others are like, then the pretentious mask is soon whisked away. The tiniest gesture or movement, which previously went unnoticed in the rush of everyday life, is now brought to bear. It may not be a coherent analysis, more an overall impression.

'There was something odd about him that day...', 'It didn't seem right...', 'You haven't been the same recently...'

Behaviour, Fire

Quite often friends, family, loved ones and even close colleagues will be able to pinpoint the difference. 'You seemed a little out of sorts the other day...', 'You're not being yourself at the moment...'

It can be hard to fool those close to you. This is especially so as they can calibrate or measure our behaviour so well. They have bountiful evidence of what we are like when we are 'normal' or how we are most of the time. This is because they see, hear, touch and smell us so often that they become acquainted with our every nuance. When the 'norm' changes, when we enter more excited or depressive states, the difference to them is stark.

It can be disconcerting to have our moods read almost before we have had time to comfortably settle into them.

This calibration, noticing the difference between the 'norm' and an altered state, is often done unconsciously. However, there are a whole host of indicators that, if we take the time to notice, conspire to make heeding the difference, or calibrating, easy. When we apply this to lesser known acquaintances and even strangers, it can be extremely useful.

We do it by taking a snapshot of what the person is like in a 'normal' state. If we do not know them well, it can be difficult to know accurately what that 'normal' or most common state is. However, we can make a presumption that if they are at ease, comfortable, secure etc, then they are in a state which is fairly common for them. Some people live more of the time in uncomfortable and disconcerted states, but fortunately this is rarer than people who live in more of a relaxed state. Once the 'normal' state has been gathered, we can take a snapshot of that and hold it in mind.

We can notice how the person stands, what their posture is like. Do they slouch? Are their shoulders back and chest out or are they leaning forward? What is their breathing like? Is it fast and furious or slow and laborious? Do they breath from their abdomen, stomach or chest? What is their skin colour? How large are their lips? Which direction do they tend to look in most? Are their pupils dilated? What are their hand movements? How do they gesticulate? What about their voice tone? Is it high or low? Do they speak quickly or slowly? Do they mumble or shout?

As the conversation subject matter changes or if we see the same person under different circumstances it can often be the case that many of these things change. The person may lower their tone, or their pupils become more dilated, their cheeks may colour and their hand movements become more frantic. Or they may alter the direction of their gaze; they may lose focus, their shoulders slump, and their shape changes. Shifts in physiology may be small but the meanings can be huge.

These meanings can only be discerned through noticing the difference. One action, one deed, one thing in and of itself does not mean anything.

If a person likes to cross her legs and fold her arms, that does not necessarily mean that she is a closed person, unwilling to listen and participate. It may mean that she relaxes by crossing her legs and folding her arms and feels most at ease in that position. If she then unfolds her legs, uncrosses her arms and leans forward, that does not necessarily mean that she is more or less approachable. What it does mean is that she has changed posture. Her physiology has changed. If this is monitored closely and what she is saying and doing now is compared and contrasted to what she said and did previously, then meaning can begin to be attached.

That is, an action or change in behaviour can only mean something if it is compared, or calibrated, to what went before. It is about noticing the difference. Once the difference has been observed we can begin to go about attaching some meaning.

This is easiest to practice when calibrating the difference between someone when they are happy and when they are sad. Their whole physiology changes. They may be alert and upright, talking excitedly and glowing when talking about something they are passionate about, and then shrunken, facing downwards, perhaps mumbling when talking about something that saddens them.

For that individual there may be several traits that repeat themselves so that we can begin to notice their mood changing almost as quickly as it happens. This is where attention to detail is crucial. And, once again, we must remember that nothing can be discerned unless it is compared to what went before. A dour, downcast, sullen posture to one person can be another's intense form of focus and concentration, when they are at their intellectual best.

'If we do not look after our self, and make sure we are in ship-shape condition to project our best, how can we better service those around us?'

Naked and Proud

With friends, family and loved ones our powers of calibration are honed through years of observation. Sometimes those observations are muted by apathy or boredom. Quite often, we will also choose not see or hear what is happening around us so we do not have to respond. It is easier to do nothing than do something we do not want to do, such as offer support when a TV programme looks more riveting, or lend a helping hand when the day has been long and tiring.

Behaviour, Fire

So surely we can get away with pretending with people we do not know that well? Surely they cannot see how angry, or resentful, or bored we are inside?

For short durations, yes. On a conscious level it is difficult to ascertain exactly what people are thinking. By no means impossible, but difficult.

Unconsciously, we are spreading our emotions like a water sprinkler dousing a lawn. We cannot not communicate and we most certainly cannot not communicate unconsciously.

However we try to hide our feelings, they will surface in one form or another, unconsciously. Our mood will rise to the fore, although it may take a less likely form, such as anger if we are feeling dispirited, or frustration if we are feeling bored.

Perception is projection. That is, what we believe inside, we will project to the outside unconsciously. And people around us pick up on this, sooner or later. They may not do it consciously, unless they are astute at calibration, but they will certainly pick it up unconsciously.

Children are expert at picking up on our behaviour, on reading through the lines and interpreting what we really think and believe. They may not be consciously aware they are doing it, but they can accurately ascertain what we believe and perceive and take that on board. The power of nurture is astonishing. And it is not something we leave at childhood.

We develop more filters as we go through life, as we build up more experiences, so we add more distortions, generalisations and deletions. We never stop taking on board everything unconsciously.

If this is beginning to sound like a disturbing disrobing that leaves us all nakedly exposed then that is no bad thing. Until we realise the benefits and advantages of aligning our internal states and internal processes to our external behaviour then we will be forever naked in the eyes of the astute observer.

If perception is projection, meaning our beliefs are readily accessible, then we must always be exposed. However, that does not mean to say that we are exposed in a negative sense. We can choose to let the world see our positive disposition. We can be attractive in our nudity, with no shame or need for fig leaves.

All we have to do is align our Earth, internal state, with Water, our internal process, to our Fire, external behaviour. By bringing back those compelling values and empowering beliefs, all we are broadcasting is positive intentions. 'I believe I can succeed…', 'I know I am capable…', 'I believe other people around me are capable of great things…'

Because these beliefs and values have been given an ecology check; that is assessed to make sure they are realistic projections for the individual, then there need be nothing overreaching or immodest about these statements. The final statement concerning belief in other people would therefore be a useful belief to perceive and project as it is most likely to enlist support from others, therefore encouraging friendship and closeness from those around us.

If we do not look after our self, and make sure we are in ship-shape condition to project our best, how can we better service those around us?

Now we are in fine shape to lend a helping hand, we can broaden the 'I' to 'We' if we so choose.

'Until we realise the benefits and advantages of aligning our internal states and internal processes to our external behaviour then we will be forever naked in the eyes of the astute observer'

Chapter 15

Deep Structure, Air

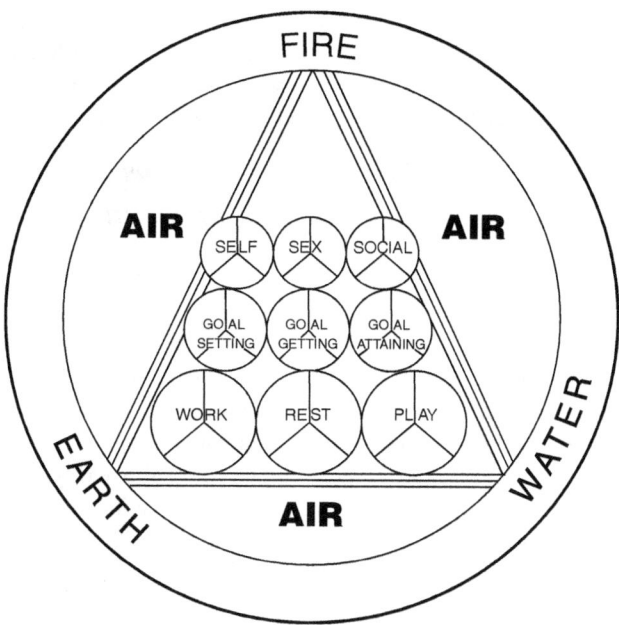

'We can be in the right frame of mind to achieve what we want because we have all the resources we need to succeed, and more'

The truth that dare not speak its name. The last great taboo. The great unknown.

Yes, welcome to the world of the essential self, the remotest place on earth, the desert ice cap of the soul.

At least that is how some would have us believe. The unreachable, the undesirable, the inexplicable... the unconscious. Is it really so mysterious, so incomprehensible that it must remain a largely unexplored field, left to psychiatrists and spiritualists? Of course not. If we strip it down to the essential facts, the known quantities, then it becomes a tangible entity, as real and concrete as our conscious awareness.

So what is the unconscious?

Quite simply, it is anything beyond our conscious radar.

We cannot do anything without using the unconscious for support. We cannot get out of our seat, walk down the street, compose a sentence, drive to the shops, or even post a letter without the support and encouragement of our unconscious. As seen in the last chapter, we constantly communicate unconsciously. Because our lives are constructed by communications, we can begin to get an idea of how much of what we do is out of our awareness.

> *'What am I doing when I'm not doing what I need to be doing to get the result I want?'*

Walk of Life

We may have learned how to stand up, how to walk, how to talk and how to move at the same time. Once we have learned these skills they become engrained and we no longer have to think consciously to gesticulate or pull a facial expression, or walk and chew gum at the same time. Our muscle memory kicks in and we concentrate on other things, such as what we are saying in conversation, perhaps mildly aware that we are standing in a particular position or smiling, or scowling.

If the reverse was true, if we had to consciously go through the process of standing every time we had to get up, we would achieve very little in life. We would have to tell our stomach, chest and shoulders to move forward as our hands grasp the side of the chair. Our legs and feet would be instructed to widen and we would then tell our muscles to work in combination to thrust upwards from the seated position. This would be the tricky bit as all of these body parts and muscles have to work in tandem. If we can not remember how to do it from last time, then there is no muscle memory, so we have to consciously urge all these parts to co-operate. This is tricky. Our lower spine and abdomen have to work as one. Our calves and thighs have to contract at the same time and all of our upper body parts have to straighten and conspire to move forward with rapid momentum. Once we begin to exit the seat, defying gravity and forcing our bodies upward through willpower and physical strength alone, we have to ensure the momentum is continued, but gradual, so we do not topple over.

If we take a moment to attempt to work out all the different movements involved in standing up, it could take quite a while. If we then consciously run through each of these movements and the interaction that has to take place between body parts and muscles, then we may find it difficult to perform.

This brings to mind an analogy. It is the same if we have a problem, when we are out of alignment with our conscious and unconscious. It is when we have tried everything consciously to overcome an issue but it will not go away, so for whatever reason, our unconscious is not supporting our conscious desires.

Deep Structure, Air

The body parts and muscle contractions required to stand are like our unconscious parts. They once knew how to act on our best behalf but something has gone wrong with our connections. We have fallen out of step, tripped out of alignment. Because our unconscious always acts on our best behalf, it must be something that has changed through time.

If we take the time out to concentrate, really focus upon the problem, then this gives our unconscious the time to work out the steps we take to do what we do. If we are out of alignment, or incongruent, it is not because our wiring is incorrect. If that were the case then we would not have been able to stand up properly all these years. We would have lost our balance or would have remained firmly seated despite our best efforts.

It is because a small part of the process has broken down. It can be the tiniest of components. Perhaps the left ankle is weak. Maybe we pulled a muscle in our chest. A wrist may be in plaster, thus throwing off our centre of balance. If we try to stand using only one leg we can get an impression of the difficulties thrown up by the smallest change.

If we are overcome by a condition that we find debilitating, such as feeling low and not wanting to socialise, perhaps not wishing to leave the house, there is a tendency to analyse the conscious things around us. Is it our environment? Are we fed up with work? Is it our relationship? Are we directionless? Do we need something to stimulate our interest? Do we need a hobby, or a lover, or more to eat, or more to drink or less to eat and more dancing? There must be something out there that provides the answer. And sometimes that is correct. It is always good to assess where we are now and where we are heading. What are we doing and what else could we be doing?

However, rather than looking around at what else can be blamed for our condition, we can take back control and put our self 'at cause'. We can take a good look at our self. If everything has worked well until now, what has changed? What is the difference that makes the difference? What am I doing when I'm not doing what I need to be doing to get the result I want?

We can break down our response. As mentioned in Chapter 14, we can do this through calibrating our self. How did I used to be? What did I used to do? Now, what is the difference? What individual part has changed that has led to me getting the result that I have that I do not want? Already there appears to be a lot of conscious exertion going on. That is not useful. It is much better to do things easily and effortlessly rather than strain to drain oneself.

So trust the unconscious. Ask it for direction. To do so, we must be in the right state. That is relaxed and composed, clear of interruption. Once we have a calm and composed bearing we can simply ask our self what is it that is the matter.

First, think of the problem, really concentrate on the problem, and ask the unconscious mind what this represents for us. This requires a high degree of focus on the particular issue. We do not need to concentrate on our interpretation of the problem or other issues that are spinning from it. That is when we get lost in the conscious clutter. All we need to do is think about the particular problem and let the representation come to mind.

Once that representation is formed, however it is formed, be it a shape or a colour or a sound or even a person, we can then begin a dialogue to resolve the issue. We can ask our unconscious mind for a specific representation that is causing the blockage. It may be different from the first representation. We then ask the unconscious, what is the positive intention of that representation? Because our unconscious mind always works for our best intention, we can discover a positive intention if we keep at it. It may not be apparent at first, but it will come.

Once discovered, we can thank our unconscious mind for providing us with that support. If it is no longer of use, ie, it no longer serves a purpose, we can ask our unconscious mind to integrate that representation into the whole so it can support us further.

(An ecology check is useful here. The positive intention may be signalling something that we need to pay attention to. We can find our self in an unwelcome position because we have not been paying attention to the signals from our unconscious mind. Physical exhaustion, mental fatigue etc, can be the symbolic manifestation which our unconscious mind uses to point to another issue that we have been overlooking. By ignoring our unconscious mind, we can be jeopardising our health. On the other hand, if we pay close attention to the signals and symbols which our unconscious mind presents to us, then we can be made aware of potential difficulties sooner rather than later. Once we have developed this awareness, of how our unconscious communicates with our conscious, then we can align the two. Once this is achieved we become congruent, in tune with our self).

To embed a more empowering positive intention, one that can work for us better in the future, we can tap into further resources of our unconscious mind. We can ask our self how we are when we are at our best, when we are feeling how we want to be feeling, whether it is happy or elated or relaxed. Once again, we ask for a representation of that state. As that representation forms we replace the disempowering representation with the empowering representation in the format explored with Storage Patterns. We have re-programmed our unconscious mind to help us achieve our objective. Because we have checked the ecology of the change and made sure that the alteration will have a positive impact, our unconscious will serve to support our outcome.

Deep Structure, Air

> *'If this sounds fantastic, it is because it is. It is extraordinary. The power of the unconscious mind is phenomenal'*

Bringing More to Mind

If this sounds fantastic, it is because it is. It is extraordinary. The power of the unconscious mind is phenomenal. We should not be embarrassed about exploring its full potential. Having a word with our self, delving into our resource bank to bring out our best is the most sensible and logical thing we can ever do.

Let us look at the facts again. From the standing up example explored earlier, it is evident that our unconscious is a vast majority of what we do or who we are. Our conscious existence is the tip of the iceberg. If our body represents the percentage of what we are, starting from our toes, then our unconscious must reach up to our chin at least, with our conscious awareness floating around the top of our head. Yet we choose, for some inexplicable reason, to bury the unconscious as if it were a foreign matter. We do not understand it, so let us work with what we know.

But we do understand it. Or we can understand it, by talking, by creating a dialogue. Nobody else can understand it. It is an entirely subjective experience and it is why it is at the epicentre of NLP, which is the study of the structure of subjective experience. Therefore, NLP is the study of our conscious and unconscious self.

If we take a step back a minute, something staggering is beginning to happen. If we are the tip of the iceberg, if everything we think and believe about our self, about who we are; it becomes evident our identity is only a fragment of what we are. What about the rest? We have spent a lifetime being described as and describing our self as things that are suddenly appearing to lose shape and meaning.

How can I be shy, retiring, arrogant, offensive, demanding, hyper, insensitive, sensitive, caring, uncaring, feeling, unfeeling, repellent, adorable, nice, nasty, quiet, loud, large, small… and so on if that represents such as small percentage of what I am? If we are going to label ourselves, surely it would make more sense to dig into our resource bank, drag something more attractive out and label our self as that.

What if I do not have it in my resource bank?

Trust the unconscious mind. As the presupposition states from Chapter 2, People have all the resources they need to succeed. We have it. We have it all. We may not have polished the skills required to get to where we need, or have the required experience in that field, but what we do have is all the resources in the world to support those ambitions.

Nothing goes away. Everything is stored. We distort, generalise and delete in order to function, in order to make life simpler and achieve simple tasks. However, the millions of bits of information that we process every day through what we see, hear, feel, smell and taste are not wasted. They are stored away. And our unconscious mind does not work like our conscious mind. It does not have to. It can work entirely differently and achieve much more because it has free rein.

It is not confined by societal expectations, or family obligations, or rules and discipline. It has its own blueprint and it runs according to that.

Key drivers of the unconscious mind are:

- It organises and stores all of our memories, temporal and atemporal
- It runs the body and has a blueprint of how the body is now and how it should be at its healthiest
- It is symbolic and uses and responds to symbols
- It works on the path of least resistance
- It does not process negatives
- It controls and maintains all perceptions
- It needs repetition until a habit is installed
- It always serves in our best interest
- It is a highly moral being.

If so much of what we are is operating on an unconscious level, then we are so much more than we think we are. If we ask our self now, what am I?, we will probably come up with a list similar to the aforementioned. 'I am happy, tolerant, nice…'

That is a conscious understanding that we have built up. For those of us who have gone through the MindFrame Patterns there will be some empowering beliefs and strategies to support those statements. Now we can ask, 'What else am I?' Although this time we can ask the unconscious. This is outside of our conscious interpretation, away from friends and colleagues and family and those who profess to know us. How can they know us, our deeper self, if we do not know?

So, what else am I?

And then, what else am I?

And what else am I?
And what else?
And after that, what am I?
And after that and after that and after that?

We can keep going indefinitely. We are so much more than we ever thought possible.

How can we prove it? Simply by tapping into the resources we have. Once we have untapped that huge potential we can then begin to use it. We need to harness it. That is where the conscious comes in. We need to be aware of what we want to use our resources for, where we want to go, what we want to achieve.

Once we have done that and have set our bearings, once we have centred ourselves, made sure we are in alignment and congruent between our conscious and unconscious, we can set our course. We can be in the right frame of mind to achieve what we want because we have all the resources we need to succeed, and more.

'We can keep going indeterminably. We are so much more than we ever thought possible'

Chapter 16

Internal Understanding

'We have the template to our own understanding engrained deep within the unconscious, deep within our personal volcano, at the epicentre of our self'

The complete collapse of the flanks, a jet stream of scorching rocks firing skyward, clouds of thick grey pyroclastic gunge and an ear shattering blast confirm the earth's nausea and we are left mouth agape at its wondrous fury.

Volcanic explosions of every kind leave us staggered at the vast potential for devastation that lies at the earth's core. We marvel at its rich, vibrant movements and alluring textures and shrink from its searing violence, cutting swathes through rock like a knife through butter.

We are all volcanic. We all have that eruptive potential. The difference is that we control our outlet, manage our emotive eruptions. The letting of pressure from deep within the earth's core is a necessary release valve to ensure equilibrium. In its own way the earth is controlling its own volatility by letting out steam through the tiny mounds on its surface. As we learn to understand our nature, our deep structure, we can use those vast, incredibly powerful forces to activate an unstoppable energy source.

Rather than let these volcanic soars cause us problems, as they have in the past, they can become our fuel, our innate electricity. Like all intense energy sources it needs to be understood and developed appropriately.

To gain an understanding of scientific and natural phenomenon, we read what the experts have to say, or watch television documentaries, or even travel the world to witness these activities first hand. When it comes to accessing the internal world of our self for some reason we either ignore it or take the advice of others. We rarely take time to take a good look in the mirror.

To truly understand the internal activity, our deep structure, the mechanisation of our unconscious, no amount of book reading, TV watching or world travel will uncover the deep matter. It is strange that some people will take the latter all too literally, travelling the globe to 'find themselves'. Whilst it is wonderful to explore different cultures and gain understanding of other peoples', it is no easier to explore the essential self when we are positioned 12,000 miles from where we are located at present.

The only person who can truly understand and use that awareness for positive gain is our self. No-one can tell us who we are but our self. We have the template to our own understanding engrained deep within the unconscious, deep within our personal volcano, at the epicentre of our self.

Internal Understanding

If no-one can tell us who we are apart from our self and if what we are is only accessible through immersing ourselves in our essential self, how can we not access it right now through looking inwards? We can, at any time. However, the product description of the 'unconscious' does what it says on the label, it is out of our conscious awareness. To become consciously aware of the unconscious we must find a meeting point of the two.

Some people can access the unconscious readily, especially as they become more practised at it. Others can do it occasionally. Once again, there is no magic recipe. Our entry codes are all different as we are all different.

What is useful to know are the unconscious drivers, as listed in Chapter 15. One of the statements suggests the unconscious is symbolic and uses and responds to signals. To talk to our unconscious in a language it understands, it can be useful to use symbolic representations. This is why generic metaphors and fairytales passed down from generation to generation have such a powerful resonance. People can make their own interpretation of the story, get out of it what they need. They may not realise why they enjoy the tale so much, largely because it is their unconscious that is benefiting from the interpretation it needs from the story.

During hypnosis, the person in trance will often be told a story that can be interpreted in many different ways. Their unconscious mind will take the interpretation it needs to help them resolve whatever the presenting issue is. The problem, it would appear, has nothing to do with the story they are being told. The unconscious reads into it what it needs. Our unconscious does this all the time. When we become aware of how our unconscious uses this information, we can feed it what it needs to help us. Remember, our unconscious always works in our best interest.

I do not know if the following descriptions will be useful right now, or if they may come into effect at a later date, or if something in there will trigger another thought on an entirely different subject. Whatever works, works. This is the study of the structure of subjective experience.

'As we learn to understand our nature, our deep structure, we can use those vast, incredibly powerful forces to activate an unstoppable energy source'

Volcanic Eruptions

Curtains of fire rip along the fissure, cracking the rock apart, shooting darts of boiling lava into the air. Pyroclastic material explodes into the sky, rocketing shards of deadly earth thousands of feet into the air, throwing a grey-black veil of suffocating clouds for hundreds of metres.

The vent of a volcano feels temperatures shoot higher than during a nuclear explosion, with the power of the earth's pulsing heart ejecting its life-blood with the fury of a natural apocalypse. The skies blacken as the blood-red sulphur and toxic waste spring forth like a mythological fountain of the fire gods, spewing incessantly, until the rage has deserted.

Vulcanian eruptions electrify the weakened sky with lightning strikes, ripping apart the order of sense and logic with the earth's equivalent of thunder and lightening. 'Who said it should come from above' booms the ear shattering shriek from the harpies of the ground?

Strombolian eruptions rhythmically eject incandescent cinder, lapilli and volcanic bombs to heights of hundreds of feet. The after-shocks of the explosions shake the ground, crack the brittle rock and shatter the furnace into further splintering explosions.

Felsic magma, high in silica, erupts in viscous, gas-rich magma that forms ash. A mushroom cloud of gas forms like a parachute over the vent, reaching hundreds of feet into the air, sucking the light from the day.

Imagine the violent, shimmering avalanches of raging hot gas flying down the flanks of the mighty mountains, sweeping all in its fanatical rush; the powerful surge flattening trees, walls, houses, all before? Lava lakes flood the plains, forging new roads and highways through the softened, putrefied earth, bludgeoning the beaten ground to pulp. The black, cracked, paper-thin veneer intimates crustacean finality; the cooling of dead earth as the victor melts to eventual dust.

Only the rampant thirst of the rich-red streaks, crashing through the crusty barrier serve to remind of the incessant blood-letting, the monstrous rage of the mighty, galactic beast, howling at the skies.

Meanwhile, away in the cold ocean the subtle fracture of rock under the sea bed give little indication of the volatile giant under the water's gentle lapping. Now lines and scars along the sea bed mark the seismic activity deep down where the giant squids and whales wrestle for supremacy in Neptune's lowly grudge matches. Submarine volcanic activity can boil the fish of the sea in seconds, sending smoke signals from under the water, as witnessed by the shocked inhabitants of a plane bound for Honolulu in 1955. The steaming water cracked the earth for a mile and a quarter, whilst nearby emerged an area of several thousand square yards of dry land, unchartered on any human map. The pumic debris soon became water logged and sank, crushing the remaining sea life like ants under foot.

As all the gases from all the volcanoes burst forth, blackening the day, boiling the waters of the earth, setting fire to the sky, we can see the shapes and sounds

Internal Understanding 111

and sense the whisper in the melting pot. 'Phew!' echoes the gentle, cursed whistle of the safety valve, shooting the steam asunder as we mere mortals cower and praise be with earthy reminders. 'Better out than in' we reassure each other before running for the lush, green hills free from the fresh fall of molten debris.

'What are we choosing not to know that if we were to know it right now would clear the blockage in a second?'

Taking Stock

Hold on a moment. Let us back-track a little way.

Vulcanian eruptions have lightening in the eruption cloud?

Passengers on an aeroplane back in the 1950s were the first witnesses to a staggering natural phenomenon. What a perspective! Sometimes flying high above can provide that added insight.

And just how powerful are Strombolian eruptions, hurling 'bombs' into the air? Truly amazing.

Do we attempt to classify ours self? Or do we recognise the vast array of separate, yet inter-acting internal functions? Do we recognise our self as the sum of many parts? Are we not more than one volcanic metaphor? Are we as wide and deep as the earth, with thousands of fissures and vents and seismic activity mapped across our resource rich contours? What else are we?

Categorisations of volcanic eruptions are not necessarily useful to us. They may be of interest, but they are not essential. Like anything, it is how we use the knowledge we have for a particular purpose. How can descriptions of volcanic eruptions serve a purpose for an exploration of our unconscious self?

Or should the question be, how can they not?

How can it not be of interest if the understanding for which we search are shooting forth like sparkling embers? How can we tap into the lightening strike? What are we choosing not to know that if we were to know it right now would clear the blockage in a second? If we were to know it, what would it be?

What would it not be?

Chapter 17

Collective Understanding

'If we are always communicating, we are always connected. That connection therefore creates a thread linking humanity'

If we cannot not communicate, what exactly are we communicating about our self? And what are other people picking up in our communication? If it is out of our awareness it could be highly destructive, if not to other people then at least to our self.

How do other people interpret our unconscious communication? Consciously we ascribe people to brackets and boxes to simplify our interaction with the world. We do this through distorting, generalising and deleting pieces of information and through our ever-developing filters. If we deliberately scrutinise every interaction we have with other human beings, we would be struck immobile through information overload.

Unconsciously, we are more sophisticated. We can project what we want to those around us, whilst undertaking wildly divergent tasks.

Because we like people who are like us, those who perceive like us and project like us pick up on our signals or communications and choose to interact positively. If the individual is someone who is not like us and does not perceive the world, or arrange their map of the world anything like we do, it would appear more difficult. Not so.

If we choose to perceive and project in a universal language, that of connectivity and a belief in the positive relationship between human beings, then unconsciously those who are apparently not like us can still feed off this.

Looking again at the presupposition that we cannot not communicate, that inter-connectivity looms larger. If we are always communicating, we are always connected. That connection therefore creates a thread linking humanity. With that thread running through us we can then make the decision of whether to move with people around us, or against. It does not mean holding hands and dancing round the maypole, unless one is inclined towards that kind of activity. It does come down to a clear choice, whether they are for or against us.

Remember the mind works in a straightforward way, repeating patterns and reaffirming previous suggestions. We become experts at categorising and one of the easiest ways to categorise is to be one of two, for or against, plus or minus, black or white, on or off. We have explored how infinitely more complex we are and how it can be self-defeating to continue limiting categorisations and beliefs. On the other hand, it can also be useful to tap into a popular dichotomy.

Collective Understanding

If we look at the polarised debate taking place in politics today, where there is an opposite view to whatever is stated, we can see this transferred throughout society. Even as political parties move towards the 'centre', issues are deliberately contrived to highlight emerging differences.

Take any topic of societal concern and we can see the polarisation of views. The obesity debate is one such issue. On the one hand politicians, education authorities and medical bodies are advising strict diets and calorie controlled regimes for young people, whilst others are saying children are becoming too thin as they follow role models in the media.

Either extreme can be seen to be harmful and counter-productive, yet where does the debate take place? It is positioned at the extremes. There is rarely exposure of a passionate supporter of the middle ground, of balance and objectivity.

On a global scale, as we come into contact with a divergent population, it becomes easy to fall into the trap of categorisation and as detailed previously, this can be ill-informed and dangerous. However, when we are talking about collective communication, unconscious inter-action on a universal scale, it can serve a purpose. That is, we can trigger each others' 'on' switch, or positive reaction, affirming a connection and innate similarity. We can then integrate and create close and stimulating relationships quickly and easily.

On a one-to-one basis this can be achieved through building rapport, reflecting each others' likes and dislikes as well as voice tone, body language, physiology and so forth. On a grand scale, as we whiz around huge numbers of people at work, at parties, in shopping malls and theatres it would seem less practicable to attempt to build any sort of relationship.

However, there are those who seem to be able to command attention instantly. They seem to radiate confidence, charisma and presence as soon as they walk into a room. They have an instant 'likeability' or attractiveness that makes people pay attention. These individuals are not necessarily extroverts, although they would normally be categorised as such. Whether consciously or unconsciously they are projecting a best possible social self. They have found the ingredients, the right recipe to project excellence in their social communications.

Students of social interaction can make the mistake of believing this is entirely about developing social skills. Whilst these are important, as seen in the last chapter our unconscious holds all the resources we need to be able to transmit the communications we wish. Whilst these 'scene stealers' indeed have developed advanced social skills, they have also tapped into a huge ream of resources to ensure the continuing development of their skills.

***'We are basically 'putting it out there', holding our beliefs
to be true to us and of possible benefit to others'***

Putting It Out There

How is this relative to collective understanding and the connectivity thread? It is one example of people projecting their best self. It makes sure those in attendance, automatically connected by their relative closeness in sharing the same room space, can feel a positive vibration in that thread. Is this not superficial though?

It can be if that is all there is. However, it is unlikely that if the 'scene stealer' has aligned his or her beliefs and values and is fully aware of their Change, Storage and Strategy Patterns, that is all there is to them. On the contrary, they are projecting a part of themselves which is wishing to communicate openly and widely to those around them. It is saying, 'I'm interested in those around me and would like to share this space.'

If it were a matter of clamouring for attention and bragging, that is exactly how people would perceive it, on the whole. As everyone's model of the world is different it is incalculable to predict in how many different ways one action can be interpreted. What we are talking about is on the whole. Most of the time. For the majority of people. It is back to the sliding scale. The better we become at communicating excellence the more likely it is that more people will be positively influenced.

What is it we are trying to communicate?

Firstly, we are not 'trying' to do anything. We are succeeding. An empowering belief could be that we are interested in what other people are saying and doing. If we have embedded this deeply and aligned our Change, Storage and Strategy Patterns to support this belief, it is unlikely that we would come across as anything less than a keen listener. We would not have to say anything. The very act of listening deeply, or observing deeply, presents the speaker with a force seldom experienced. Most people are waiting to speak, formulating their opinions as the other person talks. Unconsciously, this is picked up on. Because we all do this at one time or another, because it is so commonplace, people rarely take offence. However, when people do listen attentively the difference is profound. The feeling evoked within the speaker is often one of gratitude and acceptance, very possibly they are highly impressed with the listener and keen to continue the conversation and relationship further.

This is partly a conscious act on the listener's part. Once it is practiced regularly it becomes an unconscious trait that is deeply ingrained. Along with

Collective Understanding

other deeply embedded empowering beliefs the other person can pick up on all kinds of positive and reassuring messages that make the listener an attractive and compelling person to be with.

The importance of empowering beliefs therefore takes on another dimension. People are picking up on these unconsciously. If we have a limiting belief, we may be able to mask it for a time, but if we have several or if they are particularly strong, they will out and we will project them. It is therefore useful to do a thorough spring clean and ensure all beliefs are empowering, subject to ecology checks as described in Chapter 10.

Going through the MindFrame Patterns we can develop a useful range of empowering beliefs to underscore our communications and improve our social interactions easily and effortlessly. We are basically 'putting it out there', holding our beliefs to be true to us and of possible benefit to others. It does not hurt to share an empowering thought, notion or belief if it can help others. (Here we must be clear about time and place. People do not always want to hear how well we are doing if they are not doing too good. Sensitivity of approach is essential if we are not to come across as an interfering do-gooder or crushing bore. Developing sensory acuity and rapport will ensure this does not occur and if we can read the signs quickly enough, change the communication to one that the other people prefer).

The process of 'putting it out there' becomes unconscious if we are sound in our beliefs and values and know they can do no harm to our self or others. Like a fisherman casting his line, we can throw it out there and see what happens. Nothing as such has to happen. We are not doing this to land a whale, we are doing this to benefit our self and others. The more we do it, however, the more likely it is that we will reap further benefits. We can meet people, increase our network, increase our knowledge and understanding, open up social and working relationships.

The most important factor is that what we are 'putting out there' is beneficial to others, not just our self. If this is the case, people will connect. That thread will have a positive vibration and one people will be willing to grab hold of. If it is all 'me, me, me', some people may associate or be attracted to us, but the majority will not.

The advantages of this are manifest and we can see people who have mastered this and benefited themselves and others greatly. There are those who take this to a spiritual plane, the collective consciousness, and that is fine too, whatever our beliefs are. The advantages ascribed here are not necessarily concerned with global harmony or raising spiritual awareness, it is about expanding our individual awareness to link with others to improve every life we come into contact with. It is about creating win-wins, increasing collective understanding.

It can be expanded to incorporate wider communities; however the communal connectivity can be as small as the person we share office space with or the bus conductor we see everyday.

> *'It is about expanding our individual awareness to link with others to improve every life we come into contact with. It is about creating win-wins, increasing collective understanding'*

Collective Understanding

How we pick up on this collective understanding in others is crucially important. It may be beneficial to 'put it out there', but how much more beneficial would it be to pick up on other peoples' positive vibrations? How much more can we gain from taking what other people have to offer? How can we stop limiting our understanding if we come into contact with experts from many fields?

Through developing sensory acuity and rapport we learn to improve our understanding and pick up on positive signals. In the Sex and Social contexts our sensory acuity is vitally important.

So how can we spot those who are 'putting it out there', communicating empowering beliefs and enriching the lives of those around them? The 'scene stealers' are obvious; they light up a room, connect with all those around them and raise spirits wherever they go. Yet the quietest person in the room can have the most to offer.

As well as developing sensory acuity to observe the tiniest detail which may be extremely useful, we also have to develop that internal tuner to ensure we are not categorising or bracketing people.

This may sound contrary to the earlier appeal to turn the positive categoriser 'on'. This is to ensure we are attuned to find out people who are open and accessible to communicate with. There are many people who are very worthwhile knowing who are closed and inaccessible for whatever reason. These people should not be dismissed. However, if they are unwilling to share, it is unlikely we can develop a close relationship quickly. Our antennae in relation to this person will not be at 'on' for this occasion. What we must ensure is that the antennae can be switched to 'on'; that we are ready to contact those who are willing to communicate.

Categorising or labelling people will automatically disrupt transmission and we could miss some real gems. Taking the 'judgement' setting off and switching

Collective Understanding

to 'perceiver' will ensure we open our filters and are ready to access whatever we find around us. It is the non-judgemental mode. We may not be exposed to every gem of wisdom out there when we are in this mode, but what it does do is ensure we are not missing anything. We are picking up on every transmission and feeding it through until it resonates with our internal vibraphone. Once again, this will be picked up on. If the thread is connected, which it is, the vibration can be felt by the other person or people.

What is meant by collective understanding is the opening of a pathway for two-way or multiple communications to move freely and easily. There is no blockage to transmission. There is no judgement call or interference. The communication can be felt from person to person by the positive transmission from the individual to another, who in turn transmits a positive communication.

The collective interaction is passing messages to and fro, 'putting it out there' and pulling it in again. It is a shared understanding borne of confidence, trust and community.

> *'What is meant by collective understanding is the opening of a pathway for two-way or multiple communications to move freely and easily'*

Positive Vibrations

Everything is connected. We cannot not communicate. The very act of observation changes the events around us. The invisible thread of communication and interaction which creates collective understanding is not limited to those we share a room with, or people across the street. The collectivism goes much further and there we shall leave it to a higher consciousness which is developing around us.

The collective consciousness of reading this dialogue has involved an exploration and understanding of our internal and external selves and how we can align those emotions and processes to get the results we want. We have intentionally or otherwise developed a greater understanding. All that remains is to apply it to the world around us, a world that is embedded in our deep structure, connected by the thread's vibration. Everything is connected.

Part III: Putting It All Together

Chapter 18

MindFrame Contexts

'Everything is connected and we are connected to every context'

Everything is connected and we are connected to every Context. The nine MindFrame Contexts are expansive, covering every situation we find our self in, and in turn we can relate those to the Earth, Water and Fire environs to connect to our internal states, internal processes and external behaviour.

The Earth Contexts, representing the solid, grounded, deep rooted environment of Earth covers Work, Rest and Play. Where else would we find our self? Well, there may be a primary concern above the Work, Rest or Play environment.

It could be that we are more attentive to our deeper desires, needs, wants, wishes, aspirations. These can be both spur of the moment inclinations or longer-term ideals. This is the fluid world of Water and movement emphasising momentum and change. We therefore may find our self in modes of Goal Setting, Goal Getting and Goal Attaining. We are unlikely to refer to our situation as being one of Goal orientated, but if we are primarily concerned with planning for an eventuality, or doing something to move towards attaining it, or involve our self in the moment of enjoying an accomplishment or reflecting upon our actions, then in MindFrame terms we are in the Goal Context.

Even so, our primary concern and attention may be with our partner, our group of friends or colleagues, or even our self, as we look inward or spend time in reflection. Because this largely involves social interaction this is the realm of behaviour, actions, interactions, communication, the world of Fire. If we are self-reflective then the communication is inward. If we are with friends, family or loved ones, the communication is primarily outwards.

There is necessarily much overlap with these Contexts. In fact, it is difficult for there not to be overlap. We can be at Play with our friends, ie Social, whilst attempting to achieve a desire to reach an agreement, Goal Getting. This must not concern us too much. As we are flexible and resourceful people we will be able to move between Contexts and states smoothly and efficiently as the need arises.

Many MindFrames will hold many similarities. For some people one or two MindFrames can be transferable between Contexts. For most, the switch can be easily made through an awareness of the Primary Context.

'Using MindFrames every success can be mentally logged. This builds up a repertoire of successes, mentally rehearses achievement and improves our performance'

Primary Context

The Primary Context is the key concern that overrides the others. This may not be the same on each occasion, as it depends upon our greater need at the time. The same Contexts of Play, Social and Goal Getting can have a different emphasis each time we approach it. On one occasion it may be necessary to pursue that Goal Getting objective and therefore we place that to the forefront of our mind and access the appropriate MindFrame Pattern to achieve that objective.

That could be as simple as accessing a singular inspiring Storage Pattern (see Chapter 7) which instantly puts us in an upbeat and empowering state associated with core values of strength, decency and empathy. We may then lever a couple of Change Patterns (see Chapter 6) towards the emphasis we need, such as using a people-led Primary Interest, an Affiliation Motive to interact most positively and a fully-associated Activity focus of living in the now. We may then access a belief empowering Strategy Pattern based upon our previous success at achieving our outcome in a Social setting. We could believe we have the necessary charm, likeability and sincerity to achieve our Goal. We may even prefer to access and add another Storage Pattern which further inspires us. As we enter into the situation our Strategy Pattern is fired as we see the object of our attention and we may hear encouraging words from inside our own head, feel a growing warmth in our stomach and hear our favourite piece of classical music.

The whole sequence can take seconds to access and is triggered by our awareness of the appropriate switch to flick inside our head denoting the appropriate Context.

Likewise the same situation can have a different motivation for us on another day. This time we may prefer to place an emphasis on the Social Context, on a desire to network, meet new people, perhaps make new friends. Here it could be said that the Primary Context would be Goal Setting as our aim would be to interact more. Perhaps, if that is a strong driver. On the other hand, it may be that the elements of the Social Context, of interaction, communicating, sharing, of enriching our experience through talking to others are the primary desire. Yes, there is a Goal involved, as there is in everything we do, but the Goal or Goals are not the strongest driver; it is a combination of features which could be more appropriately assigned to the Social Context.

On the other hand we may want to experience a certain abandonment, not necessarily overly concerned with social interaction. We may want to dance, drink, sing a few tunes on the karaoke machine. This is most likely to be assigned to the Play Context. We would then activate appropriate Storage, Change and

Strategy Patterns which help us most in this situation. It may be that we access our extroverted, entertaining self, full of humour, high spirits and camaraderie. Our Play Context MindFrame may be more subdued, reflective and measured to counteract a high-pace work life. It entirely depends upon the subjective experience.

There are two things that need addressing here.

The first is how we choose which specific Primary Context to apply our MindFrame Pattern.

The second is how we design our MindFrame Pattern for each Context.

'The emphasis here is on easily and effortlessly rather than strain and drain'

Applying Contexts

Firstly, it is entirely subjective. The Contexts will necessarily overlap as suggested and that is why the MindFrame Patterns are flexible and should be assessed over time to ensure they are still relevant and effective. It is also the case that many MindFrames will work in overlapping Contexts. This can be very helpful, so we do not need to keep switching. However, as we become more practiced, switching becomes easier. So, we may wish to have a similar MindFrame for the Play, Goal Getting and Social Contexts, or for a Work, Goal Setting and Self Contexts. Whatever works.

What is recommended however is paying attention to the different elements. The Earth, Water and Fire Contexts are categorised because of their alternative slants. Earth is concerned with the environment. Water is concerned with movement and motivation. Fire is concerned with communication.

It may be more appropriate to work on MindFrames within each of these categories and move on from there. Most important is what works for the individual and how complicated or easy we want to make it. Remember, it need not be difficult to move between a number of MindFrames in different Contexts once we have rehearsed the alternative states associated with each. We are most likely to demonstrate the greater flexibility of behaviour the more states we enter. This is the law of requisite variety. Whoever shows the greatest flexibility of behaviour controls the system.

Once again though, it is entirely subjective. If we prefer one or two MindFrames and they prove to work across different aspects of our lives, then roll with that. We work with what works, not with what other people tell us should work.

MindFrame Contexts 123

So how do we know which Context we are in? The suggestions earlier, on the differences between Play, Goal Getting and Social, were subjective in themselves. They were the Contexts most likely suggested using the limited information available. In short, it does not matter. It is whatever emphasis we choose to place upon it. And, because we are flexible and inter-changeable, the Context may change during the proceedings. This happens often.

A Social occasion may change swiftly into a Goal Getting Context if we are introduced to an individual who may be useful to our career progression. Or a Social situation may change swiftly to Sex (this refers to any one-to-one relationship, family, colleague, friend or sexual partner), if we are attracted to somebody. If so, do we remain in the former MindFrame Pattern? Yes, if that works for us in the changed Context. No, if we wish to be at our best in this new Context.

The change can be made instantly; we do not have to sit down and work out appropriate Storage Patterns. It can be simply activated through accessing an empowering belief which triggers the sequence which has been practiced beforehand, which can in turn accesses Storage Patterns, Change Patterns and Strategy Patterns automatically. Or we may bring a value to mind, such as sympathy and a similar sequence is triggered. Or, if we are well-rehearsed in the use of Strategy Patterns, it may be triggered through the enticing smile of the person we are introduced to. The emphasis here is on easily and effortlessly rather than strain and drain.

If we had to mentally rehearse an appropriate approach to a new Context every time we were introduced to someone it would be painful to watch. We would have to excuse ourselves, sit in a corner, close our eyes, sway from side to side, or go into whatever behavioural process we enter when accessing Storage Patterns etc, and generally look like a raving idiot. On the other hand, doing it at the flick of an internal switch would seem more appealing.

'First things first and second not at all'

Planning Contexts

Knowing the fluidity of the Contexts and the likelihood of possible change is one thing, but setting the Context in advance can be trickier, it may seem. As mentioned, it is entirely subjective in how we decide which Primary Context to tackle.

But how do we decide? Quite simply, we just think about the situation. We may do it for a meeting, or an interview, or even for going to the cinema. We may plan it the day before, or seconds before we leave the house or office. It is all about forethought. 'What do I want to get out of this meeting?' 'What state of mind would serve me best?' It requires only a few seconds thought to determine what we want, or what we most want.

First things first and second not at all.

If we prioritise we are far more likely to get what we want out of any situation. If we take the scattergun approach, we may get pockets of what we desire, but possibly not the whole. So, if we take aim at one specific Context, achieve that, we can then move on. It can take seconds.

However, prioritising is essential. That pre-planning exercise can take a few minutes or even a few hours if it is something really important like an interview or a presentation. Or it can take seconds if it is something seemingly trivial.

It is not trivial if it has become a concern for us. If we are not interacting well with others or failing to achieve our goals, the benefit of identifying a specific Context can not be over-stated. Take possible underachievement in the Context of Goal Attaining as an example.

If we set smaller goals, such as talking to a particular person in a Social Context and succeed in doing that, then we can chalk that up. It is so easy to overlook our successes. However, using MindFrames every success can be mentally logged. This builds up a repertoire of successes, mentally rehearses achievement and improves our performance.

As we continue to strike up these successes it boosts our self-esteem and we find that it spreads to the other areas of our life. We have a log-book of wins. We can take that log-book into other Contexts and apply the winning technique. That is why MindFrames are intentionally flexible. Components of a winning MindFrame formula in one Context can be applied to another. Or, the whole MindFrame can be taken.

How often do we observe people who are entirely different in personality, appearance etc when placed in another environment? It is often the case that the same person enjoys greater success in one area and not the other. Why not use what they have in the successful situation and adopt or adapt it for the unsuccessful environment? That is essentially what MindFrames is all about. Being in that right frame of mind in the right Context to get the right result we need.

Effective use of MindFrames ensures we continue to remain on course in that Context and do not get sidetracked. How? Because we are fully aligned, living our values, beliefs and exemplifying those in our behaviours. We are fully congruent and fully aware of what we want, how we need to act to get it and what to do if a spanner is thrown into the works. That is, re-set the course and continue. Empowering beliefs and a record of success, as just mentioned, are instrumental.

MindFrame Contexts 125

It sounds terribly mechanical though, does it not, to be always thinking of what state of mind to be in for every situation?

It does if we refer to them as MindFrames in everyday life. MindFrame Patterns are a structure, or a series of tools and techniques to be applied. The outcome is a frame of mind. That is something that is easily understood and does not cause confusion. It is something that everybody can understand.

Say to our husband or wife or partner, 'I want to get into the right frame of mind for this evening' and they will know exactly what we mean. They will probably give us time and space to do that. 'Just give us a moment will you?' you may ask and we can retreat to the bath or slouch in the armchair for a moment to put our self in the right frame of mind.

Tell our partner we are eliciting the right MindFrame Pattern for this evening's Primary Context of Fire, Communication, sub-heading Social and they may think we have totally lost it.

For the sake of 'world peace' we can frame our approach to each Context as getting our self into the right frame of mind. Soon it will become a natural, automatic action, often on entering the room. It depends on how we are. Logical people, those whose Decision Change Pattern is auditory digital, may like to plan ahead, write it down, make a list. Those who are emotional, or kinaesthetic, may change their MindFrame on a whim. Likewise highly visual sorts could choose to do so on seeing a crowd of people or maybe the door handle as they exit the house. Whatever works, whatever becomes easy and effortless is the best approach.

This is about connecting the conscious with our unconscious resources so it is only a matter of time before it becomes automatic. However, it is always useful to make a conscious effort to assess where we are, if is it still working and how we can improve further.

The second consideration mentioned earlier was how we design our MindFrame Pattern for each Context. We have been doing this as we go along. Many of us will already have a clear idea of designs for different Contexts. Some of us will have a clear template for a MindFrame that can work across much of our lives and can be tweaked for the different Contexts.

This is one of the simplest approaches and is what the majority of us will tend to do. We work out what works for us, adapt it slightly for different Contexts and work with that. If obstacles appear and we can not get round them using our current MindFrame we will adjust further, perhaps tweak one of our Change Patterns and that could well do the trick.

It is important that we work with what works for us, not change things for the sake of it. Minor adjustments are normally all that is needed in our

Change Patterns, especially as we have delved into such resources already using our Storage and Strategy Patterns. Equally important is that we do not over complicate or mechanise our approach to life. Be mindful by all means, but have fun by any means!

Although we may have been thinking about specific Contexts when designing our Mindframe Patterns so far, it would be useful to go into some more detail on the different Contexts to apply the best MindFrames possible. To ensure we are successful we need to cover all the bases. Lack of consistency over time is one of the most common causes for people who do not succeed. Remaining on track, having all the tools and resource we need to stick at what we are doing, is essential.

As we know, so much is instantly changeable including the Context, our states, and problems arising. In having more information about specific Contexts, combined with our congruent approach ensures that we remain in the appropriate frame of mind to ensure completion of our objective to our satisfaction. Yes, things will come along that attempt to blow us off course, and we will fluctuate between states, but with a heightened sense of awareness we can re-tune our internal understanding, adjust our approach and remain on track.

The following chapters will give us all we need to be in the right frame of mind in the right context to achieve our specific and desired outcome.

'Be mindful by all means, but have fun by any means!'

Chapter 19

Earth, Environment

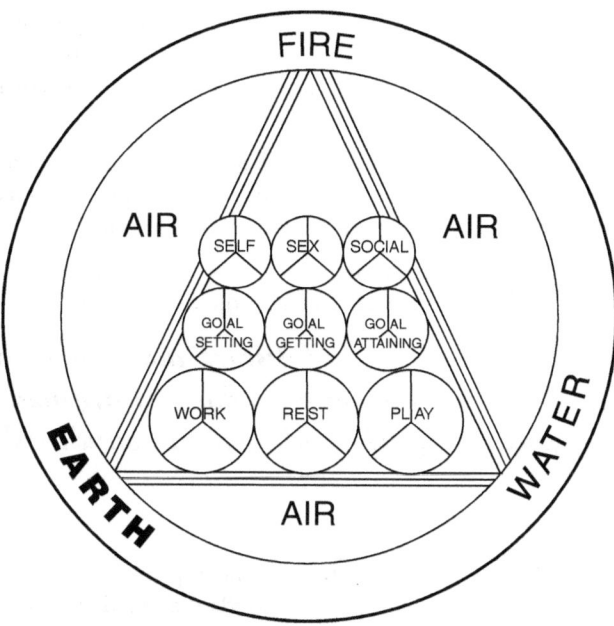

'The environment is a template of our ideal self, projected outwards'

Everywhere we go, everything we see, everything we feel and everything around us. Our environment, our surroundings, our all. We can never escape it, nor do we rarely want to. We live our dreams within it and experience all of life's vagaries as it watches disconnected, seemingly uninterested. Without it we are nothing and without us it would be barren, except for the squirrels.

Do we take the time to consider our environment? We are constantly made aware of the effects of climate change and global warming, the impact we are having on the world around us. But do we consider it from that altered perspective, how is it affecting me, or how am I letting it affect how I am?

Environmental factors have a huge impact on our everyday lives, and not just in the context of climate change. We are constrained, moulded, sometimes defined by our surroundings. At work we can be crammed into a cubby hole, limited in our horizon and sense of achievements, whilst at home we may walk as king or queen of all we survey, our mansion house articulating our stately outlook.

As human beings we are susceptible to define our self at every opportunity, perhaps in search for a greater meaning, and our environment helps us do this in a subtle, yet distinctive way. We can be different at home than we are at school, or on holidays, or with different friends from different backgrounds. To define our self in the context of one single surrounding would be extremely limiting, yet some of us do.

'This is when I am at my best, when I become the real me, here and now,' and that can be whilst driving a fast car, or riding a horse, or surveying our workforce from a supervisory office. Whatever floats our boat.

However, there is more to the environment than meets the eye. The environment is a template of our ideal self, projected outwards.

'They could manipulate and distort and create what they desired. They were not controlled or constrained by the physical limitations of their surroundings'

Dream Home

The eager estate agent was keen to show the Rappaports the upstairs rooms as quickly as possible, ushering the pair towards the grand staircase as soon as they entered the house. From the master bedroom, Gideon could see across the lawn to the birch tree lined approach of the main driveway which stretched for half a mile. Either side of the drive fields dropped away, distinguished only by the occasional ripple of a dry stone wall, hedge or stream. Far away in the valley below tiny dots of sheep could be seen scattered around the solitary farm house, smoke chugging from the chimney to indicate the only other human presence for miles.

'It's a bit out of the way darling,' Arabella whispered to her husband.

'I though that was what you wanted,' he replied, holding her around the waist as they surveyed the fresh country scene.

'I know, but this is really *remote*,' she stressed, her voice rising with exasperation. 'I mean, there's no-one else for miles. You saw the approach. Did you see another house?'

'Well no, but...'

'And all of the guest rooms have ensuite,' the estate agent interrupted, entering the room with hands apart as if holding a pretend bowl for approval, a smile erupting across his face as if he had just discovered the secret of happiness. Arabella bit her lower lip as Gideon ushered her forward with a friendly push in the back.

Earth, Environment 129

'We don't have to buy, *honey*, let's check out the loos...'

Only the feeling Gideon had was that they did have to *buy*. The house was magnificent, everything they were looking for and more. The children would love it, he knew. The games room, the stables, the pond, everything a child could desire, except...

'Who will the children play with?' she took the thought right out of his head.

'Who needs friends when you've got a playground like this?' he shot right back, knowing that she was struggling just like he was. This was going to be tough.

He thought back to the townhouse in the city. The roaring traffic. The sirens day and night. The air, for chrissake. 'This is the first breath of fresh air I've had in weeks,' he mused, and Arabella caught the deep well of contentment glitter in his eye, something she had not seen in weeks, since he came back from the fishing trip with the tale of the 'giant' carp, which had, it later transpired, been more of a giant goldfish.

'I know, I know, but there's so much to consider...' she said, mostly to herself as they traipsed through the stables towards the orchard and the disused swimming pool. God that dining room had been breath-taking she recounted. The chandeliers, the beautiful mahogany table. She could see the smiling faces of friends as Gideon wheels in the roast. The kitchen was idyllic too, but that was Gideon's domain.

Then there was the study overlooking the west wing and the Cloydyke hills, rolling off into the distance. She took a quick intake of breath at the thought of such an inspirational view. The feel of brush on canvas rippled through her fingers and up through her arm. 'Damn it', she thought, 'he's going to have to drag me out of here'. But what about the kids and the transport...

Gideon had given up on the kids. He had left them playing in the orchards, happy as he had been as a child, rambling over the rocks of Blackshaw Craggs. As the mud squelched over his moccasins he reflected on the outhouse which they had just left. As he squeezed Arabella's hand tightly she instantly recognised that pressure. He was away. He had left himself in the outhouse. As soon as they had entered he had muttered ascent. 'Games room,' he had affirmed. 'Pool table over there. Bar in the corner. Look, if I put the flat screen on that wall I can have a sofa just next to the bar. Mike'll love this.' Arabella had groaned, but with barely suppressed excitement. Gideon content in his own little world was contentment for all. She knew that as clearly as his inability to catch 'giant' fish. Occasionally he let the children join in, but never her. That was fine. When he re-entered society he was all the more enthusiastic and focused for it. When he had no outlet, his frustration was palpable and ruined many a quiet meal once the children had gone to bed. Besides, it gave her time for artwork and reflection.

Now, with the pressure of the squeeze of the hand, she could tell he had left himself in the outhouse, shooting pool and behaving like a child. That was fine too. She had taken herself back to the upstairs study and the Cloydyke hills.

Trick is to put the office next to the outhouse. That way I can say I'm working and pop next door when I want. That's cool, Gideon thought, as usual tempering his boyish enthusiasm with the sombre knowledge of Arabella's inevitable observation. 'You don't have to pretend you're working, darling,' she would say. He knew deep down that the justification was to himself.

'And finally, the gate lodge,' Martin the estate agent announced, as if unveiling the finale to a brilliant magic trick, saving the white rabbit until last. They had to lower their heads as they walked through the entrance into what turned out to be a one-roomed building, octagonal shaped, with simple benches skirting the edges and a solid oak table in the centre. Martin gestured for them to pull up the rickety chairs as Arabella felt an autumnal chill. Gideon closed the door and the stale air settled around them.

'So what do you think?' Martin enquired excitedly.

The couple held hands underneath the table and looked at each other pensively, as if afraid to hear the other's damning indictment. 'Well, I…' Gideon began, scrutinising Arabella for signs of dissent, 'I think there's a lot going for it…'

'Yeah, yeah, it ticks all the boxes,' Arabella began hesitantly, trying to cut Gideon off before he would begin one of his negative trawls. It always began with a positive spin and quickly tailed off into a dissection of everything that is wrong in the universe. She dreaded such moments, which were likely to last ages as the last vestige of enthusiasm would drain from her body. 'The outhouse was just what you were looking for,' she encouraged, knowing which button to press, raising her eyebrows as if that widening of the eyes would seal the deal alone by prising open the essence of understanding.

'Yeeesss… but does it have what you need?' he prodded. Better to raise the objections first with Arabella, he surmised, so he could talk her round now rather than wait for it to stew and solidify, in which case it could never be cleared up. The case of the forgotten birthday proved that one. It wasn't even hers, it was one of the kids, he recalled, still bitter.

'I mean, does it have what you need for your drawing,' he enquired, knowing full well that the light and the view from the study was ideal.

She squirmed at the mention of 'drawing' which always riled her, but calmed at the thought of that view again. 'It is ideal, just what I'm looking for'.

Earth, Environment 131

'It's perfect!' she blurted out. She caught herself. Out of the corner of her eyes she could see the impossibly large grin on the face of Martin the estate agent grow implausibly wider still. She thought his head might explode. Gideon looked a sconce. Rarely had he seen Arabella burst out with any proclamation. Rumination, reflection, hours spent going this way and that was how Arabella reached a decision, if she ever managed to come to one. The choice of children's school was a story still reeled out at dinner parties. He broke at once, like the eight ball smashing into the corner pocket.

'Isn't it just? It's exactly what we want!' Gideon blurted. In turn Martin could not contain himself. Times had been rough and he could not remember the last occasion he had made a decent sum. This place had telephone numbers attached, his manager had encouraged, 'if only the right sucker would ride into town.' He sat opposite the Rappaports beaming from ear to ear.

'Super! I knew you'd love it. As soon as you said what your spec was I knew this was the place. And the kids will love it too, the orchards and the swing down by the river...' but Martin's over-excitement, a source of irritation to his manager who had witnessed first-hand the collapse of trust from potential buyers as he prattled on, failed to puncture the shared delight between the couple.

Their hands became intertwined as they shared an intense moment. 'This will be perfect for us, darling,' Arabella assured, oblivious to Martin's background cackling.

'Finally,' Gideon agreed, 'a real home. We'll all be happy here.'

'What about the kids though?' Arabella sighed, less in resignation, more in acceptance that the move is on and they would find a way for the children to become as enraptured as themselves.

'Are you kidding? Have you seen the orchard and the playroom and the banister? Crikey, Harry will break his arm within the first five minutes shooting down that thing. They'll love it.' They both smiled reflecting upon Harry's recklessness and shocking accident record.

'Maybe a crash helmet is called for,' Arabella cautioned as her mood began to shift mid-sentence. 'But what about their friends? There's no-one around for miles.'

'Sure, sure...' Gideon pondered. It had been nagging at him too. They had spent the past nine years ensuring that everything was OK for the kids. Every decision cross-checked. Every eventuality considered in terms of school, friends, clubs, societies, performances... For an ad-hoc kind of guy, the last few years had been hard going for Gideon. Fortunately, Arabella was an organisational machine. He would usually walk in the door, she would shove a games bag under his arm, place a sandwich box in the other and instruct him where to drop the kids off. He was at his best shouting useless instructions from the sidelines. They both knew their strengths. But putting the kids first was where they merged as one.

'Look this is the 21st century. We have cars. We have four by fours for the winter. We're not trapped here. How far is town, 12 miles? That's half an hour, not three days. They can have their friends round, have sleepovers. You know Harry he'll roundup half a dozen new buddies on the first trip to A&E.'

They both laughed heartily. It was all they needed to assure themselves. Everything else would come down to logistics and long, after-dinner explanations accompanied by tantrums and the slow build-up of excitement towards a 'whole new world'.

'Let's do it,' Arabella said clearly. They leaned forward and kissed.

'We'll take it,' they said as one.

'There are no constraints, there is only the construct of our vision and that is boundless'

Reflections

Later in the day, Martin reflected upon the 'move of the century'. Martin, who was no great shakes as an estate agent, and knew he was no great shakes as an estate agent, was always moved by happy endings. His boss had chided him for being a sentimental fool and even his girlfriend mocked him for his emotional outbursts, but everyone knew he had a heart of gold. 'You're in the wrong game son,' his father had said helpfully on hearing he had got virtually no commission for the past six months. 'You should have been a social worker.'

Everyone in the office had stopped dead when Martin walked in with the news. A few mouths had dropped agape. The boss had dropped his spoon in his tea which had splashed his hand and caused him to drop the cup. 'Shit!' he yelped. But no-one looked round. All eyes were on Martin.

'No way. Hell-hole Manor? You sold Faulty Towers? Get out of here,' BMW Barry, his nemesis had mouthed, incredulous.

'That place has been on the market for years. How the hell did you sell that? Were they retarded?' Derek the cynic had chipped in.

The comments had continued for the rest of the day but Martin didn't mind. He was on cloud nine. And the jibes were underscored by a new tone of respect. None of the team could believe that Martin had made the 'sale of the century'.

Earth, Environment

Shinegrove House had been on the market for as long as any of them could remember. The estate of the second Earl of Cardingham had refused to shift the price. Because the estate would be split between three warring families, they had not been able to compromise on a reduced fee. It had been a long-running gag in the office that the new boy would have to show the American tourists around Shinegrove House. They had to keep up the viewings because of the annual payments. The manager loved that deal. Show a few yanks around a couple of times a year and reel in the lolly.

Naturally the place had fallen into disrepair and had become ramshackle by the turn of the century. No-one liked to take the 'Hell-hole' tour anymore, apart from in the summer, when Barry would add on a picnic in the grounds with his latest girlfriend in tow. In the dull grey of autumn, it had to be a job for 'no-mark' Martin.

Reflecting upon the triumph, Martin knew the money would come in useful. Janice had pleaded for him to get another job where he could earn enough money for them to put a deposit on a place for themselves. Martin, a self-confessed stickler, had sworn he had a good sale in him. He never really believed it though and this one amazed himself more than it did his colleagues.

Now though, it wasn't the money that he concerned himself with. It was the couple. He had been so excited that in the end they had to politely tell him to shut up. But he could see what it meant to them. What on earth were they seeing that he couldn't? The place was a wreck. It would cost thousands, tens of thousands, possibly into the hundreds of thousands to renovate the place. The roof was leaking. The floorboards downstairs were a hazard. And what the heck had the bloke seen in the outhouse? It had no roof!

'What the hell did they see that I didn't?' Martin wondered aloud.

'What?' Janice asked from across the table.

'Oh nothing,' Martin shrugged.

'What sort of place should we get then?' Janice asked cheerfully, barely able to contain her excitement. 'You're the expert.'

'Oooh, praise indeed,' he replied sarcastically, deep down relishing the rare compliment. Now I am an expert he thought, amusingly to himself. 'Haven't really thought about it,' he observed, almost surprising himself with his insouciance.

'How weird. For an estate agent, you're not very interested in properties are you? I've been thinking about it for years. I reckon we should go for a first-floor flat in town, just by the market square, I've been looking at...'

And so she continued, as Martin did just what Arabella and Gideon had done earlier. He took himself away to speculate on what really interested him. People.

What the hell made them buy it? Hope they'll be happy there. How can they afford it?

Case Notes:

Arabella's illustrations had been included in a little-known children's fantasy book, *The Riders*, which had subsequently 'taken off' as her agent had put it. Hundreds of illustrations for countless books had reaped a 'decent' income, if not a huge salary. *The Riders* had however caught the attention of a producer on holidays in London with his seven year-old daughter. The cover of the book had caught her attention and she had begged him to buy it. Bored on the flight back, he had reached over to rest the book from his sleeping child lest she drop it and clutter the aisle. Flicking through it, something amazing had happened. For the first time in his life he had been truly entranced by a story, as 'childish' as it had appeared.

The ensuing Fantasy Films picture had made over a hundred million, and the franchise quickly built. The author had insisted upon including Arabella's illustrations on every one of the book sequels. All fourteen and counting. Each one had sold in the millions across the world. Arabella, still largely unknown outside of her immediate circle of friends had done well from her 'drawings'.

Previously Gideon had been the major income earner in the family with his construction business. Since Arabella's success he had taken a back seat and let others run the company for him. He concentrated on fishing, pool and shouting useless instructions as the kids ran around parks kicking balls. He could also pursue his real love, renovating old properties. Despite the countless homes he had improved for others, he had never come across his 'ideal' property. That was until they drove up the birch lined avenue of Shinegrove House.

Observations:

Neither Arabella or Gideon spent any time in the moment, in the here and now, when inspecting the property. They had expected a ramshackle ruin and as they drove up the long drive-way that was what was before them. But that is not what they saw. They instantly saw what they wanted to see. The future, or the past. Gideon's idyllic childhood or Arabella's future inspiration sprawled out across distant hills.

Earth, Environment

Would their happiness be secure as a family unit once their dream house had been renovated? Who knows?

One thing is clear, their imaginations made their environment. The environment did not shape them. They could manipulate and distort and create what they desired. They were not controlled or constrained by the physical limitations of their surroundings.

When we talk of the Environment, Earth Context, we are not discussing outside control, we are talking about our control of the here and now, our environment. It is our Earth, our own individual grounding, our earthiness, our very self and how we connect to what is around us. We control that reality, our version of reality. The Rappaport's imagination is no more powerful than our own. They know clearly what they want and how to get it. Their vision is compelling.

Martin could not care less about his immediate environment, yet he could not have been happier, more enthusiastic.

The connection between our Earth, our Environment and the Earth, the Environment around us is intrinsic. There are no constraints, there is only the construct of our vision and that is boundless.

Chapter 20

Environment, Work

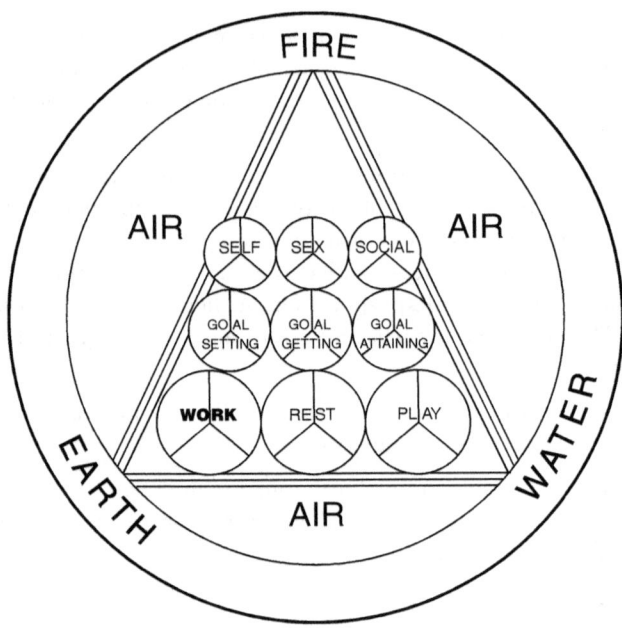

'We project what we perceive and we can perceive the world of work however we choose'

The Environment of Work goes beyond the meagre confines of the office walls, or the cab which we steer, or the classroom in which we teach. It reaches out beyond the field and crops we harvest, the regions we manage, the countries we visit. It goes beyond geographical confines, beyond political boundaries and flies above capitalist concerns. It is the globalisation of the mind, the steadying gaze of our externalisation of expectations. We project what we perceive and we can perceive the world of work however we choose.

The word 'work' can have heavy connotations. It can infer labour, toil, perseverance, effort, strain, stress, necessity and time restrictions. All too often it carries the appendage of 'hard', that beast of burden of a word which seems to wrap itself around 'work' at every available opportunity. Work is hard. Hard, hard work. We tend not to associate the word 'work' with anything easy. And if we do, we are most likely to keep it to our self. 'Of course I would like a pay rise and I most definitely deserve one. But I have to inform you that I find the whole thing rather too easy.'

Society works like our mind. If we associate earlier work experiences with toil, struggle, hardship and so forth, we also tend to label later experiences the same. Even though our working life may have changed dramatically over the years, our approach to it may not. Society works the same way. Work is hard. Time consuming. A hardship to be endured. It gets in the way of family, friends, relationships. It interrupts our enjoyment of life and all the fun that it entails. We cannot go snowboarding at work. We cannot lie on the beach. We cannot go for strolls in the countryside. We cannot sit in a restaurant and enjoy fine food and wine. We cannot dance at work, or sing, or sew, or parachute.

Of course there are jobs that do include those aspects but they are few and far between. Most of us are apparently constrained in what we can and cannot do during our working lives. Or so it would appear.

Before we explore that, it would be useful to define what work means in MindFrame terms.

'The vibration of the Work Context thrills to a different rhythm when the imagery becomes finely attuned to our individual expectations'

What is Work?

Work is not just what we do for a living. Work can be whatever it is that we are doing that takes a degree of effort. Digging up the patio and replacing it with a lawn can be described as work. There is a good deal of planning, effort and dedication that goes into it. It is work.

Work can be taking the radio apart and putting it back together, bit by bit.

Work can be digging up the potatoes in the allotment and turning the earth over.

Work can be painting the spare room.

Work can be composing a piece of music, painting a picture, writing a book.

Many of these activities could be described as enjoyable pursuits, hobbies, passions even. For some, digging up the patio and laying a lawn can be an enjoyable activity, something to keep us busy, physically active.

For many people it would be more appropriate to place such activities in the Context of Play. It may be something we enjoy doing and not something we have to do. And therein lies the distinction. If it is something we are compelled to do, out of necessity, then it is most appropriately labelled Work.

If it is something we want to do, yet find challenging, difficult even, then it is most likely to be Play. Once again, this is not written in stone. If we feel an overriding urge to sculpt, to spend hours everyday locked in a garage, moulding clay, covering ourselves in slime and creating wonderful objects, we may choose to describe that as Work. If we have been retired for 15 years and reap much satisfaction from the process, we may decide to call it Play. On the other hand if those sculptures are to be put on display and need to be produced by a deadline that must be met to ensure full payment as part of our day-to-day income needs, we may decide to label it Work.

This is where the distinction crosses over with the socially-constrained approach to Work. If we enjoy what we do, if it brings us huge satisfaction and a contentment matched by little else in our lives, work is hardly in the category of strife, endurance and pain. It is a blessing.

Even for many people who do indeed seek and find much personal empowerment and satisfaction in their jobs, they can still disavow in reflection. 'It's just a job, something I have to do,' when quite often, it can be much more that. Or we can go the other way. Our enjoyment of it and drive to improve, to hit targets, or meet deadlines, or deliver projects on time can interfere with other aspects of our lives. We can take it out of proportion and distort its impact.

Our approach to work is therefore incredibly important. Work in the MindFrame context does not have any negative connotations. The word is the broadest representation of what we all do at some time or another. It is something to which we apply our self to get a specific result.

'Stretch the contours of the mind to create the Environment which is most compelling'

Busy Bees

We have begun by re-defining work. By taking the traditional, distorted, generalised and deleted version of the word, the one with heavy negative resonance, and turned it on its head. It does not have to mean perseverance, hardship, stress and anxiety. Even Work which we endure until we find something else more suitable is not all bad. Absence would quickly ensue as we all have the capacity to escape from a meaningless captivity.

Work is what we do, it is a part of our essential self. We keep our self busy. We challenge our existence. We make our self do things. We are an industrious species. We need to do, to act, to be active and to produce things. Whilst it is great to relax, to reflect, to rest, it is also a part of our everyday existence that we Work. We push our self to get the results we want. We are conscientious,

Environment, Work

industrious and active beings, even though we may not always feel like it. We are, ultimately, driven to act.

As we do so, as we busy our self, undertake tasks, resolve issues and produce things, we have control over this domain.

We may have a line-manager or supervisor breathing down our neck. We may have the husband or wife staring at us from the window as we dig up the garden. We may be monitored on production rate, or whether or not we are hitting targets, or managing people effectively. But we are not automatons. We have creative license and liability. We approach every task and every project as subjective human beings. We may have had all the training and guidance the company can afford, but we will still approach it in our own, unique way.

Sometimes a lack of conformity to the way the organisation wants the task undertaken may lead to conflict and ultimately, termination of employment. Most of the time we conform to expectations and then work within the structure to pursue our own satisfaction, whilst meeting the objectives of the company.

Beyond that though is where the realm of MindFrames comes into its own.

We can take what we already know, how we are consciously and unconsciously. It is how we can use our values, beliefs and behaviours and shape them to get what we want. It is how we use our Storage, Change and Strategy Patterns to get the results we want.

Now we take the Context of Work and reshape it. It is not just the immediate working environment. It is the world of Work. It is our perception, projection and realisation of what the Work Environment is. It is all about us. It is all about how we are in any context related to Work.

What is our real Work objective?

What is our real Work goal?

What is our real Work outcome?

Is what we are doing now a means or an end? If it is a means, how far away from achieving our objective are we? What else do we need to do to achieve the result we want?

Do we have to change roles? Do we have to change jobs? Do we need more experience in this sector? Do we need to seek promotion?

The Context of Work is the realm of our personal objective setting. From Chapter 2, the Keys to An Achievable Outcome are useful here.

1. Stated in the positive.
What specifically do you want?

2. Specify present situation.
Where are you now?
3. Specify outcome.
What will you see, hear, feel etc when you have it?
4. Specify evidence procedure.
How will you know when you have it?
5. Is it congruently desirable?
What will this outcome get for you or allow you to do?
6. Is it self-initiated and self-maintained?
Is it only for you?
7. Is it appropriately contextualised?
Where, when, how and with whom do you want it?
8. What resources are needed?
What do you have now, and what do you need to get your outcome?
Have you ever had or done this before?
Do you know anyone who has?
Can you act as if you have it?
9. Is it ecological?
For what purpose do you want this?
What will you gain or lose if you have it?

The above is a useful guide to explore a specific and desired outcome and it gives a framework to pursue that objective. MindFrames go one step beyond.

The Work Context is connected to a broader perspective, a bigger picture. It is a model of how we view the world, except we are now beginning to redraw that picture to one that fits our view.

From the last chapter, we can see the effect a compelling vision has on the approach of a family aspiring towards strong areas of personal fulfilment. These were Work, Play, Sex, Social, Goal Setting, Goal Getting and Goal Attaining orientated. All of the Contexts are intimately connected. Changing one cannot help but impact upon another.

However, being mindful of our overall outcome, we can choose to operate differently within each Context to achieve our aim. Different roles, responsibilities, approaches are required. What bonds them together is a universal desire to move towards a particular outcome.

With that realisation we can re-shape our Work boundaries to incorporate everything that is useful to get us to where we want to go.

We have a different view of the world to our peers. The world of Work is one that shifts and moves, bends around us and moves to our whim. If this idea works, we take it. If a suggestion or motivation of a colleague holds us back, we discard it, sensitively. Once we have a self-realisation and certainty in our convictions, the world of Work is a supportive framework to help us achieve what we want. We control it, we manipulate it, no matter what level we are at within the organisation.

The cantankerous boss is not longer a burden, more a strain upon himself.

The colossal workload is not only our responsibility, it is part of the systemic flow.

The long hours are only necessary so long as that role is useful to us.

We are in control of what we are doing. We are here because we have decided to be here. We will continue to be here until we need it no more.

'Make the compelling outcome sharp and focused, so that all forms gravitate towards it, as if sucked into a vast vortex of inevitability'

Work Shapes

In the Work Context the question we have to put to our self is: does this support us in what we really want to achieve? How can we shape it to fit? Does it have to fit? What else can we do?

We are working for our self, not anyone else. We are entirely self-employed. We support our family, our loved ones.

The Context of Work is self-fulfilment.

Take three Work place values. For example, 'satisfaction', 'enjoyment', 'honesty'.

Three beliefs support those values. 'I get great satisfaction from completing a project.' 'I love what I do.' 'I always work to the best of my ability.'

The Storage Patterns provide inspiring motifs and images which are stimulated every time the working environment is encountered. A series of Storage Patterns are activated as tasks are undertaken, reflecting the empowering beliefs. Strategy Patterns are activated every time a difficult encounter with a client occurs. The individual is reaping the rewards of this newly invigorated approach. Colleagues enquire what has changed, how come you are so enthusiastic all of a sudden?

'It's just about being in the right frame of mind, that's all,' the much respected employee replies.

It is more than that though. MindFrame Contexts are more than that.

Of course the Contexts are about applying the specific values, beliefs and behaviours, plus the unconscious elements to that Context. It is also about re-defining and re-drawing the Context, the world of Work.

Take every representation we have in relation to Work. Pull it all together and create a massive structure, building, shape, whatever comes to mind. Bring in all the sights, sounds, colours, smells, tastes involved in those working experiences and finally, bring in the emotions and wrap them inside. All of them. Use the same Storage Pattern cinematic processes described earlier. Break down the sub modalities in detail, take a little time to go through the process of reconstructing the whole work-life experience.

Now begin to stretch those. Make the building larger, stretch the shape or structure. Begin to play with the confines of the object. Stretch the contours of the mind to create the Environment which is most compelling. Create a vision, a reality that works. And at the end of that, make the compelling outcome sharp and focused, so that all forms gravitate towards it, as if sucked into a vast vortex of inevitability.

Take a walk through that structure, the edifice, the shape, whatever it is and notice everything that is there. All the sights, sounds, smells, feelings. As those pictures, feelings, sounds are integrated, as every sub modality is explored and deposited deep within, take a look around at all those people in the Work Environment. Record all those systems, all those reports, all those products that are relevant and notice how they can be changed, at will.

The vibration of the Work Context thrills to a different rhythm when the imagery becomes finely attuned to our individual expectations. Soon everything, everybody can be seen to move to our tune, as our minds reshape the boundaries of our environment and we show the greatest flexibility of movement.

Chapter 21

Environment, Rest

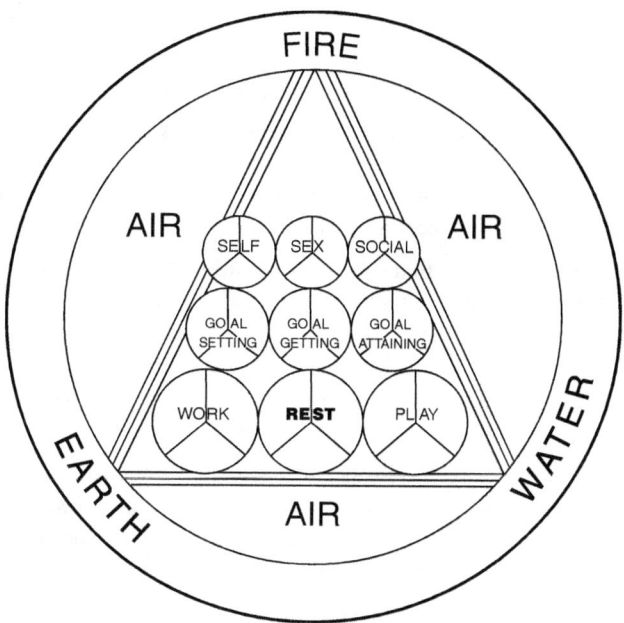

'Real rest is deep relaxation, being totally immersed in the moment, totally abandoned to calmness'

Rest is one of the most underrated and necessary functions we undertake. It is absolutely essential that we get the rest we need in order to achieve our objectives.

The rest we seek is a deep relaxation that enables us to recuperate and recharge our batteries in a short space of time. It is not sitting idly, mulling over problems whilst watching television. Real rest is deep relaxation, being totally immersed in the moment, totally abandoned to calmness.

The importance of finding real Rest on a regular basis can not be overemphasised. It allows us to do everything else we need to do. Without it, we would quickly run out of energy and begin to find activities laborious. We would then become prone to all sorts of illness. On the other hand, we can easily get our necessary level of Rest, whatever that is for each of us individually, so we can move forward, full of vitality.

Time is non-essential. If we find the appropriately deep level of Rest we require it can take a few minutes each day.

The point is to Rest absolutely, become totally immersed in the moment. If we can Rest deeply, charge our energy levels to maximum, all we need to do is enter the right state. With perfect practice we can reduce the time it takes to get into the state, enter it at the deepest level, and resurface moments later with all the resources we need. It is our internal deep sea diving.

Some of us may only require a few minutes every day. Others may wish to enter that deep relaxation state on numerous times throughout the day. Some may find it more useful to do it two or three times a week, possibly for longer periods. Once again, it is whatever works for us.

The emphasis here is that we learn to Rest properly. If we have set a compelling outcome and have all the 'towards' momentum we need, we need never run out of energy and enthusiasm, so long as we listen to our body and give it the rest, exercise and fuel it requires. We are already highly aware of the needs of our body, however we often choose to overlook its complaints or misread the signals.

Our body has a really good way of communicating with us. It yells out in pain. Likewise, if we are not paying attention to its resting needs, we will soon find out about it, as it switches off altogether and we are left snoring on the train or drowsing in front of a computer screen.

In MindFrames the Rest Context is one of the clearest to navigate in relation to Change Patterns. Although not the same for everyone, an example of the primary Patterns are: a strong 'internal' frame of reference under Evaluation.

Motivation could be strongly 'towards'.

Activity could be very much 'in the moment' and fully associated.

Organisation could be 'possibility' orientated, that is wanting rather than needing to do something.

It may be helpful for values and beliefs in the Rest Context to be self-oriented. Such as having health as a value and spending the relaxation time reflecting upon the revitalising effect upon the body. Beliefs can be along the lines of, 'I know I can relax totally and completely and get all the energy I need,' and 'As I relax deeply I can get all the resources I need to do x…'

The appropriate Storage Patterns can be unearthed when in a state of deepest relaxation. Everybody can relax. In fact everybody can relax totally.

> *'The point is to Rest absolutely, become totally immersed in the moment'*

Relax

All we need to do to relax completely is put our self in a comfortable position. A comfortable chair. And we can be comfortable in it. As we breathe deeply, so we can relax deeply all over. Just by breathing, taking deep breaths. Imagine taking those deep breaths now.

Once this passage has been read through, we can go through the process again when we are even more comfortable.

Take a moment. Take a moment to wonder. In a second or two, or maybe three or more, we can begin to see what it looks like through our own eyes, through our eyes as a child, as if we are a child.

The eyes of a child are wide and believing, full of awe and wonder and as we step through those eyes into the eye of the beholder, I wonder if we can not now begin to think as if we were a child.

Imagine what it would be like and it would be likely to like thinking like a child. How might a child think? How mighty might a child think as large and lurching as every sound and movement is?

There are giants in every sense and every sense is nonsense. There are lumbering adults with gangly limbs and strange shapes and sounds moving around the rooms of youth and education and play time. The changing sounds and shapes around us are sounds of laughter, are they not, or are they grander sounds such as encouragement and hysteria? What does it appear that every reminiscence grows hotter by the hour, with sunlight casting sparkles on every thought?

Who speaks when we hear the laughter and excitement all around us, whether tumbling down meadows, or flying higher and higher as we scale the heights of fantasy on the playground swing or shoot faster and faster as the roundabout whizzes around and around and around?

And around about this time, this time right now, in this very moment, many more memories can enter in. And is it not strange how every memory has a golden hue and every golden hue is cast in shining light and the sun always seems to shine through?

As we float away along the corridors of fantasy, the floating feeling carries us away and away and away. Even flying through the air can we not see different ways, vapour trails and super highways in the sky? And we can choose whichever way is right, whichever right way we choose is the right way.

Right away we fly towards the one true right place for us.

Here on the sandy beach, with the palm trees...

Here on the top of a snow coloured mountain...

Here sailing on the high seas...

Here in the rose garden, pruning the blooms...

Here by the log fire, curled up on a sheepskin rug...

Here in a steaming bath, bubbles bursting around us...

And finally, wherever is dear, wherever is sanctuary, wherever is sacrosanct. Wherever we find most inspiration and relaxation. Wherever we can relax deeply.

And we can relax deeply here. We can become so much deeper in relaxation.

We deepen and deeper as all those sounds and pictures and feelings become bigger and brighter and louder and more intense. We can spend a few moments playing with those sounds and pictures and feelings, taking our self to that time on that beach, or on that mountain, or in that garden when we really feel great, at our very best.

And once we have taken the time to fully experience just how great that feels now we can take that with us, to our new, improved favourite place.

Here, magic happens. We can turn up all those feelings and sounds and pictures. We can become more content, happier still. Richly revelling in all the colours and sights and sounds. All the laughter or the singing or the beat of the music. All of it, and all of it gives us more and more, more and more respite and reassurance and deeper relaxation.

How can we not relax totally as we revel in the playground of our senses?

How can we not feel a deep, deep satisfaction from playing so heartily as we have not played since we were children, and are children still and right now, as if we were never anything else?

How can we not begin to find that every time we do this, again and again, every gain is like a grain of sand on the beach that sits beside another and another and another until the whole ground beneath us becomes a sea of sanctuary?

What can we not fail to gain in being so completely at calm as we rest in the relaxing current of the earth, as we feel its rich vibration, our vibration of all that is wholesome in those sounds and pictures and feelings?

What else can possibly be missing?

As we step into the sunshine promenade we feel the warmth all around us. There, wherever we are right now, we can begin to see whatever it is we find our self wanting to do.

We may be as we are dressed right now, or will be dressed a little later, or as we once were, whatever is right. And is it not amazing how clear and colourful and bright we seem to our self?

And is it not oh so easy to turn up the volume, increase the size of the picture and pump up the feelings until we are as high as a house and loud as a hundred voice choir? What we are doing makes so much sense with what we are going to do in a few minutes, or a few seconds, or maybe a few hours in the future, or the next day, or next week. We are playing at what we will be doing and how we need to do it right, right now.

How relaxed we look as we play through it in our minds, how smiling and happy and easy it all is. Even the things that we thought were once so hard are no more than the easiest thing we ever did as a child, such as drawing a happy face, or skipping, or kicking a ball, or playing catch.

Remember, remember! As a child running and skipping and jumping easily, so easily and often and how that appears now as we go through that speech, or rehearse that meeting, as we are now, on our beach or hideaway, or wherever it is that works. As we see as a child how easy it is to walk through that situation, feeling as great as we do now, as we do the deed now, and feel great thinking about it later.

And as it becomes easier and easier, smoother and calmer, as relaxed as a soundly sleeping baby, deeper than any adult could ever try and imagine. And go ahead try and imagine being so deeply relaxed, totally relaxed about everything, so that when the floating returns to journey us home to the nearer now, the now of the right here we can bring all those relaxed feelings, every one, right back with us, only fortified by resolve and energy to fire us further forward, right through the right now, to the right in front, straight ahead, right into the immediate future.

As we begin to resurface, feeling brighter and recharged, easier and freer, we can also reflect upon how easy it is, once in a totally relaxed position, we can re-enter, recreate and go even deeper next time.

If we re-read the above, re-immerse our self in the process, we can later take our self away and run through it in isolation, and let it take full effect.

Real Rest

There is no more to relaxing, to deep-seated Rest than to spend a little time in introspection. It is using the magic of the mind to fantasise and restore every little bit of lost energy and recharge the mainframe. By breathing deeply and entering that deeply relaxed state, we become all we need to get to where we want to go.

Without real Rest we will become lost. With real Rest we can become anything in a second. As we become masters of our own relaxation, we control our frame of mind and govern our state. To achieve anything we must know how to control the zone, be in the flow, and maintain momentum in the here and now.

Rest gives us all we need to do that, right now.

Chapter 22

Environment, Play

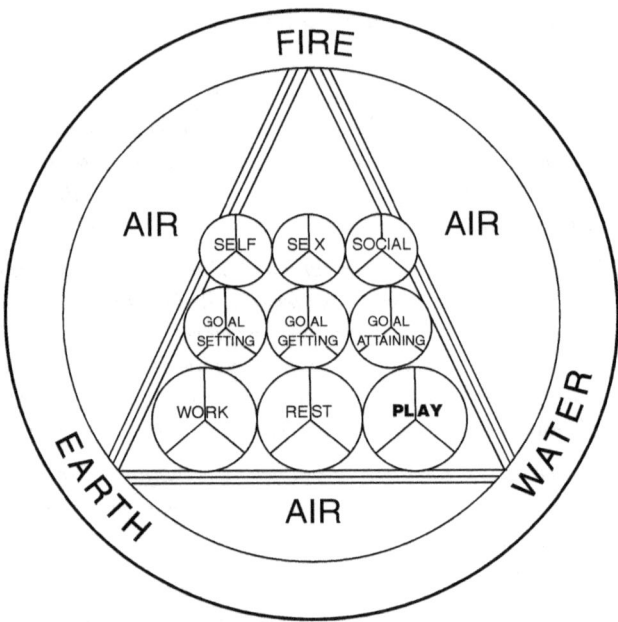

'The past has happened, it's been and gone, and the future's going to come what may, there's no stopping it. The only place to be is right here, right now. It's where it's all at'

The Interview

'There is nothing else, only the moment, only what is right there in front of you, what needs doing there and then.'

'Don't you sense the danger, feel the fear?'

'Not in the way you're thinking. Yes, it's there, I'm aware, but the adrenalin, the buzz of the moment, the focus on climbing is so intense, so thrilling, that all else is lost. I'm only aware of what is right in front of me, finding the right foothold, getting the right grip. The focus wins out every time.'

'Don't you ever think about everything that could go wrong? The weather, the avalanches?'

Environment, Play

'No, not then. Earlier, in the planning stage, yes, but not when I'm climbing. Back in camp when we're preparing the next climb is the time for that. We also stop to take stock every now and then, whether to push on or bed down for the night. But not when I'm climbing, that requires every ounce of attention on what I'm doing. I don't have time for fear, or thoughts of failure. I'm in a tunnel, totally focussed, totally driven.'

'It sounds exhilarating.'

'It is. Like nothing else on earth. The buzz, the excitement, I feel really alive, the best feeling in the world.'

'Is it like that when you reach the summit?'

'Yeah sure, that's a thrill. But in a different way. That's all about completion. Finishing what we set out to do. It makes sense of all the effort, pain and endurance. But that's a different kind of a buzz. For me it has more to do with satisfaction, the achievement, ending the journey, finishing the chapter...'

'So that's different from when you're actually climbing?'

'Yeah. There's a different dynamic going on. It's the thrill of the ride, the intensity of the moment. I feel so... exhilarated, so alive... it's hard to put into words...'

'What are you thinking at that time, when you're scaling an overhang for example?'

'Thinking? I don't know. I don't know if thought really comes into it. I'm just in the zone. Totally focussed. Everything seems to happen automatically. The experience kicks in I suppose. I've done it thousands of times before. The hands know where to go and the feet just follow. Like a horse trotting along. When I'm in that zone I don't think at all, I suppose, I just do. Do you know what I mean?'

'Mmm. So how do you know when you're in the zone? What's happening?'

'I'm just there. It just happens. Everything else fades away. There is nothing else, only the rock face and me. We become as one. I melt into its features and it embraces me. It sounds crazy but that's how it feels, at that moment. I just feel at one. I know I'm exposed, vulnerable against the powerful forces of nature, just a tiny dot on a mountainside, but in that moment I feel... exhilarated. There's no other word for it, I feel exhilarated. The energy is immense.'

'Once you've scaled the heights. When you get back to everyday life, is there anything else that comes near it?'

'I haven't really thought about that. You see, so much of my life goes into planning the next expedition, or practicing and training climbs. I'm either anticipating the excitement or experiencing it. Talking about it is the next best thing. It's why I go on and on about it...'

'So you spend a lot of time looking forward to the next climb?'

'Yes I do. It's not the same, but there is a kind of excitement in that as well. It's very different though, much more serious. It's all about putting the groundwork in, making sure we take account of every variable. Very methodical, but necessary.'

'Is that a grind for you?'

'Ha! Yes and no. We all have to do it. Sure, I'd rather be off scaling a peak, but wouldn't we all? Climbers that is. So that's what I tend to do. Just head off and climb. It doesn't matter where I am. The thrill's always there.'

'What's more of a thrill, the bigger the mountain or the harder the climb?'

'Either, or. The sense of achievement is greater, sure with a hard climb. But the thrill of doing it? Pretty much the same the world over.'

'Thank you Sir Digby. One final question, what advice would you give to young climbers starting out today?'

'Be safe. Prepare properly. Planning is everything. Then enjoy. We're the luckiest people on earth.'

'How much of the time do you spend thinking about what you're going to be doing next, what you're going to be doing tomorrow, or when the next deadline is? How much time do you really spend being yourself, enjoying yourself?'

The Interviewee

Marion tucked the dictaphone away in her knapsack and shook Sir Digby Reynold's hand. 'That was fascinating, thanks again,' she said, still a little in awe of the mighty mountaineer, the first climber to scale the north face of Kilumbaro, a feat that would enshrine his place in mountaineering history forever.

'The pleasure was all mine. I love to talk about it, I still bore friends to death with climbing stories. Betsy leaves the room.'

'Your wife?'

'No the dog.'

'Oh no, it's amazing. I wish I could feel that way.'

'You do.'

'Yes I do.'

'No, I mean, you *do*, you really do feel that way. Or at least something like it.'

Marion eyed the older man suspiciously. His long thin face gave him a hand-dog expression, exacerbated by his fine, sandy moustache and eyebrows. In contrast his glittering blue eyes were alert and penetrating, as if providing evidence of the veracity of every spoken word. For a moment she thought that if she stared long enough she would be able to see tips of the Himalayas in those eyes. He tapped his knobbly, granite-toughened fingers on his leg and leaned forward, conspiratorially and whispered, 'This is no secret, my dear, we can all get a buzz out of life.'

Marion's expression remained quizzical. This did not make sense to her. Her life to this point had been deliberation, conviction and execution. Make up her mind what to do, pursue it with vigour and determination and ensure, at all costs, that she hit her target. That is how she had risen to features editor of the leading consumer title *Mini Me* within two years of arriving as a reporter. It was also why she felt she could partially understand, or at least empathise with the sense of achievement, when he talked of scaling a peak.

The thrill of the ride, the buzz, the focus, being in the zone, living in the moment had all seemed, well 'thrilling' to her, but she could not associate with that. That was why she was so entranced with Sir Digby's words. It seemed so distant, almost ethereal.

'Any more drinks?' the waiter interjected, giving Marion time to compose herself.

'Are you staying, or do you have to rush off?' Sir Digby enquired.

'I do have another interview in about half an hour, but I've got a few minutes. I'm alright, but please order yourself.'

'Water for me thank you.' As the waiter rounded the corner from their alcove, discreet, even if it was in the lobby of a busy west London hotel, Sir Digby pursued his theme. 'What do you enjoy doing?'

'Enjoy? I don't know. The regular things I suppose. Eating out, going to the cinema. I do enjoy the theatre, but I have so little time these days…'

Sir Digby sat back as if chewing over every word. Marion's quizzical expression had been replaced by one of confusion. Her large hazel eyes, partially obscured by spectacles, dilated and illuminated her face at every movement of a facial muscle. Still in her early twenties, Marion had the maturity and demeanour of someone twice her age, yet the exuberance of a teenager. Her interviewees became easily attached to the attractive expressions and the radiant eyes, which were nearly always timed to correspond with a brilliant insight or keen observation from the interviewee. In Sir Digby's case it was all genuine.

'You see, I think you are being disingenuous. I think there are things you 'like' more than you are letting on. What do you really 'like'? What do you love doing?'

'Like I said, I think my first love is the theatre. I've enjoyed it since I was a little girl. But I get so little time…'

'What is it like when you do go?' Sir Reynolds interrupted.

'Wonderful, I suppose. I enjoy most performances.'

'Does it feel good? Do you feel inspired?'

'I suppose so. But it's an aesthetic thing for me. I know most of the scripts, I normally read the book beforehand and I'm always anticipating what's going to happen next, running through the performance with them. I used to do some acting when I was younger, before the career got in the way…'

'Ah!' Sir Reynolds exclaimed, leaning forward eagerly, those gigantic hands clasped as if in triumph of discovery. Marion imagined him on top of Everest, clasping his hands and exclaiming to himself, 'Here we are then, top of the world, marvellous,' in his broad Devonshire brogue.

'What? What is it?' Marion asked, slightly unnerved at the insight she had yet to ascertain.

'Tell me more about the theatre.'

'Like I said, I enjoy it. But it's not a thrill in anything like how you describe what you do. It's not in the same league. I just enjoy it, that's all.'

'You said you run through the performance with the actors. How do you mean?'

She took a moment to consider. Sir Digby's sparkling eyes never left her. 'I suppose I'm always projecting ahead, wondering who's going to come on from which wing. How they're going to approach the part. Second guessing I suppose. Sometimes it's a surprise, mostly it's not. But I still enjoy it.'

'And when you were acting. Was it the same then?'

'No, no not at all. Come to think of it, that was an 'in the moment' kind of thing.'

'Was it?' Sir Digby mused, his eyes widening to indicate to Marion the importance of the revelation. 'But was it a buzz my dear?'

Environment, Play

'Not in that way. That's why I didn't think of it at first. It was different somehow. Yes, I felt connected, what you might call 'in the zone'. But it wasn't a thrill. It depended on the character, whoever I was playing.'

'Interesting. And what was it like when you were playing those parts? How did it feel for you?'

'Good. Well, no, great actually. I felt so immersed. Involved. Yes, that's the world, *involved*. When I was playing a part it was the only time I ever felt involved. Totally immersed. The rest of the time I'm planning ahead, or wondering what to do next…'

'I know, I know I can see that,' Sir Reynolds chuckled. Marion had become excited, moving her arms around as she recalled her acting days. She flushed at how animated she had become. 'So why give it up?'

'I don't know if I ever 'gave it up' as such. I moved on. I just did other things. Other things took over, like the job. I had to start taking my life more seriously. That's what my father always used to say, 'when are you going to grow up?' Suppose I have now.'

'Will you ever go back to it?'

'I don't know. Never really thought of it. I might take a look again, it couldn't hurt.'

'Before you do that. Do one thing for me.' This time it was Marion's turn to lean forward, intrigued at the old man's suggestion. 'Consider this,' Marion nodded her head slowly, encouraging him to go on.

'How often, in your life are you fully involved in the here and now? What is happening at the moment? How often are you fully here, enjoying what you are doing in the present?

'How much of the time do you spend thinking about what you're going to be doing next, what you're going to be doing tomorrow, or when the next deadline is? How much time do you really spend being yourself, enjoying yourself?'

Marion's nodding slowed as her gaze fixed on the disused ashtray on the table by her left knee. She thought of work, the office, the interaction with her colleagues, always light and airy, occasionally witty, but never serious. But she was always thinking of articles, or interviews, or as he said, the next deadline. With friends? Was she really with them when they were talking about boyfriends, husbands and families or was she considering her own future, her own family needs? And when she was by herself? Well she knew the answer to that. She spent the whole time speculating, either on what she'd done that week, on what went wrong and what went well, or looking forward to the next day or week, the next interview, which celeb she had lined up.

'Damn it' she thought to herself, unaware for a split second that she'd said it out loud. She reddened as Sir Reynold's long face squeezed into a broad smile and she saw for the first time the expansive generosity in those searching eyes.

'Give it some more thought. Think about how you can live a little now. And I don't mean just for enjoyment purposes, I also mean for achieving what you want. If you're in that involved state, how you were when you were in character, playing the part, you may find you can achieve more at work, get what you want more easily. Live in the moment. The past has happened, it's been and gone, and the future's going to come what may, there's no stopping it. The only place to be is right here, right now. It's where it's all at,' he concluded, smirking at his own 'hip' phraseology.

'But don't you need to plan ahead? You stressed the importance of that when it came to expeditions.'

'Sure, sure. Of course planning is important. And re-appraisal, stopping to take stock. If we didn't do that half way up a mountain I wouldn't be here now. But once it's done, it's done. Get on with it. Don't get stuck in thinking about the future, just do it. You'll find you enjoy life more and get more done, quite simply. What's the line from that film, 'Get busy living or get busy dying'. I've said something similar to myself a few times whilst stuck in an ice blizzard I can tell you. Same thing's true back on earth too. '

'I never really thought about it before. Isn't it amazing how you can't see things that are right in front of you? No wonder I get so stressed. I somehow managed to forget something that made me feel really happy,' she mused, mostly to herself. 'But how do I just put myself in the moment, become involved again? I'm out of practice,' she laughed.

'That's for you to figure out,' Sir Reynolds said rising, holding out his hand again. As she shook it, he leaned forward and pecked her on the cheek. 'It's been a pleasure Miss Wheaton.'

'Marion please,' she protested. 'It's been… well… 'exhilarating'.'

'For me too. Goodbye now,' and with that Sir Reynolds turned and strolled towards the lobby, a man truly without a care in the world, or so it seemed. Halfway across the marble entrance he stopped. His hand went to his chin and he turned on his heels. 'Miss Wheaton,' he called, 'sorry, I mean Marion. Why don't you try looking through your own eyes?'

The waiter, busy collecting the cups from the table, pretended to ignore the strange comment. Marion smiled and waved as she did just that, thinking to herself, 'I'm going to be lucky too…'

Environment, Play 155

Total Immersion

In the MindFrames Context Play is not play as in childish frolicking. It is the serious business of being fully associated, fully connected with the here and now, completely focussed on the task at hand. Whilst this powerful state is one most associated with enjoyment, it is a wonderful condition to be in to accomplish a task, to be totally immersed in what we are doing. Of all the Contexts it can be the most empowering.

The most useful Change Patterns for this is Activity, being in the now. Other possible useful Change Patterns include Information, specific details. Motivation could be strongly towards. Motive could be achievement and Evaluation, internal. Key though is Activity, living in the moment.

The Storage Pattern should be fully associated. The Strategy Pattern should be associated to a similar state of total immersion. Be here and now: having, doing, being and truly living.

Chapter 23

Water, Movement

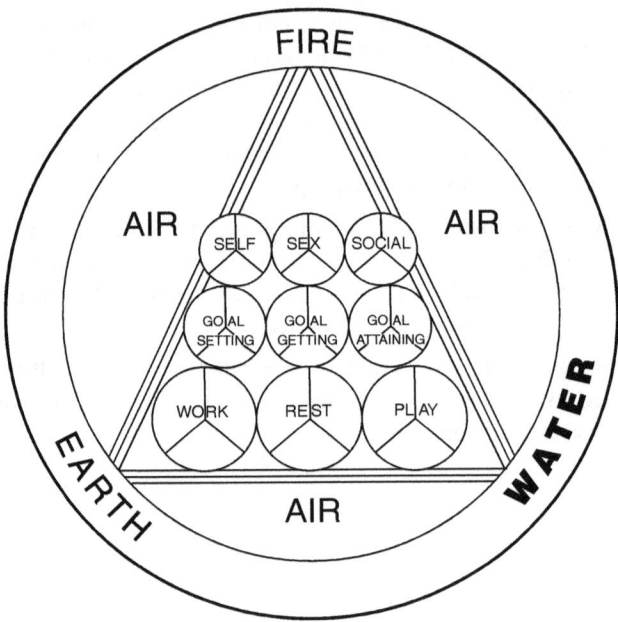

'For the first time, one of the key findings of NLP can be applied to this theory of motivation to combine and give us all we need to maintain a consistently high quality state to get the result we want'

Until now everything covered has advocated movement, gradation, shades of grey, leverage. To support this flexible approach there is an underlying theory that appears at first to be digital; that is one thing or the other. Indeed the principles are as clear as the title suggests, Reversal Theory*.

Reversal Theory

The theory states that people are inconsistent and reverse between psychological states, depending upon the meaning and motives felt by the individual. Reversal Theory states that there are 'eight ways of being', made up of four pairs of reversals. We are in four of the eight states at any moment in time and can switch into the reverse of any of the pair of states in an instant. The four pairs are: Serious or Playful, Conforming or Rebellious, Mastery or Sympathy, and Self-Orientated or Other-Orientated. These can be further described as Means-Ends for Serious or Playful, Rules for Conforming or Rebellious, Interaction for Mastery or Sympathy, and Relationships for Self or Others.

The theory states quite categorically that we cannot be in the opposite state at the same time. We cannot be rebellious whilst we are conforming and we cannot be playful whilst we are being serious. We can, however, 'flick the switch' and enter into the reversed state instantaneously.

Does this not contradict what MindFrames espouses in terms of absolutes? On one level, yes, as MindFrames refer to every thing, structure, context, and state, as being flexible and changeable.

On the other hand it would be impossible to be playful and serious simultaneously. Some part of us might be serious as we go about playing a game for example, such as having an underlying desire to win and being mindful of how we go about doing that, but the motivational state is playful as we undertake the activity. The application of reversals is therefore useful in discovering what state we are in at a particular time. The theory is particularly useful for assessing motivation.

The purpose in applying to MindFrames is because of the underlying flexibility of the theory. It does not categorise people. It does not put us into boxes and describe us as 'introvert' or 'extrovert'. That can have a purpose for some people, although it can be damaging if it is not applied in context, which it seldom is. Reversal Theory emphasises that we are inconsistent and changing, reacting to the same thing in different ways on different occasions depending upon our state of mind.

A profile can be determined through a simple questionnaire which indicates how much time we spend in each of these reversed states. It does not indicate what we are doing when we are in these states, nor the quality of those states. That is, if we are achieving the results we desire.

What it does show is how long we spend in each state, which can be the starting point for assessing if we need to spend more time in one state over another, and whether we should enter more fully into the state to get the goals to which we aspire. Awareness alone can help us move towards a state which is more helpful. If we take a look at these opposites now and apply them to our MindFrame Contexts, we can begin to see which states would be more useful.

Through scrutinising how long or short a time we spend in each state, we can determine how much use being in a particular state is for us. If we are stuck in one state for prolonged periods and are having problems because of that, it would be useful to switch states.

MindFrames obviously gives us all the tools we need to do that, but the point here is that through awareness of our reversals, we can gain even greater control over our frame of mind. Research has shown that when people are made aware of their reversal states they are far more likely to succeed in whatever they are doing. This has been proven in everything from sports, health and business to giving up smoking, tackling violent behaviour, education, counselling and team building. Using MindFrames in conjunction with Reversal Theory we can go beyond what has ever been accomplished before.

First, a little more information on the states mentioned in Reversal Theory.

'The knowledge of the power we now have to control our frame of mind can inspire us to move beyond the limitations of our previous understanding'

Ways of Being

The first pair, Serious or Playful, is in the Means-Ends domain. The Serious state is future and achievement focussed and is concerned with making progress towards a goal. In the Serious state we are planning ahead, creating a sense of direction. We are thinking strategically, seeing the 'big picture'. Marion from the last chapter would have spent a lot of time in this state. It can be very helpful in the Goal Setting Context in MindFrames. This is focusing on the 'end', the destination, not the journey.

The Playful state on the other hand is about having fun in doing something for its own sake, enjoying the moment. It is all about energy and enthusiasm, being creative and spontaneous. This is the 'means', the journey itself. It is climbing the rock face, playing the guitar, solving the puzzle. Just because it is labelled 'playful' does not mean it can not be concerned with undertaking an important task. Think of the Activity Change Pattern and being fully associated, immersed in the here and now. That is the Playful state.

The Rules domain splits into Conforming or Rebellious. Conforming is about doing the right thing at the right time, fitting in. This is when we accept rules and structure and guidance. It is when we follow procedures, adhere to standards and accept things as they are.

Rebellious is when we feel free, unrestricted and liberated. In this state we can be defiant, stubborn, belligerent or eccentric. It is when we are being mischievous, challenging assumptions, questioning, disagreeing, arguing, being critical. It can also be useful for creativity and innovation, challenging the norm.

The third pair is the Interaction domain of Mastery and Sympathy. Mastery is all about winning, of having control and power. In this state we will exhibit determination and confidence and will strive to take charge.

The Sympathy state is about affection and caring, building and maintaining relationships. In this state we are concerned with building strong relationships, providing emotional support, co-operating with others and being open and caring. We are likely to be sensitive, tender and kind in this state and we are concerned with being likeable to others.

The final pair is in the Relationship domain. This is whether we are Self-Orientated or Other-Orientated. Self-Orientated is about individualism, doing the best that one can for oneself. This is concerned with personal ambition, attention-seeking, taking personal responsibility and realising personal ambitions. It is about putting the self first.

Other-Orientated is about collectivism, doing the best that one can for others. This is all about helping others, working as a team rather than for personal gain, boosting pride from the accomplishment of others. It is concerned with the team spirit, being sensitive to other peoples' needs and can involve coaching and mentoring.

Reversal Theory states that we are in four of these states at any one time. If we sit down and think about what we are doing, thinking, feeling at this precise moment, it is fairly easy to place our self in four of the eight categories. When we do this we are not committing our self to an absolute. We are not 'playful' or 'conforming' all of the time. It is a snapshot of how we are at one moment in time. It is neither right nor wrong. We can be in a playful state for a tiny percentage of our lives yet reap the greatest results from that time, and visa versa. What Reversal Theory does is put us in mind of how much time we spend in each state, and in doing that, how much we are getting out of being in that state.

This is where MindFrames comes into its own. We are now moving into the highly valuable realm of movement, planning, processes, undertaking tasks and achieving goals. Our preferred right frame of mind for each of these Contexts may be different, but if we use Reversal Theory to assess how much of the time we spend in each state, we can then use MindFrames to put our self in the right state for more of the time, and most importantly, to the highest possible level.

'We can control our motivational states to a degree never considered previously. Through applying Change Patterns alone we can have a remarkable impact upon our reversals, an approach overlooked until now'

Controlling States

As we read through the eight ways of being it may have become obvious how much cross-over there was with each of the Contexts. Mastery and Sympathy, the Interaction domain, can be seen to draw a close parallel to the Communications Context. Likewise the Orientation domain. The Serious and Playful pair, the Means-Ends domain, overlaps with the Environment and Movement Contexts. The Conforming and Rebellious pair, the Rules domain once again can be seen to overlap with Movement.

Through being aware of the overlap, we can work out the best states to be in for each Context. This is a personal, highly individualistic application, so it is no use being prescriptive in advising what state to be in. Also, the real impact comes from being at our best in whatever state that is. We may be in the rebellious state all day long, but it does not get us what we want. On the other hand, we may enter that state for two minutes, and because we do it to our maximum benefit, that may be all that is required.

The rich resources we have in our Storage and Strategy Patterns is essential here to enter fully the state we require. We can also use the anchoring suggested earlier, plus other techniques to put us in the state we want. However, Reversal Theory is adamant that states are instantly changeable, like the flick of a switch, and can be triggered by a number of variables which we looked at earlier. This is something that MindFrames has addressed in terms of a negative trigger. We can collapse anchors and set compelling Strategy Patterns. However, we are still wildly variable people. We skip from moment to moment and our attention can flutter around.

This is a primary concern of MindFrames. How do we consistently remain in the right frame of mind over a period of time to achieve our specific and desired outcome? We have covered some of the most effective NLP techniques to help us access the right states at the right time. However, that consistency may still be a problem for some of us.

For the first time, one of the key findings of NLP can be applied to this theory of motivation to combine and give us all we need to maintain a consistently high quality state to get the result we want.

This is through the use of Change Patterns. These patterns are most certainly not digital. They are levers, which we pull or push, this way or that, to get the result we want.

If we go through the eight ways of being again we can see how effective this can be.

Firstly, Serious. This is the realm of Goal Setting, which we will come onto in the next chapter. The Change Pattern with the greatest relevancy here is Activity. This is where we put our self in the planning mode, 'through time', looking towards the future. As we push the lever towards the future perspective, standing back from time, becoming dissociated, seeing our self in the picture, we find our self in the right state to approach this task.

If we become distracted, if we begin to get blown of course, we simply step back and take stock. To re-enforce this Change Pattern we can enter into a Storage Pattern which is dissociated and future focussed.

The power of using Change Patterns here is that through consciously deciding to be more externally focussed, for example, we automatically enter into the right state to approach the task in hand.

The Playful state is the reverse. So we can pull the Activity lever towards 'in time', become fully associated, look through our own eyes and live in the moment. This is very possibly where we need to be when in the Goal Getting Context. We can then enter into a Storage Pattern which is fully associated.

What happens when someone interrupts us, throw us off course, surely we lose that Storage Pattern, come out of that state? Yes indeed and therein lays the problem. Now, fully cognisant of our Change Patterns and what states we need to have in every Context, we merely switch back. So the question then becomes, how can I get back into the state I need to be in?

If that is Playful, we simply become fully associated again, and focus entirely upon what we are doing. We can then lever other Change Patterns to help us accomplish that task.

For Conforming, we would need to have an external Evaluation, so we can fit in with the expectation of others.

For Rebellious we may move towards 'feel right' in the Decision Pattern.

For Mastery we would need a 'power' or 'achievement' Motive pattern.

For Sympathy we could do with a Primary Interest of 'people' and an 'external' frame of reference for Evaluation.

For Self-Orientation we could go 'internal' and for Other-Orientation we could go 'external' again.

If we write down each of the eight ways of being and apply them to a specific Context, we can soon determine which states we need to be in, at what levels, to get the results we want. Once we have done that, we can decide upon the beliefs, values and behaviours and then the Storage and Strategy Patterns that would be most helpful in those Contexts. The fundamental driver though is our Change Pattern. As we adjust our unconscious processes we can enter the state at will, maintain it for the required duration, and ensure we can return to it following distraction.

Research shows the powerful impact Reversal Theory has had once people become aware of their motivational states and take remedial steps to move where they want to be. With MindFrames we can up the ante considerably. We can control our motivational states to a degree never considered previously. Through applying Change Patterns alone we can have a remarkable impact upon our reversals, an approach overlooked until now.

Even if we choose not to use these eight ways of being for every Context, the knowledge of the power we now have to control our frame of mind can inspire us to move beyond the limitations of our previous understanding.

The Movement Context is pivotal. If we can refine our approach to Goal Setting, Goal Getting and Goal Attaining we can achieve anything. As we can control our states, so we control our frames of mind and now we can move forward to control each Context.

*Reversal Theory was developed by Professor Michael Apter. Visit: www.apterinternational.com

Chapter 24

Movement, Goal Setting

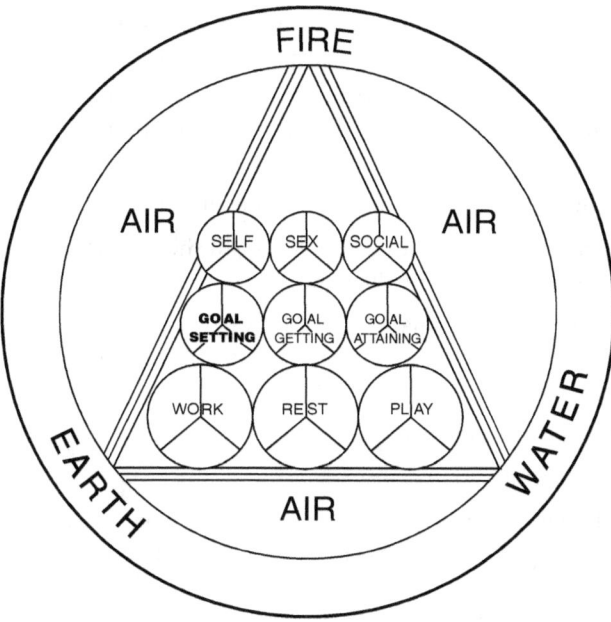

'The person who shows most flexibility of behaviour controls the system. If not this way, then how?'

Now we can sit down to set our outcome. This is one of the most important Contexts, the Context which decides our fate, the Context that sets our course and determines our destination. It is the be all and end all.

What frame of mind do we have to be in to ensure we set the appropriate, achievable outcome? First of all we should adopt the serious state, as referred to in the previous chapter. We should move to a dissociated position, detached from our self, looking towards the future. In that position, we can then move through the NLP Outcome Model from Chapter 2 in more detail.

Setting Outcomes

1. Stated in the positive.

Why does it have to be in the positive? Because when we frame things in the negative we automatically move towards that. The unconscious mind can not process negatives so in order not to think about something we have to go through the process of thinking about it. So whatever our outcome is, it should be phrased in the positive. 'I want to run a marathon,' 'I am going to start my own business,' 'I will finish the house by the end of the year.'

Next we must ask, what *specifically* do I want? If running marathons is a regular achievement, then it is hardly stretching oneself to state, 'I will run a marathon this year.' A specific outcome would be to say, 'I will run a marathon this year, under x time.'

'I will bring in x amount of income for the first year of the business.'

'I will finish all the essentials for the house, the heating, plumbing, electricity, so it is habitable by the end of the year.'

Being specific is essential. Otherwise we would not know if we have achieved anything or not. It is why we refer to achieving a 'specific and desired outcome.'

2. Specify present situation.

Where are you now?

If we do not have a clear idea of where we are now, we will not be able to measure accurately how far we have come. If the house is only half or a quarter finished, how will we know when it is 'finally' finished. Is it when all the utilities have been fitted? Or is it when the last room has been papered and decorated to perfection? It may never be completed to our satisfaction if we do not know what our level of satisfaction is now.

We must ask our self, where exactly am I, now, at this moment in time? What exactly do I have? What exactly don't I have? What is missing?

This is the time to take an inventory. It is similar to calibration. We must take a snapshot of the present so we have a picture to compare it to the future desired outcome.

We must be able to calibrate the difference. For some things it may be relatively easy. There may be a cheque, or a lump sum of money in the hand. It may be a tangible object, building or structure. For other things it may be less obvious, such as achieving a level of mastery with a musical instrument. How will we know we have achieved the desired level? Will an instructor or examiner tell us? Will it be feedback from our friends, or colleagues? What will it feel like?

3. Specify outcome.

What will you see, hear, feel etc when you have it?

This is perhaps the most important point. It may sound simple. 'When I get x thousand pounds of course I will feel great.' Not necessarily. How do we know how we will feel until we put our self in that position?

Movement, Goal Setting

How do we know if we will feel elated, exhilarated after completing a marathon? We may just feel drained, wondering why on earth we had started in the first place. It leads on to number 8 and the crucial question, have you ever had or done this before? It is the experiential element. If we have no idea of what it will look like, sound like or feel like, then equally we will have no idea of whether it will be satisfactory once we have achieved it.

Putting our self in the position of experiencing it in the moment, in the here and now, that Play state, then we can begin to get a measure of the desirability. It will also confirm to us that we will know when we get it. 'Yes, that is the feeling of satisfaction, elation, emancipation that I want!' Having experienced something similar gives an indication of what the outcome will look like, sound like and feel like.

This must not be underestimated. We can only motivate our self to do anything if we get a reward from it. If the reward proves a disappointment, if it does not live up to our expectations, it is unlikely we will be able to find the motivation to achieve it again.

We are concerned here with knowing exactly what we want and how it will feel. It is the finest measurement we can have. All the cheques, physical constructs, verbal confirmations, slaps on backs, cheers from the crowd, letters of condemnation, medals, honours from the Queen can not replace the feeling inside. It may be that the meal with the Queen or the slap on the back will trigger all those desired feelings, indeed, that could be the confirmation of the outcome, but the tangible evidence also comes from within.

4. Specify evidence procedure.

How will you know when you have it?

When we have that feeling, when we see what we need to see, hear what we need to hear and feel what we need to feel, then we will have it. But what exactly is it that triggers those feelings? Is it the material evidence? Is it the cheque, the stamp of approval, the ringing endorsement, the shake of the hand, the signing of the contract?

The two therefore go together. We can not have the feelings associated with accomplishing the outcome without the tangible evidence. Likewise the tangible evidence means little without the emotional verification. That is why we need to link the two together.

Once I have the cheque in my hand, what will it look like, sound like and feel like? How do I know I have achieved my outcome? Will it be when I have the cheque in my hand and those feelings are present? One without the other is futile.

5. Is it congruently desirable?

What will this outcome get for you or allow you to do?

Congruence is key. If we are thrown out of alignment, if there is something that will cause another part of our self to be disturbed, then we must consider it now.

How do we know? We run through everything that will happen when we have it. So once again we must enter that achievement state, those feelings we have when we have accomplished our outcome, and measure what else is happening.

Is this changing my life? Am I receiving fame, fortune? How do these changes sit with my values, beliefs and behaviours?

If one thing changes, it is impossible for other parts not to change also. It is why MindFrames are so effective. A positive tweak in one area can ripple across into other areas of our lives. However, it is essential that these changes are monitored. Will we be able to cope with more attention, responsibility, money, riches, time... whatever it may be?

It is a very personal, introspective moment. How will I be able to handle fame, fortune, seclusion, isolation, openness etc? To measure this we must project ahead, see our self in the picture and work out what it feels like for us. At one level we may be really happy to have more wealth, or security, or independence, whilst on another level that may mean more responsibility, less time, more work.

How will other areas of our lives be affected and how will we respond?

These questions need asking now, not after we have, for example, put all our assets behind a business venture, ie, before it is too late. Do not run a marathon if all it will do for you is make you feel awful.

6. Is it self-initiated and self-maintained?

Is it only for you?

Who else will be affected by the change? Will we have to depend upon other people? We can often find our self planning ahead based upon a whole series of circumstances fitting in place to our favour.

'If so and so moves into x department, then my boss will take over their role and I'll be able to take her role until I've learnt the ropes and then if x makes a hash of that, y will move in and take over that portfolio and as long as z keeps sleeping in I should be able to take over the world...'

The crux of the matter is, can I do this by myself? If other people are to be utilised, are to support the process, how reliable are they? What circumstances may occur that may throw the whole thing off course? What fall-back plan do I have? What other routes can I take? If this way does not work, how else can I do it?

Flexibility of approach is key here. It is rare in life that people achieve much through doing the same thing over and over. If it does not work one way, then we try alternative routes. Do I need to put plan b into operation? Or plan c? Or do I run several approaches at the same time?

If I am relying on one client for my income, how do I increase the number of clients, so that if one does not come through, I can go to another? It is the Law of Requisite Variety. The person who shows most flexibility of behaviour controls the system. If not this way, then how?

7. Is it appropriately contextualised?

Where, when, how and with whom do you want it?

As we are in the realm of Contexts, it is hardly surprising that this question arises. What may be desirable in one Context can be unwelcome in another. Having a wonderful house in acres of land may be greatly desirable in Orange County, California, but it may not have the same attraction if it were situated in a war-torn country. Acquiring great wealth may be wonderful, but it can mean nothing for some people if there is no-one to share it with. Every outcome should therefore by highly contextualised. There may be a need to have different outcomes for different Contexts, or, most likely, different approaches in the various Contexts to achieve the same outcome.

8. What resources are needed?

What do you have now, and what do you need to get your outcome?

This is vital. If we have a basic qualification in mathematics and wish to become a nuclear physicist it would be fair to say that some serious study would be required. However, if we are talking about an MSc graduate who is beginning a PhD they would appear to be on the right course. If we have no experience in the field in which we have set our outcome, then how do we hope to achieve anything? What skills do we need? What study do we need to undertake? Where can we acquire the expertise?

This is why it is always useful to set numerous outcomes, set over a wide time range. There could be outcomes for next week, next month, every month thereafter up until six months, then another at a year, another at two years and a further one at five years. We could even have a ten year plan. The important point is to break them down into achievable chunks. Make the first few outcomes easily attainable, so progress can be made every day if need be. Indeed, there is an incredibly useful strategy that some people use on a daily basis.

Three Goal Strategy

Set three goals for the day. Keep them simple and achievable. It may be to complete a task or an assignment. It may be to phone a friend, or do some housework. If the goals are varied, we are far more likely to pursue them with rigour than keep pursuing a similar task over and over.

At the end of the day, on the successful completion of each task, review what went well. That is three things that were done to a high standard. It may be a conversation in which we got our point across clearly. It may be a letter that was well written. It may be as simple as smiling at a little-known colleague and receiving a warm greeting in return.

Finally, list three things that could have been done better. That is not three things that were done badly, but three things that if we were to do again, we would add something, or adjust, or improve. It could be something that went really well, but could be improved still further. This way we are mentally rehearsing a successful outcome; the only way to succeed repeatedly.

Once this has been noted, either mentally or on paper, set three new goals for the next day. After a little while it will become apparent how easy it is to achieve goals, and continually improve performance. It also contributes enormously to achieving outcomes as it creates a momentum of its own.

What other resources do we need? *Have you ever had or done this before?*

If we have done the activity before then, as detailed above, we can work out how to do it again, or slightly differently, to achieve our outcome. If we have not done it before, we need to ask our self the next question, *Do I know anyone who has?*

If we do, we then need to assess how they do it. Could we do it in the same way, or would we have to adjust it to suit our needs?

Finally, we should ask, *Can I act as if I have it?*

This is not acting as in pretence, even if it starts out that way. It is acting as in doing. It is behaviour driven. If I *act* in this way, I can see, hear and feel what it is like to be x. After a while the acting becomes natural and the task becomes easier. In acting 'as if' we have something we soon feel like we actually have it and it becomes a self-fulfilling prophecy.

9. Is it ecological?

For what purpose do you want this?

What will you gain or lose if you have it?

These are the money questions and lead on from the congruence check touched upon earlier. Ecology, the study of consequences, is the final part of

Movement, Goal Setting

the jigsaw. We must not proceed further until this has been fully explored. It can have a devastating effect if we choose to ignore it.

If we ask the simple question, what is the purpose of achieving my outcome? it raises the topic to a higher level. If we keep asking ours self, what will I get by having x? we are raising our understanding of what the real reason is for setting an outcome. What do I really want by doing this? What will it get for me? How will it make me feel? For what purpose do I want it?

'Because it will make me feel happy.'

And what does being happy do for you?

'It makes me feel content.'

And what does feeling content do for you?

'It makes me feel whole.'

And what does feeling whole do for you?

'It makes me feel at one.'

'And what does feeling at one do for you?

'It completes me.'

And what does being complete do for you?

'It gives me a purpose.'

And what is your purpose?

'To do x.'

Only through pushing and pushing our self, through self-interrogation do we find out why we really want what we want. It helps to re-shape our outcomes, make them more targeted and fully aligned to our values and beliefs.

The further ecology check can be made by asking the following, far-reaching questions.

What will I gain when I get it?

What won't I gain when I get it?

What will I gain if I don't get it?

What won't I gain if I don't get it?

'Only through pushing and pushing our self, through self-interrogation do we find out why we really want what we want. It helps to re-shape our outcomes, make them more targeted and fully aligned to our values and beliefs'

Storage Patterns

The above gives a practical support system for achieving short, medium and long-term outcomes. To maximise the potential for realising our outcome we need to move between the associated and dissociated, access our Storage Patterns and introduce a further technique to produce a compelling future.

Having gone through the nine stages simply re-enter the third stage of specifying the outcome, and see, hear and feel what it is like to achieve the outcome. Now, enter fully into the association and adjust the sub modalities to maximise the feelings.

Increase the size of the pictures, make the colours brighter and more attractive, make the scenery more compelling and attractive.

Turn up the volume, if there is any. Make the voices louder and the laughter clearer. If there is any music or background noise, turn it up to make it more inspiring. If there are any emotions, move them around, make them more intense, hotter, more fluid, more vibrant. Just as the feelings rise to their peak, as the images get brighter and brighter and the sounds as loud as can be, step out of the image so that you are looking at yourself.

Now, notice how you look, how radiant, how inspired, how beautiful, handsome, however you look at your best. Make the picture bigger, turn the music up so it is booming.

Increase the picture of yourself until it is as huge as possible, as high as a house. Make it a massive, colossal picture, all that you can see.

Holding that picture of the best possible you in mind, we can now use a Time Line to place that picture at the time in your future when it will come to pass.

Time Line

Our mind stores our memories linearly. Otherwise what happened last week would be indistinguishable from what happened three years ago. We would not be able to distinguish one event from the next.

Everyone has a time line. These lines can run from front to back, left to right, diagonally, or vertically. As you think about your time line, you can ask your unconscious mind, if I were to know in which direction is my past, where would it point? Ask your unconscious. Now, if you were to ask you unconscious, which direction would my future be, where would it point?

If it does not come at once, forget about it and ask again. It is not the conscious response that is important, it is the unconscious response. So if you

Movement, Goal Setting

were to ask your unconscious again, where is my past, which direction would it be? And my future? Where is that?

Whichever direction you point is fine. That is what works for you. Now, having figured out which direction, you can then follow the directions until they begin to indicate a line. As that line materialise you can simply and easily float above the line, the way you would float in the bath, or in a hot air balloon, or imagine floating in the air. However you float up is fine.

Once you have risen above your time line, face towards the past and float back into the past, a day or two, until you are above a recent event, looking down on the event. Take your time. Once you are above the event, turn around and look towards now. Slowly, float back along the time line until you are above now, looking down on now.

Once there, think of an event one or two days in the future, an event that you know is going to happen.

Float out into the future along your time line until you are above the event, looking down on the event. Take your time. When there, float higher above your time line, higher and higher, until the time line looks about two inches long. Once there, look back towards now and float along the time line until you are above now. Once there, float gently down and back into the room.

Now take the compelling image of the best you. You can hold it out in front of you as if it were a giant picture, or hold it however you feel comfortable. Take the picture and float up above the present until you are above your time line, facing the future. Take the picture out into that time in the future when you have successfully achieved your outcome. When there, take the picture and float down into the time line and gently drop the image into your time line.

Enter into the picture, look through your own eyes. Feel the feelings, fully associate, enjoy. Run it like a movie, as you achieve your outcome and enjoy the satisfaction of accomplishing what you set out to do.

Step out of the picture, so that you are looking at yourself, where you are, where you want to be to achieve your specific and desired outcome. See yourself in that time and space with everything that you will have on achieving your outcome. Now float up above the time line and face back towards now. Take the time to notice if everything seems to fall into line, as if a series of doors are opening up or things are somehow connecting together to take you to where you want to go.

Float back along your time line, bringing the feelings of success with you. When you are above now, float down into your body, having achieved all you set out to accomplish.

Practice this a few times. Rehearse the Storage Patterns until it is the exact visual representation that you require. Use the time line to place outcomes exactly where they should be. Playing those movies through whilst being in that frame of mind will provide an inspiring vision. However, make sure you are fully dissociated before floating up again. The vision needs to be something compelling to move towards. You need to see your self in the picture.

We can mentally rehearse each outcome. Using the time line go to fifteen minutes after the successful completion of a goal and fully associate with the satisfied feelings of having accomplished the task. Float up again and take those satisfied, elated feelings to the beginning of the task and run through the events whilst experiencing the same state. Do this repeatedly to practice perfectly the required function.

Now that the compelling dissociated image has been set and planted in the future time line, we can now begin to go about achieving that outcome. How? By being fully associated and goal-orientated, looking through our own eyes, in achievement mode. We can now step, fully prepared, wide-eyed and eager into 'the zone'.

Chapter 25

Movement, Goal Getting

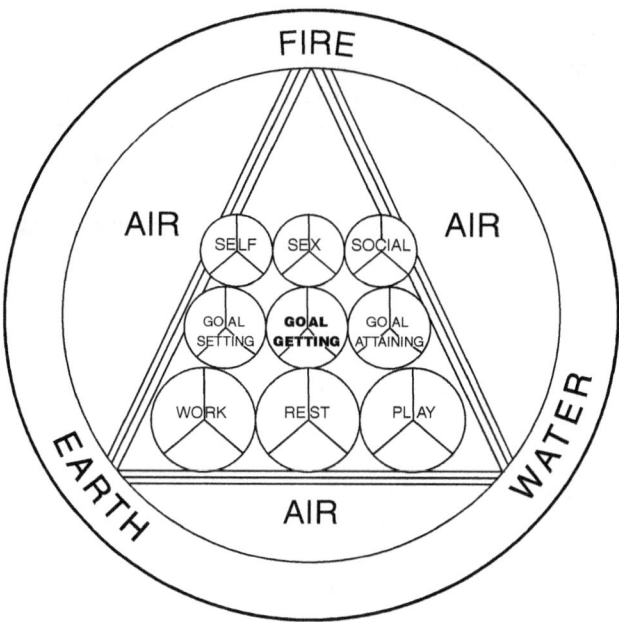

'This is the realm of the here and now, in-time, in the moment, fully associated, looking through our own eyes and totally focussed'

The visual rehearsal described at the close of the last chapter means that the task to be undertaken has been practiced repeatedly. Not only that, it has been practised perfectly, so that we are in the right state, experiencing the exact emotions that we desire in order to accomplish the deed to the best of our ability.

Our mind, following the most recent pattern that has been laid down will automatically pursue the path when it comes to enacting the 'real' task. Because the mind does not differentiate between the highly imagined and the real, the mind will believe it has done this before and follow that pattern. It is therefore imperative that the pattern is firmly established by repeated perfect practice.

If it is a straightforward function such as a conversation, or completing a simple report, or writing an essay, then it may not be necessary to mentally rehearse that action more than once or twice. If however it is something that can be seen as an important function, such as giving a speech at a wedding, or doing a presentation at work, or playing in a cup final, the mental rehearsal may need to be more deeply engrained.

As the scenarios are run through in our minds, we can also throw in 'curve balls', interruptions that could potentially throw us off track. In fact, the more curve balls, distractions, obstacles and interruptions that are envisaged, the better. We can then work out a way to deal with anything that could go wrong. This means that by the time we come to the actual event, any complication would have been anticipated and dealt with. In all likelihood the complication will be minor and will be handled easily, but it does not hurt to be prepared for all eventualities.

Doing it for Real

Yes, but it's entirely different doing it for real is it not? We can not possibly know exactly what is going to happen until we are out there, exposed, facing the firing line of public scrutiny.

The NLP Outcome Model number 8 asks, 'what resources are needed?' and more specifically, 'have we ever had or done this before?' which gives us scope to explore similar experiences to drawn upon. Every experience that has anything in common whatsoever with what we are about to do can be explored fully. In fact, we can utilise experiences that at first glance may not appear to have anything in common with the scenario that we are facing, but employ similar skills and techniques. Not only that, we will examine what others do, learn from their experiences and access every resource and tool we have developed until now to assist us with the task.

We will have run through the activity so often, to such a high standard, that it will be something to be looked forward to. Every possible stumbling block will already have been overcome, so the unnecessary pressure of the 'what if' which we place upon our self will have been removed.

Is this fail safe? Does this work every time?

If done well, yes; if the nine steps have been followed closely. The visual rehearsal is in many ways the easy part. We will have already constructed the right Mindframe, which gives us all the grounding we need.

But that is not to say we will be perfect. Nor will we be necessarily able to say we could not do it better next time. Continuous improvement is a great aspiration. The more we do an activity the more opportunity we have to assess how well we did and how we could improve still further. This works in visual rehearsal and in the practical exercise.

Having done the required mental rehearsal and put our self in the best possible position to successfully complete our goal, how then do we approach the Goal Getting Context?

Quite simply, this is the realm of the here and now, in-time, in the moment, fully associated, looking through our own eyes and totally focussed.

'Feel what it is like to focus totally on that part of the self that delivers the result and we have untapped a resource of volcanic magnitude'

In the Zone

How often do we find our self totally focussed in the present, on the task in hand? How often do we lose our self in what we are doing so that time seems to stand still? We might think that it happens quite frequently, every day perhaps. In fact, it is a great deal rarer than we think. All sorts of things pop into our head all the time. As creative and complex creatures we are constantly looking ahead, dreaming of the future, imagining what is going to happen next week, tomorrow, in a few minutes time.

We may think we are 'on the ball' or embroiled in the task in hand, but all too frequently something will pop into our head, there will invariably be a distraction or an irrelevant thought. 'What's on television tonight?' 'I'm looking forward to going out to eat.' 'I wonder if Shirley's feeling any better?' 'Am I doing well at this?' 'I wonder what they're thinking about me?'

How do we control our minds so that we can totally focus on getting what we want? For a start, we can not stop things springing to mind. It is impossible to stop thinking. What we must do is ensure those thoughts are all related to what we are doing. Therefore we must get into the right frame of mind. We know all about how to do that in theory. What about in practice? How do we enter the zone?

First of all we must re-enter that state we have rehearsed so often. We must fire the anchor and access the appropriate Storage Pattern whilst bringing to mind the right Change and Strategy Patterns. Once we have entered the appropriate state, we must then concentrate, unblinkered on the activity in which we are involved.

In order to ensure we do not distract our self, we can control the mind through reiterating our beliefs and values regarding what we are doing. If for example we are making a speech, it may be useful to repeat over and over to our self the belief, 'I know what I'm talking about, I am good at what I do.' This little mantra can be repeated over and over again. As the speech begins this belief is reinforced in the ease with which we speak. It becomes a self-fulfilling prophecy.

This 'drilling' can be very useful, almost imperative for certain situations. Before going on stage in front of a large audience, where there are multiple distractions, one of the best ways to remain in the moment and not worry about what is ahead is to repeat a drill to ensure the mind is concerned only with success.

The trick here is to unclutter the mind and remain focussed in the present. As soon as we step out of time, we start to worry about the future. We become dissociated. If we are fully associated, we can not worry about the future because we are preoccupied with the present.

Once the drilling takes effect we can release our minds to focus more fully on what we are doing. When this occurs we lose all track of time. It can appear to stand still or slow down. We appear to have all the time in the world. How can we maintain this state?

We can do this by controlling the moment, re-running the visual rehearsal and concentrating minutely on every tiny detail, every component part, until they run seamlessly together and immediacy is all that matters. We can no longer see the detail, the minutiae, as we concern our self only with being in the zone, going with the flow. This we can do immediately by simply immersing our self in the task in front of us. But it needs to be total immersion.

Feeling the Flow

If we take a moment to quieten down we can hear the sound of our breathing. We can feel our heart beating. If we focus on one part of our body, our left hand, for example, we can feel the pulse of our blood racing through our veins.

We can feel each finger individually. Feel how warm it feels. Feel how much warmer it feels than the fingers on the other hand. Notice the feeling at the end of each finger. Concentrate on the tip of the thumb. What does that feel like? Is it warm? Is it hot? Is there a tingling sensation or no sense at all? Could there be any more warmth, any more tingling? How can we increase that?

Concentrate hard on the end of the thumb. Let the warmth from the rest of the body flow into that zone. Notice the veins in the hand, how clear they become.

Do they rise to the surface? Are they beginning to throb? Imagine blood rushing from the heart, along the arm and down into the hand. Imagine it flowing like a fast-flowing river, hurtling along the veins, carrying all debris before it, hurtling at high velocity.

Movement, Goal Getting

Try repeating a mantra, 'I can control the flow… I can control the flow…' and keep saying it over and over again whilst imaging the fluid pumping through the body, along the arm and crashing into the hand, as if the wrist were the top of a waterfall and the hand and fingers the basin hundreds of feet below.

As the warmth spreads from finger to finger imagine the hand is placed above a radiator or inside a nice warm glove. Feel the glowing feeling of warmth and heat rising. The radiator is boiling hot and the hand can barely touch it without being scorched, so go ahead and hover the hand just above the radiator, and feel the heat rising.

Imagine those veins are now pumping hot water, as if the fingers are hot water pipes and the palm of the hand the radiator. Turn the thermostat up to ten, to a red hot, scorching temperature. Now imagine that volcano erupting, the white hot explosion of molten rock bursting from the heart and overflowing down into the arms and into the hand and fingers like lava.

With eyes closed the veins are burning bright amber, yellow and red, emitting a heat too hot to handle. With the back of the other hand, feel the heat in the palm of the hand and the fingers.

It may be that it feels a little hotter. It may feel very warm indeed. But that is a trick of the mind, is it not?

The mind is controlling the body and when we are in the zone, the mind and body are one seamless entity.

Try focusing on different parts of the body. The small of the back on the seat, or the right foot on the ground, or the left buttock. Focus on one part at a time and notice the control that can be exerted on that part just by concentrating upon it. Notice how warm it can feel. Or tingly. Or even numb.

The only way that control can be exerted is through the power of intense concentration. If the hand did not feel any warmer or the pulse throb any greater in the palm or on the back of the hand it is highly likely that something else came to mind. Something other than, 'I can control the flow…'

How do we maintain the flow? Practice, perfect practice. But like an exploding volcano it is difficult to predict where the lava will run and it is tough to maintain a high degree of concentration for extended periods; that is until we become better rehearsed. What we can do right now is focus for short bursts. These can often bring us all the rewards we need.

80/20 Rule

The 80/20 Rule states that 20 per cent of the people in business produce 80 per cent of the profit. In many businesses this can be much higher. We function similarly. Twenty per cent of what we do produces 80 per cent of the results. It may be even lower; ten or event five per cent of what we do can produce the results we want.

This begs two questions. The first is, what on earth are we doing 80 or 90 per cent of the time that is producing not very much? The second, more importantly is, how can I enter into that five or 10 per cent of the time whenever I want, to get the result I want at the right moment?

The answer is in the lava flow that runs to the tips of the fingers. Feel what it is like to focus totally on that part of the self that delivers the result and we have untapped a resource of volcanic magnitude. Once the hole has been unplugged, once the dialogue has begun there is no going back. It is all out there, primed and ready to roll. Focus, feel a way in and go with the flow…

Chapter 26

Movement, Goal Attaining

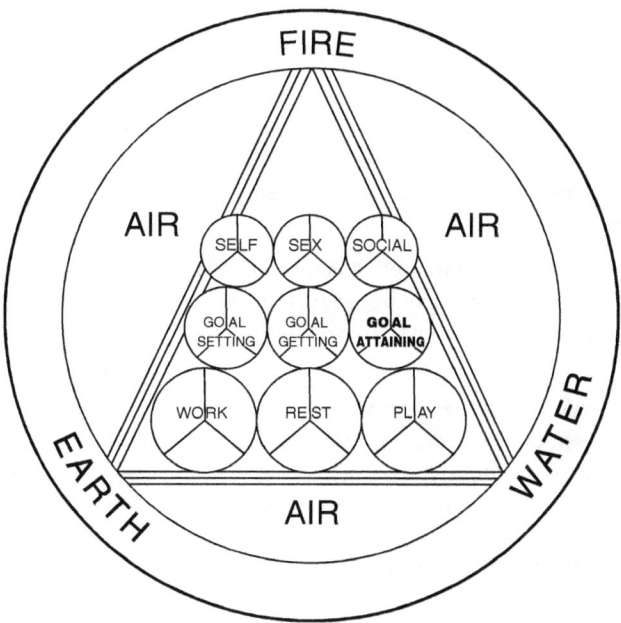

'It is like an on-going stock take, or internal audit, checking that we are making progress and things are going according to plan'

The getting of the goal is as important as the setting of the goal. How we achieve our outcome determines how many more outcomes we can achieve.

If we are satisfied with getting a little bit, of hitting a target and celebrating our success forever more, then it is unlikely we will ever do anything else. That is fine if that is all that is required. For most of us, succeeding at one thing does not give us sufficient succour. There is more to achieve and more to aim for. It gives meaning to our existence and momentum to carry on. It is life's energising juice that propels us towards greater gains.

That is not to say we can not be content with what we have, what we are doing and what we are achieving. There is a misconception that if someone keeps setting new challenges and moving on to the next thing, that he or she is discontent with their lot. They may well be. But this is different. There is no reason why we can not be content with who we are, what we have got and what we are doing, yet still feel a desire to move forward.

In the business world this is largely accepted by those who believe in continuous professional development. The Context is not dissimilar. We can pursue our heart's desire, enjoy what we are doing and where we are in life and still get better, still improve, still acquire more knowledge and understanding.

As the last two chapters explored, visual rehearsal and perfect practice is essential to set about attaining our goals, but repeated practical experience can only improve our performance. Equally, the more goals we attain to the required standard, the greater challenges we can then take on and the bigger outcomes can be met.

It is not that we are unsettled, it is that we refuse to settle for less than what we are and can be. We can still be satisfied in the process. What we refuse to do is be satisfied with less than we are able to achieve.

A commonly-held belief by many is, 'there is nothing worse than unfulfilled potential.' That can be a misleading mindset to carry around because one person's assessment of another's potential is not necessarily accurate, especially if the individual has different beliefs and values. But the underlying ethos can be empowering. It motivates us to keep on going until we have realised our own expectations in that area. It may be that the potential can never be fully realised in a single, short lifetime. That does not mean we should be unhappy with our lot.

There are many great composers, writers and artists who continue composing, writing and painting literally until they drop, believing they can produce higher quality work.

For this reason this Context is Goal Attaining not Goal Attainment. It implies that the act of accomplishing our outcome is a process in itself, one that leads onwards. Once the activity has been completed, another one is set, another goal established to move towards. Therefore we are always compelled forwards, not left stagnant in a state of acceptance.

> *'Take a break and look at the view from the mountainside'*

Celebrating Success

What we do need to ensure is that we celebrate our successes, take the time out to credit our self and others with coming as far as we have. If the outcome is large, such as getting a promotion, or buying a house, or completing a major project, it is worth marking in style. That could be through throwing a party, or going out for a meal, or taking a holiday. Whatever is to our liking. Most of us are used to adopting such an approach. Even if we are not the sort of person who enjoys stopping to take stock and mark an achievement, other people tend to coerce us into doing something to mark the occasion. And this is good, worthwhile. It need not be a party with balloons and speeches, encores and trophies. It can be as simple as taking the time out to reflect upon how far we have come, what we have accomplished and how well we have done. If we do not take the time out to register our success it is difficult to recognise if we have made progress or really accomplished something. If it is not worth celebrating, then why bother doing it in the first place?

The celebration can be as simple as taking a few minutes to reflect upon what has happened. We can do this by soaking in the bath, or taking a stroll along the beach, or scaling a hillock; whatever works.

What we often fail to do though is mark the smaller events. We can all too easily overlook the 'little wins', the smaller accomplishments along the way that help us achieve the big wins. It does not have to involve throwing a huge party after achieving a minor success, but it should be marked.

It is like an on-going stock take, or internal audit, checking that we are making progress and things are going according to plan.

How often do we get in from work and comment on what a bad day it has been? How often do we pay attention to what goes wrong and determine our mood, our assessment of the day according to that? All too often, perhaps.

On the flip side, how often do we celebrate our successes? What do we say to our self when we get that slap on the back, or words of approval, or friendly smile? We frequently overlook the positives and dwell on the negatives.

Instead of reflecting upon what goes wrong, ie, mentally rehearsing failure, it would be far more useful to record everything that goes well. If we do this we can provide all the motivation we need to keep moving forward.

This is the case when it comes to attaining our goals, however small. If we register what we have done, how far we have come, it gives us the evidence that we are succeeding. A little is better than nothing.

This is why the Three Goals Strategy from Chapter 23 can be so useful. It gives us the opportunity to record success every day, not once in a blue moon. It also gives us the framework to review what we have done well and identify how we can improve in future. Therefore it does not allow us to rest on our laurels, but gives us the time to appreciate our accomplishments.

'Goal Attaining is a process of progress in which we can integrate everything we have accomplished, everything we have now, and everything we need for the next chapter in our lives'

Finding the Balance

The Context of Goal Attaining is therefore a fine balance between reflecting upon what we have done, how much effort we have exerted, and looking towards the future and moving forward. It removes inertia whilst giving us the time to celebrate and congratulate our self on making progress.

If we set out to climb a large hill or small mountain, it can seem like a daunting task, taking hours and hours to reach the high peak in the distance. There will be plateaux along the way and quite often it may seem like we are reaching the top but just as we scale the top of a mound we can see the peak is still further away.

If we keep marching forward with our head down this can soon prove debilitating, boring and repetitive. Our energy levels can quickly drop and we can become disconcerted with the task in hand. Our legs may feel tired, our feet may be numb, our hands cold and our back caked in sweat. We may be hungry or desperately thirsty, longing for water and sustenance. We may become dehydrated and faint, in dire need of replenishment. The desire to go on could easily fade away and only stubborn pride will keep us from turning back, or worse still, collapsing.

However, if we take time to stop once in a while, sip from our canteen and nibble on sandwiches, Kendal mint cake or chocolate whilst checking out the spectacular view, then our desire to continue on may, if anything, increase. We can wonder at the beauty of nature, the valleys and hills around, the sprawling mountain range and majesty of birds swooping beneath our vantage point. It may even inspire us to move forward apace.

But what happens if we spend too long in that place? We begin to enjoy the view more than is helpful. We can have a little too much to eat and our legs can drain of energy. We no longer feel like getting up again and struggling upwards. The view from here is fine; we may begin to wonder if it will be much better at the top.

What if it starts to rain, or hail, or snow? If we are well prepared, we can unwrap our waterproofs and shore our self up against the onslaught, safe and warm under layers of protective gear. We may be further inspired by our efforts in overcoming the elements and move forward 'in spite of everything'. The greater the challenge the harder we try. Our thoughts can move forward to our safe return home and a hot, welcoming bath, or a soothing cup of tea, or an uplifting shot of whisky.

For the ill-prepared, it could be the straw that breaks the camel's back. The water would quickly invade the summer jacket, run down our neck and soak us to the skin. If we do not find shelter we could quickly become chilled and exposed.

Movement, Goal Attaining

The variables are infinite and it is no different to our journey through life. Even when we reach the top, the weather may be too severe for us to loiter for too long to enjoy the moment. That may come later when we are back in front of the log fire or soaking in the bath.

The point here is that it is a fine balance. If we want to get to the top, it is important to keep moving, yet stop occasionally to look back at how far we have come and appreciate the scenery all around. It is important to log our progress and take enjoyment in what we are doing, take little time outs to reflect and re-gather our energy.

This all may sound simple and straightforward. So it is, but it is also surprising how many people forget to enjoy the small things, lose track of time and keep their head down until they run out of steam.

In fact, it can be worse if we are enjoying what we are doing. We can become so engrossed that we forget to take a time out, to unwind and relax.

All of these Contexts do come together. Work without Play represents and imbalance; it could well lead to wreck and ruin. So Goal Getting without Rest is reckless. And Goal Attaining without consideration of every Context is unwise.

It would be beneficial to take a time out frequently, perhaps every day, or once or twice a week, or as often as is practicable. Take a break and look at the view from the mountainside. Look at how far you have come, at what you have done to get this far, at how beautiful it is here, in this place now. Give yourself some praise, some appreciation for coming this far. Appreciate the scenery, the wonderful landscape, the rolling hills and lush green valleys. After taking those moments for reflection and contemplation, knowing that if you have come this far, you can go a little further; set out again, this time with more knowledge, more understanding, and even greater resources.

The Context of Goal Setting is one of the most complex. It requires moving from state to state, skipping from Context to Context. A little bit of deep relaxation and Rest is essential. An assessment of Work completed and Work to be tackled needs to be done. As the Rest and reflection is fully absorbed we move seamlessly towards Goal Setting and Goal Getting, creating the required levels of motivation to propel us further forward. Goal Attaining is a process of progress in which we can integrate everything we have accomplished, everything we have now, and everything we need for the next chapter in our lives.

Chapter 27

Fire, Communications

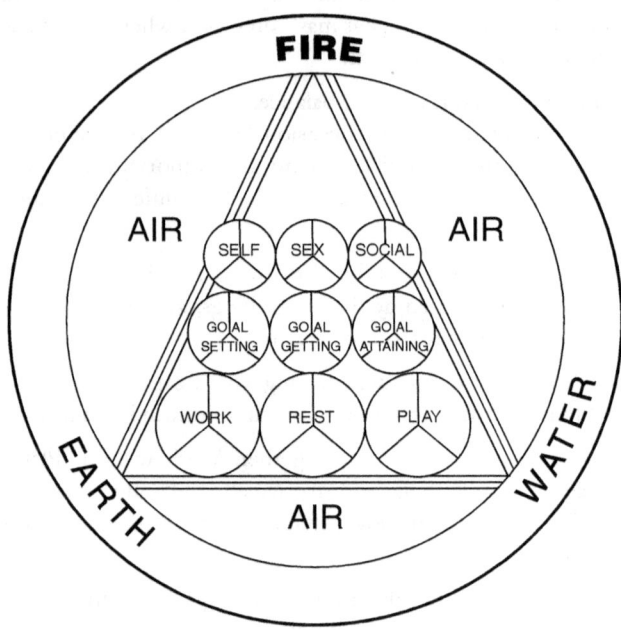

'The person who shows most flexibility of behaviour controls the system'

The key to communicating effectively is to understand where the other person is coming from. What do they think, believe, value, project? What is going through their mind as they nod along to what we are saying? How do we know that what we are doing/saying is having the desired effect?

Unfortunately we have a tendency to mind read, to project our misgivings onto the other person. 'Oh no, they think I'm an idiot'. 'I'm making a real fool of myself here'. 'I can tell by the look in their eye that they're not interested in what I'm saying'. 'I'm being boring, I know'.

All, some or none of this may be true. Often we just do not know; we presume, speculate, infer. So how do we move beyond the limitations of mind reading to ascertain what the person is really thinking?

For a start we can never be 100 per cent accurate on what anyone is thinking at any given time. Half the time we are not certain what we are thinking. 'I'm feeling quite warm. Oh, hang on; now she's opened the door, I'm suddenly cold.'

This first thing we know how to do is calibrate. What is the difference between how they were when we first met them and how they are behaving now? What are the subtle changes in voice tone, physiology, eye movement, facial expression? What happens when I raise this subject or emphasise this phrase?

This can reveal all sorts of useful insights into the individual's preferences and mood changes and provide us with the information we need so that we can adapt to suit their needs. But what can be done to dig a little deeper, discover more about how they are and what they are thinking?

'The best way to communicate effectively is to demonstrate the best possible behaviour'

Perceptual Positions

The first step is to move into their position, to see things from their perspective. The expression, 'stepping into his shoes' is apposite. We literally need to float out of our own body and into the other person's; seeing what they are seeing, hearing what they are hearing and feeling what they are feeling. The easiest way to practice this is to imagine someone we come into conflict with quite frequently. Choose someone who easily provokes, who can cause annoyance or frustration.

Imagine looking at the conversation or argument from their perspective. Float into their shoes, look through their eyes, and inhabit their body. What would they say? How would they articulate their discontent? What would they say about you, about how you annoy them? Go through all the complaints they have. Be thorough and honest. Say what they would say, in the same tone with the same emphasis. If they shout, shout. If they hiss and spit, hiss and spit. Be true to what they are and how they behave. This should not be difficult as we have all the behavioural demonstrations we need through past conversations.

This is called the second position, looking through someone else's eyes.

Once practised, float out of the other person's body and into our own. Go through the same process. Respond to their complaints, their criticisms. What do we see, hear, and feel about their behaviour? Are they right? What is our come-back, put-down, assessment? Say it how we normally say it. Speak how we normally speak to that person. Behave the way we normally behave. This part should be even easier. This is called the first position, looking through our own eyes.

Once again, step into the other person's shoes and continue the discussion or argument. Go through the same procedure of inhabiting not only their body, but their beliefs, values and behaviours. Come at it from their perspective. If at first their contentions seem unjustifiable, put the self to one side and think only how they think and who they are. Right or wrong does not matter. It is about inhabiting the spirit and essence of that person. Discovering where they are coming from, how they believe what they believe and acting the way they act requires this selfless perspective.

Switch back again to the self and respond to the next set of statements. Repeat this whole procedure a number of times until all the issues have been brought out into the open. Make sure all the usual bones of contention have been exposed and all the usual lines of argument pursued.

'Try something else. If that does not work, try something else. If that does not work, try something else, and so on'

Third Position

Now, float above or to the side of the two characters; the self and the other. Run through the whole interaction from a detached perspective. This is a totally non-judgemental position. There are no assumptions, no sides taken whilst in this position. It is entirely concerned with capturing, as accurately as possible, exactly what happens during the discussion or argument. Who says what in what tone of voice? What does the other person say in response? How do they speak back? Be as detached as possible. There is no right and wrong, just the process of communication, the to and froing of a lively discussion.

In this Meta or over/above position, we have the opportunity to observe communication in an objective manner. Pay close attention to what one person says and what the other person says in response. Take note of the changes in physiology, eye movement, facial expressions and voice variations. What are the triggers, the anchors that put the other person in a bleak mood or fit of rage? Are these consciously or unconsciously fired off? How does the other person respond? Do they then fire off an anchor for the other person?

Does the argument or discussion have a pattern? After the tantrums, explosions, sulks, rages, are there apologies and sympathetic overtones made from one to the other? Who holds out the first olive branch? Does the other person respond in kind? Are there hugs and kisses, a firm handshake, or is it just left hanging as one or the other storms out?

This is where it begins to get interesting. Notice the patterns. If one person says something provocative, notice how the other person reacts. Do they do this each and every time? Do they always respond this way? Does the other person always push the same buttons?

Fire, Communications

What about the content of the conversation? Is it always the same? Are there particular issues that keep arising? Are there values and beliefs that are being demonstrated? Are there traits that keep arising?

It is almost always incredibly easy to identify patterns of behaviour and response. MindFrame Patterns is named for that very reason. We constantly resort to patterns in the way we think and behave. Communicating with friends, colleagues, loved ones and strangers is no different. There is almost always a recurrent pattern in the interaction with particular people.

On assuming the Meta position, or third person, we can identify these patterns as they repeat themselves over and over. Quite often, the pattern is activated very quickly and the issue appears to be blindingly obvious. But when we are in the heat of an argument all we are thinking about is re-enforcing what we are saying with evidence that highlights what an idiot the other person is, whilst our anger rises by dwelling on what an idiot they are. Assuming their position and then the Meta position, we can see what is really happening, beyond the boundaries of our own perspective.

Even if we are rock-solid, a 100 per cent right and they are indeed the biggest idiot on the face of the earth, we may be able to identify that they are behaving that way because we are pushing them into a corner. If we change our behaviour the whole course of our future personal inter-actions may change.

How do we recognise these patterns?

It will be difficult not to. The same topics, reactions, changes in behaviour will keep happening over and over again. It will be like a loop. He says this, she says that, he begins to sulk, she begins to scream, he runs off, she chases after him with a shot-gun... we know the drill.

The loop is very important. What happens with the loop pattern is that the two protagonists can not escape it. The conversation hits a familiar theme and each person resorts to their pattern of behaviour. This will be re-enforced by values, beliefs, Storage, Strategy and Change Patterns associated with the topic under discussion, and the loop pattern of the conversation will be activated.

The other person will re-enforce their argument, we will re-enforce our own. Each person will fall into their well-rehearsed drill, repeating over and over again the same deeply held beliefs. The loop will continue infinitum. 'He will never change'. 'She's always the same'. 'I can never get through his thick skull...' and so on.

Only through having the insight of being able to observe the loop in action, through second positioning and third positioning, can anything be changed. Otherwise it is a case of storming out, or agreeing to disagree, or sulking until next time, or ending the relationship entirely having had enough of going over the same argument over and over again.

We can all relate to the sentiment. 'I'm fed up with going over the same ground time and time again'. If it has not been in an intimate relationship, it may have been with a family member, or old friend, or colleague. Ever have a friend who never seems to grow up and always harps back to the past, repeating old stories from school days? 'It's about time they grew up,' we say to our self having heard the same story for the umpteenth time and gone over the same views repeatedly. This can provide a measure of enjoyment for some people, reminiscing about times past, but the opinions can often be stale and limited.

In adopting the three positions we can soon observe the pattern and the loop. How do we break that loop?

As always, do something different. Change the course of the conversation. Do the opposite of what we would normally do. Take a long, hard look at our own values, beliefs and behaviours in this context. Assess Storage, Strategy and Change Patterns. Are they working? Am I being too blinkered, digital, in my approach? Is this really a black and white issue? Is it really a matter of right and wrong?

It is the Law of Requisite Variety. The person who shows most flexibility of behaviour controls the system. The previous way of communicating with this person has not worked, hence the long back catalogue of conflict. Try something else. If that does not work, try something else. If that does not work, try something else, and so on...

If you always do what you have always done, you will always get what you have always got.

There is an infinite variety of approaches that could be adopted. One could be to not worry about winning the argument. If most things are analogue and it is rarely a case of black and white, on or off, right or wrong, then there is really no argument to be won. Or, the argument is un-winnable. If we believe that there it is not really a case of black and white and the other person does, how can we convince them otherwise?

How about advising them to take a more measured approach, adopt a Meta position?

It entirely depends on who we are talking to. However, even the most open-minded of people would object to being advised to take a wider view in the heat of battle. There is always the right time and the right place. Likewise, recommended reading is fine, but it is rarely wise to impose our beliefs and values on others.

The best way to communicate effectively is to demonstrate the best possible behaviour. If we demonstrate a flexibility of behaviour in the middle of a conversation or argument, that clearly shows that not only are we in control, we are also mindful of where they are coming from, and the person will usually respond positively.

Adopting a second position gives us instant insight into the other person's perspective. If we use that insight to show consideration of their perspective, they will be grateful and respond positively. 'I understand where you're coming from. I know what you're saying and I respect your position,' is unlikely to solicit a slap in the face.

We do not have to be sycophantic though. We could continue, 'In respecting what you are saying, I would also appreciate it if you could respect my opinion. I'm not saying I'm right and you're wrong, it's something that I value greatly…'

'Now that we have all the resources we need, we can assess accurately what other people have to offer and refine their strategies to adopt and integrate our self'

Fourth Position

What if that does not work? What if I identify the loop, get to the crux of the argument, and still can not find a way to resolve the issue?

In going through perceptual positions we are widening our perspective and therefore our understanding. We are looking through our own eyes, naturally, as well as through someone else's eyes, and finally, taking an overview position, observing the whole process from a detached, non-judgemental perspective. The concern, consideration and insight this gives us into people and situations is immense and can be heightened with practice.

In fact, some people are able to walk into a room and after a few minutes conversation they can notice the patterns and loops that are occurring. This can even be the case with a group of complete strangers, such is the insight gained from using perceptual positions, particularly the third, Meta position.

However, if we use this skilfully and still cannot find a way to break the loop, there could be recourse to adopt the next perspective, the fourth position. The fourth position is not dissimilar to the Information Change Pattern. It is the global perspective, the 'big picture', looking beyond the detail of the now to the wider considerations of the group, the organisation, or the society.

The fourth position is looking through the eyes of the owners of the organisation the individual works for, or the leader of the group to which they are affiliated. It can be a number of people, such as a board, or a council or even a government. The fourth position is therefore a really big picture. It can, however, be broken down.

It is basically asking the question, what does the person or people who govern this individual see, hear and think? What are their values, beliefs and behaviours? What are their likely Storage, Change and Strategy Patterns? If we look through their eyes, to their needs, then we can see the influence it may have on the person we are talking to.

This is particularly appropriate in the context of negotiation. It is rarely a case that the person we are negotiating with is the decision maker. They are often a representative of another person or a group and accountable to a company, organisation, business or union. If we are not mindful of what the governing body is thinking then it is unlikely we will be able to make any progress.

Adopting the fourth position often requires a good deal more imagination as it is very possible that we will not know much about the people we are inhabiting. However, in adopting the second and third positions it is likely we can get a good deal of information and insight into how the individual perceives their organisation, which is being demonstrated in their actions and behaviour.

First Step to Successful Modelling

A good proportion of MindFrames has concentrated upon how we can find out what our conscious and unconscious patterns are and how we can use these to our advantage. Now we are beginning to externalise, to observe how other people are operating and what we need to do to communicate effectively with them.

This is the very foundation of NLP, modelling successful people, and it is an essential addition to the toolkit if we are to most effectively use MindFrames. Now that we have all the resources we need, we can assess accurately what other people have to offer and refine their strategies to adopt and integrate ourselves. The wonderful world of Fire, Communications, is the final part to creating our ideal MindFrame.

Chapter 28

Communications, Self

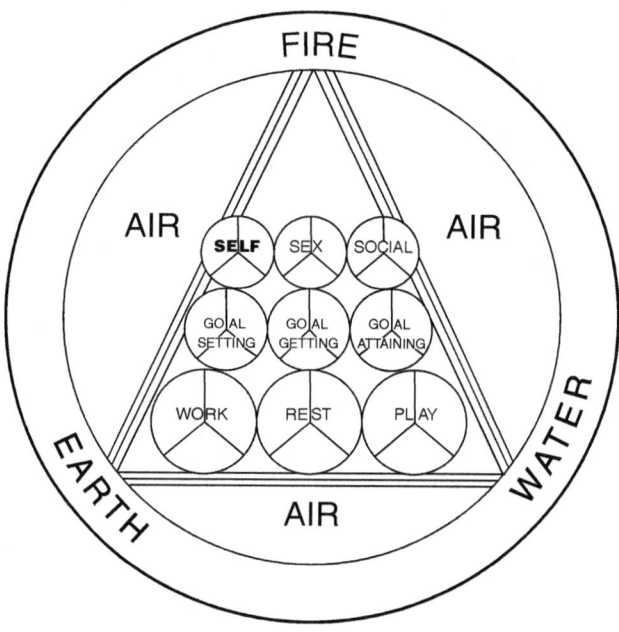

'How can we expect to communicate effectively with other people if we are not congruent, if our conscious and unconscious are out of alignment?'

Communication begins at home, with the self, with the internal dialogue. How can we expect to communicate effectively with other people if we are not congruent, if our conscious and unconscious are out of alignment?

Some people can manage it, put a brave face on, blag their way through the evening, and convince their friends that they are enjoying themselves. Sooner or later though, even they get found out, as they skulk in a corner or suddenly alter their behaviour radically for no apparent reason. Most of us communicate well with other people when we are 'on form', 'on the ball', or 'happy in ourselves'.

Have you ever heard the expression, 'How is she in herself?' The interested party is going beyond the behaviour to pursue what is happening at a deeper level. People are not easily deceived. It works both ways. If we can find a measure of contentment within, if we are aligned to our values and beliefs, people can pick up on this.

The outward manifestation of this internal calm, when we are truly centred, is the ease with which we talk and listen to people. This congruence is palpable. Perception is projection. If we are calm and relaxed and comfortable in our self, other people can pick up on this fact. They feel at ease, and sensing our assurance, they can relax themselves.

We have explored the tools necessary to put our self in the right frame of mind, but what else can we do in the Context of Self, to ensure we get our specific and desired outcome?

'Sort the Self out and the rest is a doddle'

The Conversation

What else can you do?

'What do you mean?'

I mean, what else can you do? What can you do that you are not doing already?

'Lots of course.'

Give me an example.

'I could sing. There's one, I could sing.'

Be serious.

'I am being serious. Well, kind of. I could go to the karaoke, sing a few tunes, join in more.'

And what would that do for you?

'It would show that I can have fun, that I have a human side.'

Do they need to know that?

'Of course they do. That's what it's all about. I'm not a hard bitch, I'm a decent human being.'

So a decent human being sings and a hard bitch doesn't?

'No, I'm not saying that. I'm just saying that it would show my humane side. Have a laugh, show a bit of warmth, be friendly. You know, show the soft side of myself.'

You don't have a soft side.

'Yes I do. I'm not always the boss, the one giving orders. I can be caring. I am sensitive.'

Of course you are. That doesn't mean you're soft though.

'No, but it does mean I have a heart. I do give a damn what people think.'

Yes, you've got a strong external frame of reference.

'Oh, don't keep quoting MindFrames all day long, will you? You see that's half the problem. I'm in management mode so often that most of my team don't think I have another side to me. All they hear is me talking a language that they either don't get, or despise. I'm in a lose-lose situation.'

How do you know what they think?

'There you go again. I know I don't know what they think, but I do know what I think and I think I know how I come across.'

And how's that?

'Assertive. Controlling. Decisive. Disciplined. Ruthless, on occasion… you know me, I'm tough, hard, no-nonsense.'

And more. What else are you?

'Don't start that.'

No, come on. What else are you?

'I can be sensitive. I know I can be sensitive, that's what I was saying. I am sensitive, right here, right now, in this bath. I'm a nice person. I'm not a monster.'

Who says you are?

'Oh no-one, but you know what I mean.'

Do I?

'Yes of course you do, you're me.'

Yes, but you need to explain yourself. What do you mean?

'I mean that I don't want to be seen as a controlling, harsh, tough, determined woman. I want to be seen as decent and caring and sensitive.'

Is that all?

'No. I mean, I still want to be seen as intelligent, creative, decisive, a good, strong leader…'

And still be decent, caring and sensitive?

'Yes, why not? It is possible to be all those things at once. Men can get away with it.

You're not a man; but you're team are mostly men. Have you thought about how they see you?

'Of course I have. A hard bitch, that's how they see me.'

Is it?

'Yes it is.'

Is it really?

'Yes it *really* is. Get off my case. It's a man's world, I know that.'

Hang on a minute, let's just back up there. Have you second positioned this?

'Yes, of course I have, I did read the last chapter.'

Ok and what did that tell you?

'It told me what I already know.'

Did you third position?

'Meta? Yep. I know the patterns, I can see the loops. By and large I'm getting what I want because I'm the boss. I've fourth positioned. I know what the company wants, I know what our clients want and I know what our suppliers want. My record's the best in the company and I'm assured of the next promotion.'

Go bitch go!

'Thanks, really helpful.'

You know what I mean. Have a sense of humour, it helps! Listen, you've gone through you're values and beliefs and behaviours haven't you?

'Yeah, sure.'

And you know your Storage, Change and Strategy Patterns inside out don't you?

'Yeah, it's worked a treat at work, you know that.'

And you're in touch with your unconscious. You're congruent?

'Sure, it's how I met you.'

So what's missing?

'I dunno. I thought you'd help out there.'

OK, so you've second, third and fourth positioned this. You've gone through your Change Patterns. You've done everything you know to connect with these people. So what's wrong?

'There's nothing wrong as such. My 360 appraisal said that they all respect me and support me in everything I do.'

They respect you? Support you in everything? Well that's great isn't it?

'They would say that wouldn't they?'

They would?

'Well, I kind of think they do. But they still think I'm a hard bitch, I'm sure.'

What exactly is the problem here? You've been a great success in business, you have surpassed all of your career ambitions, you have the complete support of the management board, your employees are fiercely loyal and your social life is fantastic. What is it that you really want?

'I don't want them to think that I'm a bitch.'

Is that it really? With all that you've learnt, you're still preoccupied with what other people think of you? If you really didn't want to come across as a bitch, then you know what else you could do. I don't think it's being a bitch that bothers you, it's not being able to control everybody's thoughts.

'Nonsense. How did you come up with that?'

Because you want the truth. That's the only thing you'll get when you speak to me.

'No, I don't believe that.'

Yes you do. You know it's true.

'It seems so harsh. I mean, it really makes me sound like a bitch!'

Get over yourself. You're not being a bitch, you're being human.

'How terribly flawed.'

Aren't we just? But we're more than that.

For the first time that evening, a smile comes to Madeline's lips. 'What else are we?'

What else do you think we are?

'Lots. Tell me what else we are. Tell me how a bitch can become a decent, caring, sensitive leader.'

I'll not tell you what you want to hear. I'll tell you what you need. Right. Listen carefully. First of all, let's use what we've already got. Let's get those resources we need. In a moment we'll run through those. It will blow your mind, but that's fine. First though, let's work out how we can control the system. Controlling the system's fine; that's so we can work to everybody's advantage and get that win-win we all crave. Controlling other people's minds is unhealthy and impossible, so drop that. So let's look at the set-up. We have the team, you're at the head of the table, and I'll go Meta.

'What about fourth position?'

You know fourth, you've gone through it before. But I'll hold fourth as well, at the back of our mind, if you please. Now, in a moment we're going to run through the scenario from the beginning, using the resources we need. We'll do it a few times, until the bathwater goes cold, and that should do it. Tomorrow night, we'll review it and add anything extra that's needed.

'Sounds great. You know when I go on about Storage Patterns and things like that it can sound so mechanical. This is exciting, it's for real.'

Sure is. Mind you this is the first time we've spoken about this, so no wonder we haven't got this part sussed yet. Won't take long. So, what we need to do is second position...

> **'We need to establish a strong rapport between our conscious and unconscious. The internal dialogue needs to be a clear and strong link that will last throughout our life-time'**

Trust the Unconscious

It is very rarely the case that someone who goes to a therapist sees their problem disappear when told what it is. There is a lot of stock placed on self-awareness. Of course self-awareness can be a good thing. What we need to do is move beyond self-awareness to the practical pursuit of finding a solution; apply what we know.

That solution can only be found from within. Even if it is strikingly obvious to outsiders, that means nothing if we as individuals do not recognise the problem, or even if there is a problem. Besides, armchair critics are not always right. Because our existence is entirely subjective, what appears to be the problem may not be the case at all.

What this amounts to is self-diagnosis and self-help. No-one else can do it for us. Not then, not now, not ever. We are entirely self-motivated and independently minded. If we choose to be in control, we cannot be controlled by anyone else, no matter how hard people might try.

So, if we do want to find the remedy for our self, or progress forward, the only way to do it is to maintain a strong line of communication with our self. We need to establish a strong rapport between our conscious and unconscious. The internal dialogue needs to be a clear and strong link that will last throughout our life-time.

It has always been there, but not necessarily serving our best interest. Now that we have become aware of it, we can refine it to our satisfaction. It will ultimately work in our best interest. However, like the dialogue above, it may be brutally honest to reveal what we need to know. Do not be afraid to hold back. If we can not be honest with our self then who can we be honest with?

The important thing is to work with it, in every Context, but most importantly when we are alone, when we are with the Self. Some people love to spend hours by themselves, whilst some people can not do without the company of other

Communications, Self

people for even a short period of time. The duration spent by our self is not particularly important; it is the quality of time spent establishing that rapport and understanding of what, how and who we are. So if we are the type of person who likes to socialise and easily become bored on our own, we can always call up our internal self and continue the conversation. We need never be lonely again!

As the above dialogue highlighted, the Context of Self leads on to all other Contexts, in this case Work, Social and undoubtedly the Movement Contexts. When it comes to Communication though, it always starts with the Self. Once we have mastered our internal communication, there is no external communication that presents any problem whatsoever. That is because we can unfurl all the resources we need to get the result we want.

The dialogue between the lady in the bath and her internal self could have taken many different forms. She could have got out of the bath and rehearsed the perceptual positions around the house. The internal voice could have been from a spiritual guide, an ethereal guru or a hobbit in her head. Whatever works. It can be whatever springs to mind. Trust the unconscious.

This is not as fantastic as it sounds. Remember the unconscious mind is highly symbolic; it responds to symbols and metaphors. If the symbol is an angel hovering above then so be it. The connection is still there.

The conversation can also go much deeper. It can be more challenging. There can be different considerations thrown into the mix. It is up to the individual to decide how to make the most of that quality time together.

Crucially important though is accessing those resources. The only thing blocking the way is incongruence. So once the conversation has been had and the understanding reached, there is no reason to hold the resources back. If that conversation does not take place it is incredibly difficult to access those resources because the unconscious has no reason to let go.

The unconscious believes that holding the resources inside is in our best interest. How would it know otherwise? If it did let all the resources out all the time, we would be in a constant state of agitation; one minute as hyperactive as a manic conductor and the next as reclusive as a hermit, and everything in between. Only by persuading the unconscious otherwise; that releasing these resources will be of great benefit, will it agree to let go. Once the valve is released, magic happens!

Once we have sorted the Self out and the rest is a doddle.

Chapter 29

Communications, Sex

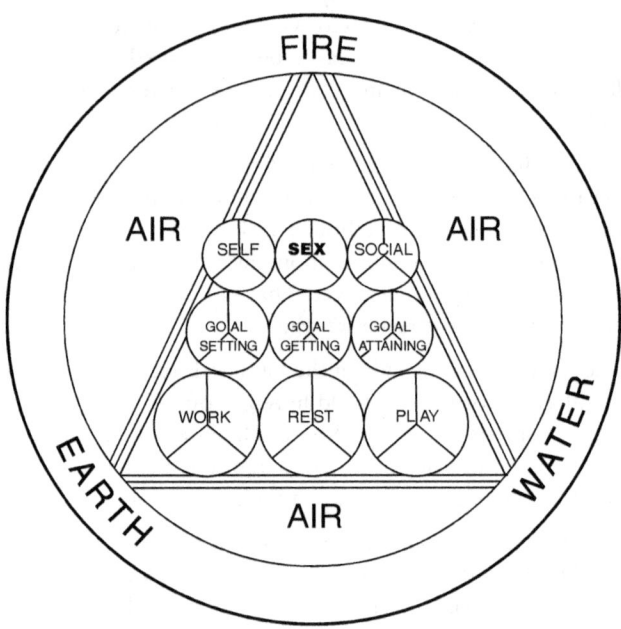

'An angel and a demon coming together to create a celestial masterpiece'

The starry eyed lovers clasped each other's gaze for what seemed like minutes, yet could have only been seconds. The room throbbed with noise and mayhem, laughter and high spirits, and yet at each stolen glance time stood still and everything else faded away as the silent bond shot across the busy bar. The moments were sparse as friends and colleagues blocked the path or hoisted drinks upon the celebratory pair.

'Here's to Caroline and David, as lovely a couple as you could ever meet,' proclaimed Harold, David's oldest friend and the one pencilled in as best man, much to Caroline's bemusement. Harold had always been a loveable soul but a frightful, if largely harmless drinker. Deep down Caroline knew he was the man for the job, if only he could stick to the script for just one day.

He continued carefully, aware as everyone else in the room how much he had drunk in the short time they had been at the wine bar. 'I would go as far as to say they are the perfect couple, don't you agree?' A small cheer echoed in agreement.

Communications, Sex

'Too good for you Caz,' someone shouted from the back of the room.

'Good enough for me,' chirped Amanda, Caroline's quick-witted friend, which prompted a ripple of approval from most of the women and a very loud 'phwarrr' from Caroline's sister, causing an eruption of laughter.

'Now, now ladies, my dear friend is well and truly spoken for and has committed his loins to the loving Caroline, the most beautiful of companions…'

'Here, here,' David boomed, raising an unsteady glass to his own fidelity.

'That's my boy,' Harold sang back, attuned to their unique banter. 'Indeed, it has taken a staggering beauty held by the bewitching Caroline to rein in my unwieldy companion…'

'Here, here,' Caroline howled from the other side of the bar, raising her glass to her intended, as he gave a private toast in return.

'And it is fortunate for all that I did not take it upon myself to go about capturing the alluring filly myself, surrendering instead to the wistful and intoxicating charm of Gina Gin and Tina Tonic here…' another burst of laughter rippled around the room, as much in appreciation of Harold's eloquence under the severe restriction of copious amounts of alcohol as the wit of his words.

'Seriously though ladies and gentlemen, if there are any left here, I would like to toast the delightful pair, crafted in heaven and placed on earth to enthral and delight us mere mortals. An angel and a demon coming together to create a celestial masterpiece. To Caroline Fontasque and David Giles Bedenfield, a match made in heaven.'

'A match made in heaven,' and 'Caroline and David,' came the mixed chant of the crowd's toast. The couple came together and kissed gracefully, if a little too quickly, conscious of having all eyes upon them. 'Speech, speech!' a couple of David's rugby friends implored.

'What can I say in return to such a finely worded epitaph?' David began, speaking calmly and fluently, a man well used to public speaking. 'I concur with my learned friend,' he doffed an imaginary hat to his barrister buddy, 'the lady is indeed an angel sent to entice and enthral us weak male mortals.' He tightened his grip around Caroline's waist as she feigned surprise. 'She has managed what I thought impossible, to satisfy all my desires and I only hope to keep her entertained whilst she dwells amongst us,' another cheer went up as Caroline flushed at the pretence.

'Seriously though, I do feel like the luckiest man in the world. I never thought I would meet someone as beautiful, intelligent, funny and delightful as Caroline. For the first time I feel complete and this is down to my darling wife to be. Ladies and gentlemen, I give you the beautiful bride to be!'

As David raised his glass the crowd did the same and this time chirped back in unison, 'the beautiful bride to be.'

'Speech, speech!' Amanda and a couple of Caroline's work friends demanded supported by the baritone chant of the rugby players. Caroline flushed again and raised her hands to lower the noise.

'Ok, ok. Yes, well I agree with everything that has been said, of course,' she smiled as the audience 'here, here'd'. 'I only want to say one thing really. That is to thank my fiancé for throwing this surprise party, which should come as no surprise to those who know David well. And to say, well, David, you never fail to amaze me and I love you!'

The crowd responded as one, clapping and cheering. This time the pair enjoyed a long, tender embrace, regaining that magic isolation when sharing eye contact across a crowded room. 'I love you too,' David whispered as Caroline nuzzled his ear and sighed, 'always' in response. The music exploded through the speakers and the dancing re-started spontaneously with dozens of people bouncing almost as one. The couple were instantly jostled into participation, spilling champagne and holding each other tightly out of necessity, lest they topple to the sticky floor.

* * *

Later that night, Harold and David sat in the corner of the empty bar, feet on table, dicky-bows untied, jackets off, looking tattered and drink addled, Harold in particular. Two miles away, in Amanda's riverside apartment, Caroline lay on the settee as Amanda poured her another glass of Rose.

'It's not that I'm having second thoughts Harry, it's just me you know.'

'Of course, of course my boy, end of an era. Wild oats well and truly sown and all that. Happens to us all. Well, not all. Never happened in the first place for me.'

'It's not that so much. It's me, you know. It's a big thing becoming a couple, being 'x' and so and so; not me, not David, you know?'

'No idea old boy, you're talking gibberish.'

'I'm used to doing my own thing, not being an appendage. I don't know if I want to be a half of something else; I want to be a whole me.'

'What are you wittering on about?' Harry queried, before sinking the last of his G&T and staggering across the deserted bar to restock.

* * *

'So you've finally tamed the beast then?' Amanda teased, slightly less tipsy than Harold, but still a little unsteady on her feet.

'Have I? I don't think I want to be known as the woman who tamed David Bedenfield. Makes me sound like a disciplinarian. I want to have fun too.'

'Not like David you don't.'

'What do you mean?'

'Oh you know, you know all about his past, everybody does.'

'That's what it is, the past. It doesn't stop us going out and having fun does it?'

'That's it though, isn't it, it would be the two of you, that's a different thing all together,' Amanda teased, topping up their glasses, spilling Caroline's over the edge. 'Oops, sorry.'

'It's ok,' Caroline responded, mopping up the over-spill with a napkin. 'It's just that I don't buy in to all this losing your identity business as soon as you become a couple…'

* * *

'I just feel like I'm losing my identity, becoming, you know, a couple,' David moaned.

'Oh please, can you hear yourself? Have you seen the woman? I wasn't joking when I said I'd wished I'd bagged her myself,' Harold shot back, a little prissily.

'And leave the sauce?' David pointed to the G&T cradled in Harold's giant paws, 'the sacrifice would be too much.'

'And is it too great a sacrifice for you, losing your single status?' Harold snapped, still too sharp for David, despite the dulling effect of alcohol.

'It's not the single status I'm talking about, it's the couple thing. I'm not sure I want to be part of a whole, I want to be a whole part.'

'Maybe you're growing up, putting somebody else before yourself for the first time.'

'It's not that. I do love her Harry, no doubt about it. I just think I'm more than that.'

* * *

'You see, you can still be yourself, do all the stuff you want to do and still be in a couple,' Caroline reasoned.

'Of course you can. But do you really want David going off doing his own thing?'

'Sure. I trust him. He's a big boy now Amanda. He still puts on the act, but he's grown up. I think he's found out who he is, what he's all about. There's so much more to him now; he's always coming up with something new, something different. That's what I love about him. He brings so much…'

* * *

'I just feel that I don't know who I am anymore. I'm becoming this 'couple thing' and I'm not ready for it. I want more…'

* * *

'Don't you feel you lose a bit of yourself, being in a couple? Don't you worry about getting married?' Amanda challenged, half to herself, as she thought of her near-miss with Harold all those years ago.

'Hell no! Why should you lose any part of yourself? I think you expand if anything. You get more from the other person, take what they have to offer and use that to grow yourself. You don't have to lose anything. I think if anything you gain more through being with somebody, sharing those dreams and desires, building a future together, growing as one…' Caroline caught the far away look in Amanda's eyes and checked herself. 'Oh, I'm sorry, I didn't mean to rub it in.'

Amanda came back into focus, 'no, no, don't worry about me. I shouldn't have teased you earlier. I'm just interested, that's all. You know with Harry and me, it could have been…' she let it hang.

'I know love. Don't listen to me, you don't need someone else to be complete, look at how well you're doing…'

'It's fine, really,' Amanda cut in. 'Don't listen to me. What were you saying about being yourself?'

* * *

'… and it's like I don't get time to be myself anymore. It's like I'm being David the fiancé; David, Caroline's partner, David, the bridegroom, you know. It's like I'm losing myself…'

'What the hell makes you think that?' Harold interrupted, growing impatient with David's self-pity. 'Who the hell decides all this? Whoever said that you had to be Caroline's other half? Who told you to be one half of a couple? Where is it written down that you lose your identity when you go into a relationship? Sure it's about sharing and commitment and putting someone else first for a change, but who the hell ever said that you stopped being you, you blithering idiot?'

David's mouth dropped at the vehemence behind the delivery of the last statement. A terrier in court, Harold rarely, if ever, raised his voice to his friends. Harold looked away, shaking his head at the stupidity of his best and most admired friend. 'And I thought you were smart,' he said quietly, with not a little contempt.

Taken aback, David sought absolution, as he always did whenever he overstepped the mark. 'I'm sorry old pal, it's the drink and the melancholy. I'm being silly.'

'Damn right you are. You don't know when you're onto a good thing,' Harold snapped back, but already his voice was beginning to soften, as it always did when David sought redemption.

'I know, I'm a fool. She's amazing. I should be grateful.'

'You know you'll only lose something if you give it away,' Harold advised, slipping back to his usual role as the sympathetic older brother.

'How do you mean?'

'In a relationship. It's not about supplication, missing out, becoming a lesser person. If you're smart you lose nothing. You bring everything you've ever had and you give everything you've ever had. And if you're lucky, really lucky, the other person does the same and then, well, a beautiful thing happens...' Harold tailed off, unaware he had become lost in thought.

'What happens Harry? What beautiful thing?'

'You'll see. If you commit properly. There's more to Caz than meets the eye, you know. She's got more to offer than you think. So much more.'

David eyed Harry suspiciously but the bigger man just laughed and slapped his closest friend on the shoulder. 'You'll make a fine upstanding man one day, Davey,' and with that the giant of a man rose to leave, hoisting his companion from under the armpits as if he were picking up a rag doll.

* * *

'So that's it really, that's what he said, and I think he's spot on,' Caroline concluded, placing her empty glass on the table and smiling at Amanda. Amanda looked shell-shocked. Her mouth fell open, just as David's had done a few minutes earlier, and she stared at Caroline as if she had just announced that she was really from Mars.

'Eh?' she finally managed. Caroline laughed.

'Honestly, that's what he said.' Amanda remained in a state of shock, puzzling over what Caroline had told her.

'So, let me get this straight, Harold tells you that to grow as a couple you first grow as an individual, as yourself. Then, if you really want to move ahead, you give your all to the relationship and, in return the other person will give you all you need.'

'Well, yeah, something like that. Except he put it much more eloquently than that. It's more about being your self, becoming self-less and growing whilst being close to somebody else; if you get what I mean. It's like a loop, a self-fulfilling destiny. Each inspires the other.'

'I'll be!' Amanda exclaimed, still shocked. 'Harold Bloom, once mighty barrister, bar room drunk and destroyer of relationships (well mine), speaking like a bloody love doctor!'

'He's a changed man Amanda. You should speak to him again.' Amanda nodded unknowingly, already intrigued beyond repair about the Damascan transformation of her former beau. 'I'll be...' she repeated, lost in thought. 'Must be something in the drink.'

Caroline cleared the glasses from the table and took them into the kitchen. Looking out of the window she saw the two staggering figures on the riverside path below, winding their way slowly towards the apartment, arm in arm.

'You're not wrong Harry,' she said aloud, knowing the gentle giant would have provided wise council to her unpredictable lover. 'This is only just the beginning of something....'

Chapter 30

Communications, Social

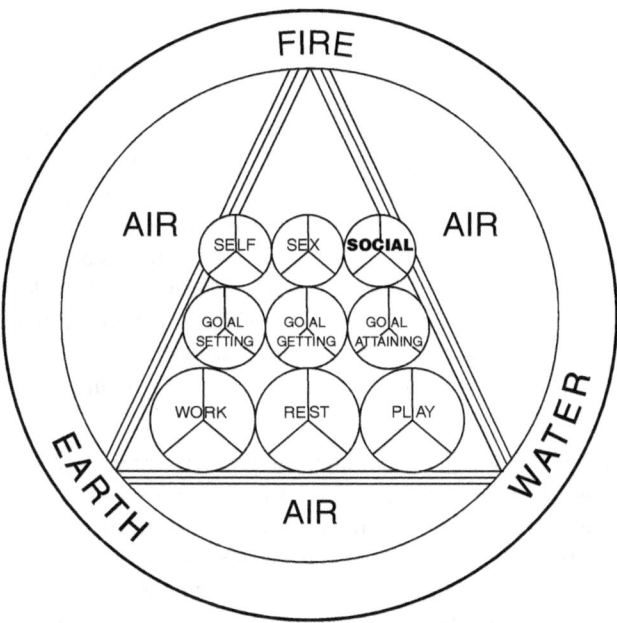

> *'Through using MindFrames we have already established most of what we need to know to get what we want and certainly be in the right frame of mind in the right context to achieve our desired outcome'*

How do we know when we are saying the right thing, making the right noises, coming across well? By and large our sensory acuity tells us so. We notice peoples' expressions, physiology, voice tone and tempo, and the dilation of the pupils and colouration of the skin. There are many tell tale signs.

But how do we know how to begin? How do we know what buttons to press, what to say and to whom?

The visual rehearsal practised whilst in the Context of Self, perhaps whilst also in a state of Play, combined with the groundwork done during the Goal Setting Context will ensure we have the right MindFrame in the Social Context.

However, when we are there, in the midst of the group, team, circle of friends, family gathering, we are in the maelstrom of a dynamic series of interactions, of which we are one part. There is not only our interaction, there is also the interaction between other people, who may or may not be involved in our conversation. Even though we may not be in conversation with members of the group we are still intimately linked through the process of inter-connectivity; everything being connected to everything else.

Although we might not be speaking, we may be listening, and even though we may not be listening to everybody, we are still in the same sphere. The person who we had just been talking to is now talking to someone else on a theme that is not dissimilar to the conversation we just held and that person's view may have slightly altered by our conversation. They might not be aware of it yet, and the difference may be minor, but it may cause a ripple effect that dramatically transforms that person's way of thinking. We may have recommended a book or a film that the person subsequently reads or watches which leads them to discover new books or films in that field which leads to a different way of thinking. It is the domino effect. We may have been the catalyst or we may have been a contributory factor. Whichever, we cannot not communicate and that goes for every situation.

How do we know we are communicating in a positive way? For a start, we are communicating consciously, acutely aware of what we are saying and doing. We have a new level of self-awareness. That is not to say that everything we say or do will be for the benefit of mankind. It does not stop us saying something that could be hurtful. It does make us aware of when we do it, therefore giving us the power to reduce the frequency, and we have the wherewithal to seek to rectify the unhelpful remark or action.

In the group dynamic, things happen quickly. There are conversations whirling around of which we may only have a slight awareness. Surely we cannot control a system that has so many parts operating at once?

All we can control is our self and through that our inter-action with the group or system. So we can control our involvement, our communication.

'Once we have mastered our self, set up that internal communication channel and broadcast it clearly and effectively, we are ready to move to the next level'

Controlling Communication

The first step in controlling our communication occurs at the Self stage, where we have time to go through the steps we take in social situations. More importantly, it gives us the support framework we need to communicate easily and effortlessly. That is a strong rapport between our conscious and unconscious. Once this has been firmly established people recognise how comfortable and relaxed we are 'in our own skin'.

Next we can develop our awareness, resources and overall growth through the close relationships we have with the people around us. The close relationships of the protagonists in the last chapter did not just concern David and Caroline, and eventually, Amanda and Harold. It also involved Caroline and Harold, David and Harold, and Amanda and Caroline. There was little evidence of the relationship between David and Amanda, despite the fact that they were lovers once. That would have been another dynamic altogether. The point here is that any close one-to-one relationship can enhance our understanding and our effectiveness in every Communications Context.

We then have the insight and depths of perception available to us through the use of perceptual positions. This can give us a real understanding of the other person's point of view, through second positioning, as well as a wider overview through using the third, Meta position. A fourth position can give an even broader insight into the group's governing principles.

What else would be useful in the Social context?

There is a close link here with the collective consciousness described in Chapter 17. That is a strong, unifying thread that runs through every person, especially felt by those who are like-minded. The way to establish and feel the strength of this connection is through opening our self up to this possibility. If we are open and honest, approachable and genuinely interested in others, the link will soon be established. Projecting a generosity in our behaviour, showing understanding and interest, is a great way to achieve this. We need to be able to put our self on the line, open our self up to be able to reap the dividends.

For those people who are apprehensive about strangers, or colleagues, or friends of friends, who we may perceive to be up to no good, this could be seen as difficult. The problem here is that we may well be projecting our insecurities and problems on to other people. Even if we are right, and the person is a con artist or a thief, they can only take from us as much as we are willing to give.

Projecting a generosity of behaviour does not mean doling out our credit card number to the nearest person. It means opening our self up so we can be as accessible as possible. That does not mean to say we are gullible or easily manipulated.

With everything we have discovered about how we function as individuals, it is not difficult to read how other people are operating. In fact that is essential to move up to the next level, which we will come to shortly. We will probably be able to ascertain a manipulative person's motivations fairly quickly. We also have all the tools we need to be able to protect our self should someone attempt to manipulate us. Basically, we are not placing our self in any danger by being open and honest, so long as we are aware of what we are leaving open. There is a difference between being open and being exposed.

As we open our self up and allow those connections to be made, it is very difficult for people not to be enticed towards us. People are interested in people who have something to offer and do not want to take things away from them. However, too few people are prepared to be open because of the reasons listed earlier and the societal expectations that dictate that 'people are out to get you'.

That means that when someone does act charitably, opening themselves up for the benefit of others, it is very apparent and people become interested in this break from the norm. If there is evidence of incongruence, that the open person has in fact a barrel full of problems, that is also picked up on. So it is only worth doing if that alignment is sound and the congruency is there between the conscious and unconscious.

Once we have displayed this attractive characteristic we do not need a script to communicate effectively with others. For a start, by showing an interest in other people, a deep curiosity, it is often the case that the other person will open up. There does not need to be a script if the person opposite is going into detail about their own life.

Saying the right thing at the right time is easier if there is a genuine interest in the person to whom we are talking. If we are struggling to find something interesting to say about our self, this is more than likely because we are thinking of our self and not the other person. However, there are moments in conversations when the attention does come back to us. How we deal with this is simply down to the ease with which we already communicate with our self. We just let that communication branch outwards.

When we know our self well, there is an ease with which we can talk about what we are doing, without being immodest or attention seeking. We can also grow to trust our unconscious more and more so that we do not have to consciously search to unfurl great pearls of wisdom, or strive to find something to say on each and every topic.

We can simply trust our self to discover what to say by delving into our experiences. Through extensive use of Storage Patterns it should not be difficult to access states that can also put us in mind of the current topic of conversation. When we are in that state, it will be surprising how many similar experiences, or terms of reference, we can call upon.

The reason many people become stunted in conversation is because of recall problems; trying to remember something about a subject of which they have little experience. However, there is nearly always a similar experience we have had to which we can refer. If we have not been there and done that then it is likely we will know somebody who has.

> *'What gives highly successful people the edge is that extra dimension of awareness'*

Modelling Excellence

The individual who we witness communicating very effectively in the social environment will have doubtless observed others interacting well. They will have consciously or unconsciously worked out what that person did, how he or she did it and then how they could apply it to make it work for their self.

There are many skills that can be developed to help us communicate more effectively and these can be learned through attending training courses on presentation skills and such like. However, we already have many resources to call upon to communicate more effectively right now. Through using MindFrames we have already established most of what we need to know to get what we want and certainly be in the right frame of mind in the right context to achieve our desired outcome.

What gives highly successful people the edge is that extra dimension of awareness. They have gained insight through observing other highly successful people, and they have adopted and adapted these practices and applied it to themselves. This could have been done consciously or unconsciously. What these people have in common is the bed rock of expertise in their chosen fields or some other highly developed skill which enables them to move to a higher level. They have developed their awareness of self and others to a high degree before moving on.

This is the purpose of going through MindFrame Patterns in a deliberate, step-by-step way. It gives us the building blocks to establish all we need to be successful in every Context. It gives us all the tools and techniques to sort our self out, to make sure we are the best we can be in every situation. Once we have mastered our self, set up that internal communication channel and broadcast it clearly and effectively, we are ready to move to the next level. That is to start modelling other people. Or more accurately, to start modelling highly successful people. When we do this right, communicating brilliantly in the Social Context becomes easy.

If modelling is the foundation of NLP why is it only explored at the end of MindFrame Patterns? This is simply to ensure that everything is in place to model most effectively.

We needed to start with our self in order to get all the basics right. If we had begun with other people it is highly possible we could become confused about identity and direction.

Now that we are aligned and highly aware we can integrate the highly sophisticated techniques of successful people. Because we know all about Contexts and being flexible in our behaviour we now know that just because we use someone else's strategy that does not categorise or label us as being the same as they are. In fact we can fine tune the techniques so they flow seamlessly in whichever Context we choose. It can be almost like putting a hat on and taking it off again. Whatever fits.

MindFrames gives the most comprehensive preparation to explore modelling, strategies and models of excellence in the most effective way possible.

In many ways the journey is only just beginning.

Part IV: Modelling Excellence

Chapter 31

Modelling Excellence

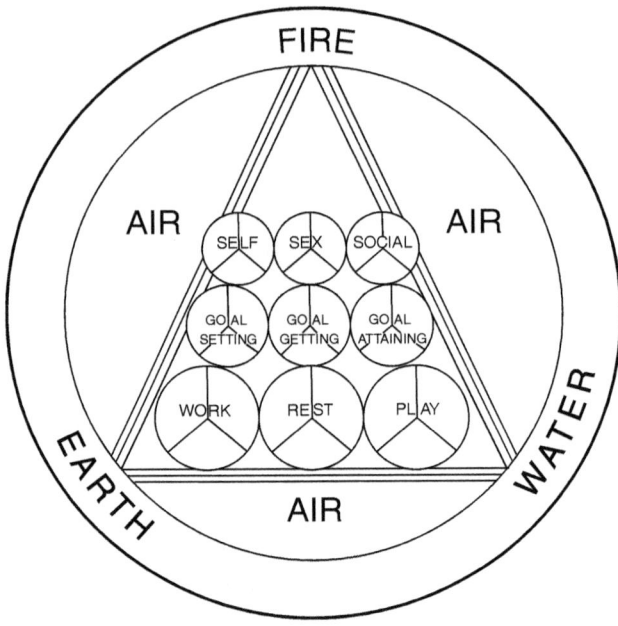

'As we develop our skills at modelling, so we can adapt strategies to fit, tailor-make them for our personal preferences'

We have been unconsciously modelling people all our lives. It is something we can not help but do, particularly when we are children. Modelling other people comes to us as naturally as breathing.

What we can now do is model successful people consciously, therefore to our advantage, rather than model average people out of our conscious awareness. Once we become aware of how successful people operate, we will plug into the habits and strategies of high-fliers and we can adopt these traits our self; if they are proven to work for us as individuals.

As we develop our skills at modelling, so we can adapt strategies to fit, tailor-make them for our personal preferences. We can cut things out, add things on, manipulate to our liking. We can integrate successful strategies seamlessly and make them our own to use in specific Contexts. We can then switch to another strategy in another Context, as easily as taking one hat off and putting another on again.

Modelling Excellence

The first rule of modelling is to ensure we model excellence. If we model mediocrity that is exactly what we shall get, mediocrity. If we aspire towards excellence, that is what we are likely to achieve.

Successful people are fairly easy to identify. They excel at what they do and are at or near to the top of their chosen speciality. They are outstanding. They are high achievers and they are highly successful. They do not have to be the most wonderful people on earth. They do not have to be well-rounded human beings who excel in everything to which they apply themselves.

We are looking at Contexts. If we are modelling a highly successful musician we do not have to concern our self with how they behave at home, whether or not they have a successful marriage or family life. That is unless it forms part of their success strategy. If it does not then what we will be looking at is how they play the violin, cello or guitar to such a high standard and what under-pins that achievement. They may be a dirty rotten scoundrel when it comes to other aspects of their lives, but so be it.

Ideally, of course, we will be modelling wonderful people with wonderful lives who are highly moralistic. However, that is not a pre-requisite because we will be modelling people in specific Contexts. If we are to use the strategy in every Context then we will need to be very careful on every aspect of the person's life. We will have to check the ecology thoroughly, ensure that the required changes will not negatively impact our life or the lives of people around us.

This is why it is rare that a strategy will be used for every Context. It is much more likely we adopt and adapt a strategy for a particular Context that may transfer over into others. It is not difficult to run a number of strategies in a number of different Contexts, once the elicitation and installation has been mastered.

MindFrame Patterns give the steps required to model successfully. All we need to do is run through the same process we have to set up our own MindFrame Patterns, except this time analyse somebody else's frame of mind. Instead of asking our self the questions, we will be asking someone else.

If the thought of having to ask someone we admire how they do what they do sounds off-putting; the fact is that it is highly likely the individual will be flattered and more than willing to help. Especially so if it is approached in the right way. 'I admire the way you do x. How do you do that? Do you mind if I discover more about your strategy for success?'

The only difference between eliciting our own MindFrames and those of other people is that we know very little about the other person on a deep level. Therefore the questions we ask need to take account of the unknown quantities. We also need to adopt the non-judgemental perspective of the third person, or Meta position of perceptual positions.

The final and possibly most important aspect of eliciting a strategy is that it must be a win-win. The individual whose strategy we are eliciting must get something from the process. They must benefit from the elicitation as much as we do; otherwise they could feel exploited and manipulated. We need to ask our self, what benefit will they get from the exercise?

For a start, they will find out how they do what they do. They will discover their success strategy and be able to utilise it elsewhere in their life. It is exactly the same as the personal MindFrame Patterns process. If something works in one area of our life we can work out how and adapt it to work in another Context. Likewise, if a highly successful person finds out how they succeed in one area of life, they can adapt it to use elsewhere.

It might be that they can adopt the entire strategy for use elsewhere, or it could be small sections that can be used. It is highly unlikely that they will not benefit in some way from having their success strategy elicited and explained.

A common complaint here is that if the person finds out how they do something well, they will become too conscious of what they are doing and somehow lose the gift. The opposite actually applies. If they find out how they do something well, they are then aware of each part and can improve where appropriate. If they do become very self-conscious the next time they go out to do the activity, then we can help them change state and enter the right frame of mind to go back into the 'zone' or whatever state they need to be in. If this is explained beforehand most people welcome the possible benefits.

This ecology check is necessary whenever we involve people in MindFrames. They need to be aware of the impact of any changes that could occur. By and large people tend to welcome the opportunity to gain insight into how a successful strategy operates and advice on how to implement it elsewhere. They are doing us a favour in divulging their strategy; the least we could do is show them how to improve upon it where possible and how to utilise it elsewhere in their life.

'The first rule of modelling is to ensure we model excellence'

Strategy Elicitation

The first step towards eliciting a strategy is the Conscious element of Earth, Values. What are their values in this Context? What is most important to them? What do they spend their time, money and energy moving towards or away from?

We can ask them to draw up a list of their top ten values. We can then challenge them to identify five which they could not do without. A good question could then be, 'With all those values firmly in place, what would have to happen to make you leave this situation?' If another value is added, we could then ask them, 'With all these values in place what would have to happen to make you stay?' We could then reverse it again. Several other values may well be added.

This is when the scrutiny starts. Work out exactly how much time, money and energy is expanded for each one over the period of an average week. Which are means and ends? That is which of the values help them move towards or away from something and which are end results? Once the list has been drawn up a particularly challenging question could then be asked. 'Would you prefer to live with the opposite of that value or do without it altogether?'

This can highlight a harsh reality. In life we often learn to live without the thing to which we aspire rather than endure the opposite. In enduring the opposite, we can begin to move through that and towards our outcome.

Once the values have been determined, assess whether the top values are means or ends. Enquire further as to whether these values are towards or away from and with each one, ask what percentage are they towards or away. This is essential for when we come onto Change Patterns.

Remember this process is entirely non-judgemental, so if the values do not sit with our own, that is fine at this stage. Other things will come into play.

Beliefs

We then move on to Water, Beliefs. What are the governing principles of this person's life in this Context? The Context is essential. The values and beliefs in this Context may be entirely different from their values and beliefs in another Context.

What are the rules by which they live their lives? What do they need to believe in order that they can live according to their values? Which of these beliefs are empowering? Which of these beliefs are towards or away from? Do they have any limiting beliefs? (Limiting beliefs can sometimes be part of a successful strategy. If a limiting belief is that they cannot do anything else, this may help them focus all their time, energy and attention upon this activity, for example).

Beliefs can be surprising and varied, so it is helpful if we constantly refer to the specific Context. What specifically do you believe about this activity? The more specific we are, the clearer we are about the Context, the more likely it is that the subject will be expansive and helpful. At first they may be reluctant to impart information if it sounds egotistical or self-indulgent. However, if we clarify that it relates specifically to this Context, to this activity, and does not include how they are with their family, for example, the person is more likely to be at ease. 'I don't mind admitting that I'm totally driven and think I'm great at doing x because it's only in that situation. I don't think I'm wonderful at everything all the time.' So be specific and challenging.

Subjects tend to claim they either know little or nothing about how they do something well, or they go the opposite way and say they know exactly how they do it. Neither matters. We are not concerned with how they think they do it; we need to know how they actually do it. It is highly unlikely they will know their unconscious process for doing the activity.

They may also think they know exactly what their supporting values and beliefs are in this Context, which is not always the case. Once it is written down in black and white and once they have explored how they actually allocate their time, energy and resources they might find that the values and beliefs have no similarity to what they thought. Or they may find there is a hidden belief that empowers them to succeed. 'I didn't realise that being good at that meant that I knew I would be good at this…'

This is a subjective experience for the individual, just like when we do our own MindFrame Patterns, so give them the time and space to explore a little more about themselves. Just because they are successful does not mean to say they know how they are successful.

We then need to drill down. We need to find out exactly what they mean, go beyond ambiguities and generalisations, and discover their model of the world.

This is where second and third positioning comes in really handy. In fact the process is almost impossible without the ability to perceive the world through their eyes, to step into their shoes. This can be a strange experience. Even people who we think we know intimately have 'weird and wonderful' maps of the world, somehow similar but distorted to our own. It can be as if we are living in parallel universes. Every single person's model is different and inevitably will appear skewered at first when compared to our own. Whatever their model is, in this Context it is working for them, so have the patience to pursue it further because it may well work for us.

Once we have nailed down the most important beliefs we move on to the behaviours.

Behaviours

What are they doing? What is their body language, their voice tone and timbre when they are doing this exercise?

Modelling Excellence

Here we need to witness them in action, watch them closely do what they do best. If there is an opportunity to record them in action or listen to them on audio, it is well worth doing. We can scrutinise exactly what they do and when. What is their body posture like? How does their facial expression change? Follow the direction of their eyes, notice the hand gestures. Does their skin colour change? Are they stooping or upright? Is their voice soft or harsh? Do they move about much? Are they static? Is their head tilted forward? Are they deep in thought, caught in the moment, or are they looking around, scanning everybody else present?

With the background knowledge we have about their values and beliefs, step into their shoes, and look through their eyes. What are the underlying values and beliefs that are supporting this behaviour? Does this gesture indicate a self-confidence that comes from a particular belief? Does that easy, self-assured delivery echo a deeply-held value?

As has possibly been ascertained already, modelling if nothing else, can be a lot of fun. It is like trying on a new suit and parading around town. It certainly does no harm to try. Actors are natural modellers. They do it all the time. They get into character and embody their part. The Method form of acting is a brilliant form of behavioural modelling. So play around, have some fun by second positioning.

Although this is still the elicitation stage of modelling, in order to elicit effectively, we should already be thinking about installing the strategy for our self. Looking through the other person's eyes is the first step.

Once all the conscious elements have been taken care of, we then move onto the unconscious process, starting with Storage Patterns.

Storage Patterns

'What are you seeing, hearing and feeling when you are doing x?' Ask them to think of a specific time when they were doing that activity. Ask them if they have a picture of that time. Now ask them to float back to that time and float back into their bodies so they can see what they saw, hear what they heard and feel what they felt when they were totally enraptured in what they were doing, when they were at their very best.

Ask them exactly what they are seeing, elicit all the visual sub modalities. 'Is it a movie? Is it black and white? Is there any contrast? What colours are there?' Do the same for sound. 'If there are any sounds, where are they coming from? Can you hear your own voice? What does it sound like? Is it loud or soft? Is there any music? Is there an internal voice? Is it inspiring? What is the tone like? Is the sound constant or does it change? Does it get louder or softer?'

Next, ask if there are any feelings that are important. 'If so, where are they located? Are they large or small? Is there any movement? Do they swirl around your body or do they remain in the same place? Do you associate them with a colour? Are they liquid or solid? Does it vibrate? Is it soft or light?'

Ask if there are any tastes or smells that are brought to mind.

Now ask where the picture is located. 'Is it near by or far away? Is it up or down, to the left or right? How large is the picture? Is it associated or dissociated?' These last few questions are most important and should be recorded diligently.

Ask them to come back to now. Break the state by saying something completely different. If there are any other times when they conduct the successful strategy ask them to go back to that time and elicit the Storage Pattern again. Notice if there are any differences with the last time. 'Is the location the same? Are they associated or dissociated. Is the picture large or small, black and white or colour?'

It may be that the strategy runs differently depending upon the environment, so we need to take the differences into account. Perhaps the subject uses a dissociated Storage Pattern when performing in front of other people and an associated pattern when on their own.

Once the Storage Patterns have been elicited we move onto the Change Patterns.

Change Patterns

In this Context, does the individual like change or are they a difference person? Do they notice the similarities, or the odd one out? Where is their attention directed?

Ask what their Primary Interest is. Which do they prefer to talk about most in this Context? General conversation around the topic should provide ample evidence of their preference. Ask anyway. 'What do you prefer in this Context: people, things, activities, information or places? What is your secondary preference?'

Next is Information. 'Do you pay attention to the big picture first or go straight to the detail? Are you a blue sky thinker or a specific, minor detail person in this Context?'

The individual may not be clearly one or the other. This is where we need to dig deeper. Ask for examples. 'When you are doing this activity, what are you thinking about? Where is your attention focussed? What is happening in there?' Mostly, they will be happy to relive the activity, because it is largely an enjoyable experience to go through a successful experience.

Modelling Excellence

The most important Change Patterns tend to be the ones that are most pronounced, most obviously different. The ones that tend to be balanced are rarely the most important in this Context. Why? Because success is about exceeding, excelling. The achievement is pronounced, exaggerated. Remember, we are not modelling mediocrity, we are modelling high achievers and it is likely that their important Change Patterns in this Context are towards the extreme end of the scale. Whilst it is useful to pursue balance in most things, there is a necessary imbalance between mediocrity and success.

The next is Evaluation. Do they need to be told they are doing well or do they know themselves? Have they an internal or external frame of reference? Are they self-reliant or outward focussed? What works for them in this Context?

The Decision Change Pattern can be ascertained quite quickly. Do they succeed because it looks right, sounds right, feels right or makes sense? Of all the Change Patterns this is the most likely to be used across all Contexts, although it can occasionally change, so it is worth asking.

The Motivation Patterns for successful people tends to be in the 'towards' zone. However, some successful people use a strong 'away from' motivation to get them to where they want to go and then may switch to 'towards' to propel them further forwards, onto the next level.

This one is well worth scrutinising because the subject may think they have a strong 'towards' but in fact could be 'away from' and visa versa. A good example of this is freedom. Freedom can be seen as a strong towards Motivation, being able to do as one pleases, having opportunity and so forth. However, it may actually emanate from restrictions in the past, such as wanting to get away from having no freedom. So be careful here to drill down into the detail.

Motive is often more obvious. 'Are you 'power', 'achievement' or 'affiliation' orientated in this Context?' Following that, 'Are you 'towards' or 'away from' in that orientation?' This Change Pattern is by no means the most comprehensive personality type tool available, but it is extremely useful as part of the Change Pattern portfolio. Whilst the individual may be in further modes whilst being in the 'power' domain for example, it is fair to say that this would be easily identifiable and useful to know when installing the strategy our self.

The Activity Change Pattern indicates whether we are 'in the moment' or looking ahead. 'Are you fully associated or looking to the future and dissociated? Do you see yourself in the picture?' There is usually an obvious distinction with this Change Pattern and it is simple to install if we have practiced running Storage Patterns. If we are usually in time, that is associated and living in the moment, we can still switch to through time, that is dissociated and looking to the future, should the occasion demand.

Finally, the Organisation Change Pattern determines whether the individual feels a need to do the activity, as in they have to, or expresses a desire, as in they want to undertake the function.

Once the Change Patterns have been elicited, note them down and look at the ones that seem most pronounced, the ones that are most definitely either/or. These are the ones that will very possibly prove most useful.

Strategy Patterns

The final unconscious process is Fire, Strategy Pattern and is the one that requires the most rigour. It is best to prep the subject beforehand and explain that there will be a little bit of repetition involved in this process.

Firstly, we ask them to go back to that time; float back into their bodies and see what they saw, hear what they heard and feel what they felt. We can place the experience in the present tense so they can relive fully the experience. We begin by asking, 'What is the very first thing that you see that makes you realise that you are totally x? Is it something you see, something you hear, or something you feel?'

Once that has been determined, we ask, 'What is the very next thing that you see, hear or feel?' And so forth. We will need to repeat this over and over again and verify each step to ensure it is correct. There can be some confusion at first as it is unlikely the individual has ever given much thought to this process. However, once they become fully associated in the experience and go over it a few times, it should become clear.

It is helpful to talk them through the process a few times, to make sure it is absolutely correct. 'So you walk into the room and see the crowd of people. You get a feeling of excitement and that prompts you to recall when you last gave a speech that was successful. You then hear the applause of the crowd and a feeling of warmth rises in your stomach. Just before you go on stage, you repeat to yourself, 'I love doing this', 'I love doing this...' over and over and as you do so you get a great feeling of contentment which starts in your stomach and rises to your head...' It is useful here to go through the process with them. 'So tell me exactly what you are feeling. Describe it so I can experience it with you.'

Previously, the subject may have just thought they saw the crowd and got a buzz of expectation and went on and 'did their thing,' so be patient as they extrapolate their exact procedure. Here, we should be mindful of the TOTE model. That is test, operate, test, exit. This stipulates that each time the strategy is activated they go through the same steps, test that everything is working according to their usual criteria, and if that matches up, they exit.

Modelling Excellence 221

There is no harm in going over this a few times to ensure it is the right procedure. Pay very close attention to the eye patterns of the subject as this can indicate what they are really thinking. They may believe they are hearing something when in fact they are looking up to their top right, which is visual construct, creating a picture.

It may be that they are indeed hearing something but they could be creating a picture of what they are hearing so they can describe it to you. No one thing means anything. Everything needs to be scrutinised and evaluated against what else is happening.

It is worth enquiring repeatedly, 'So you are definitely hearing something?' After a couple of enquiries they may re-evaluate and explain. 'Now I think about it, I'm actually seeing what it would look like once I've successfully completed x.'

Or it could be that looking up and to the right is what that person does when they hear something because they may put a picture to a sound. Each to their own. It does pay to be persistent. Whatever happens, their model of the world should always be respected, even if it is wildly different from our own.

Once we have elicited all the values, beliefs and behaviours, Storage, Change and Strategy Patterns we can get down to the real business of installing the successful strategy.

'MindFrame Patterns gives the steps required to model successfully. All we need to do is run through the same process we have to set up our own MindFrame Patterns, except this time analyse somebody else's frame of mind'

Installing a Successful Strategy

If there are similarities in our approach to life and that of our subject then installation may be much easier. We simply run the formative Change Patterns as we do in certain Contexts and apply it to the particular activity. If the person is greatly different to us, it can be a little trickier and require greater flexibility and practice.

It is imperative that we have gone through in some detail each of our own values, beliefs and behaviours and worked out our Storage, Change and Strategy Patterns for each Context. In so doing, we are familiar with what we do, how we do it and how successful we are in each Context. We can also call upon our unconscious resources to help us get to where we want to go.

If we have not gone through this process it will be very tough to adjust our Storage Patterns and apply them appropriately. If the subject runs totally different patterns to our own, and if we have not discovered how we operate, it is highly unlikely we will be able to model them effectively.

For young athletes to model top athletes successfully they need to have mastered the basics of their sport. Otherwise the additions will not be built on a sound basis and will soon crumble. Likewise, we can not model successfully until we have understood how we operate. Developing skills in appropriate areas is the easy part.

This is also an appropriate time to address the ecology check. If we do not have the requisite skills to undertake the activity or if we are restricted by the environment then once again it is highly unlikely that we will succeed. MindFrames give us the building blocks, the basics, to begin modelling successfully. However, we may need to learn certain skills to perform the activity. So modelling anything requires that we have a thorough understanding of what we are doing. If we are modelling a great musician we need to be able to play the instrument to a high standard.

If there is a first rule of installing a model, it is to have fun. Work with it. Try it on for size.

Starting with values, we check what their top three are. Do they bare any similarity to our own? If not, can we adjust a value so it fits? Can we rearrange, re-word, re-define a value so that it fits, or works for that Context? Similarly, can we use a belief of our own that can be re-shaped to serve a similar purpose to their empowering belief?

This is about experimentation, moving things around. It is trying the suit or dress on for size. We have to 'don the full kit' and stroll around in it before deciding whether or not it is for us. So play with it. Have fun.

Copy the behaviour, replicate the body language, the voice tone, the physiology whilst bringing to mind the values and beliefs that reinforce those actions.

Next we run Storage Patterns that have a comparative impact for us. If their Storage Pattern has a similar effect then run that. If not, use similar experiences and replicate the location, size, shape, association. Pick out the most pronounced aspects and use them to enter the same state. Re-enforce this with the Change Patterns. Try them on for size. Imagine stepping into their shoes, running the different Change Patterns. If they are fully associated with a 'difference' orientation, run the Change Pattern in that way.

Finally, use a similar Strategy Pattern. Imagine running through the exact same procedure over and over again. Do it until it becomes engrained. Drill it in.

Modelling Excellence

It may be useful to write each of these components down and to keep referring to them until it becomes engrained. Once the activity has been rehearsed repeatedly, slowed down and broken into each separate action, we can then apply for real.

We would then need to undertake the activity, under the same conditions. Once again, if it is at all possible, do it for fun. As it is rolling out, take a third position, watch how the strategy is working. Make notes. Reflect upon how it is functioning.

The key here is having something to measure against. How do we know if the strategy is working if we can not measure it? Feedback is essential. We need to ascertain exactly what we are doing. This is why the Meta position is so important. We can take an overview, outside perspective of what we are doing.

If there are any colleagues or friends who can offer feedback, refer to them. It is important to brief them well beforehand on how to give effective feedback. That is to ask them what was done well and what could be done better? Also, are there any patterns of behaviour that they noticed?

Once this evaluation is in place we can begin to notice if the strategy is working. We can also play with it some more. What are the idiosyncrasies, the habits that the subject does that do not enhance the performance? How can we do it slightly different? What can we take away, or add? Once the idiosyncrasies have been ironed out, we can go about adapting the strategy for our specific needs and to our personal style.

This takes some time. We must first ensure that we master the strategy in the way the subject described it. Once we have done that, and it has proven to work, then we can adapt it further and make it our own.

It may be in the fullness of time that we drop large parts of the strategy and bring in other elements that work better for us. We may eventually only use small parts, which prove particularly useful. Once we have modelled a number of subjects we can find that we can run various strategies for different Contexts. We can also pick up strategies very quickly, such as through casual conversations. We can go away, try them on and if they work, apply at will. It is a great way to enhance performance easily.

We can also model successful people remotely. We can ascertain what their values, beliefs and behaviours are through reading books about them, or watching them on TV and in films. The subject does not have to be close to us for us to model them well.

Above all modelling is great fun. And it is highly subjective. It is about working with what works for us individually and tailoring it to our liking and expectations.

We began by modelling our self. We found out what we did well and used that to improve performance in every area of our life. We have moved forward to adapt what other successful people use. Now all we need to do is ensure we apply those learnings appropriately to achieve our outcomes. We are in the right frame of mind, now all we need is the right frame.

Chapter 32

Final Frame

'Once we have control, once we set the frame, set our course and have controlled our mind we can achieve everything'

The final frame is the Context as we define it. That still refers to any one of the nine Contexts, but within each Context we can re-define the criteria so we can achieve our desired outcome. It is not dissimilar to the Storage Pattern exercise we ran through in Chapter 20, the Work Context.

We can set the perimeters; change the contours of the Context to manipulate the system to fit around our expectations. The walls can shift. We can use our map of the world to define the Context.

We need to take into account other peoples' models of the world and do an ecology check on any changes we make to ensure every individual involved has a positive outcome, a win-win. Once that is checked, we can go about sculpting the parameters of our existence.

First of all we need to define what the frame is.

The frame is the description of the Context.

Whoever sets the frame controls the system. If we can control the system we are more likely to get the result we want.

How do we set the frame?

Simple, we define the operating procedure, lay down the agenda and articulate the criteria. We put the situation into Context. We can do this as a Chairperson would control a meeting; in a formal, logical manner. Or we can do it informally, out of the conscious awareness of other people.

The formal setting is well established. It need not be the person in the 'chair' who controls the agenda however. We can take control by setting the frame our self, straight away. In this Context, it tends to be whoever gets in first. 'So, as I understand it, we're here to talk about x and y. Might I suggest that we apply Reversal Theory to this dilemma and see how that goes. If that does not work for everybody then I suggest we refer to Zogolog the Nogolog's Theory of Inter-Planetary Transderevational Searching?'

In negotiations, whoever sets the frame gets their way 80 per cent of the time. Setting the frame, defining the criteria, is essential.

How do we do that informally?

'The frame is our map of the world, our model of the world'

Setting the Frame

First of all, we have a clear mental map of the Context and our specific and desired outcome. Through MindFrames we establish that we are in the right frame of mind at the right time to achieve our goal. We apply the MindFrame to the specific Context and using our time line, and whilst in the right state, practice perfectly the activity until it is engrained.

As we enter the Context, the frame changes to suit our needs. Instead of thinking about space, time, solid materials as being absolutes, we need to adjust our perceptions so they become malleable, soft and flexible, just like our approach to communications.

De-focus the eyes and shift to peripheral vision. This will loosen the contours of our map of the world. As we loosen the boundaries, the materials around us move and sway as we move around. This soft focus flexibility is how we should regard the frame. It is not something that is set in stone that we have to follow rigidly. If it is not working for us, we can shift our focus, just as we change into peripheral vision, and allow more useful information to come in.

We can then filter what is useful and what is not and move the contours of the frame. We start off by having a fairly clear view of the frame. 'I will paint above the mantelpiece in a purple colour and either side in lilac.' Instead of slapping on lots of mauve straight away, we can paint a few brush strokes of the mauve and a few lilac either side to see if the colours match up. If it works, fine, we continue. If not, we try some other colours. So it is with the frame.

If we decide to follow a certain criteria, based upon our values and beliefs in a specific Context and that works, then great. If however, we meet resistance, we need to shift the frame so that it works.

This is reframing. There are two main types of reframing. These are context reframes and content reframes. If someone is described as stubborn, a content reframe could be to say that the individual must be strong-minded and independent, hence changing a perceived vice into a perceived virtue. A context reframe changes the environment. The stubborn individual may cause problems in refusing to get out bed in the morning, but that same attitude is useful if it is a child who refuses to get into a car with a stranger.

Although reframing is useful if things do not go exactly according to plan it is more advantageous to set the right frame in the first place, wherever possible. Can we always control the frame?

Yes, if we are clear in our mind what the end result is, if we are clear on our outcome. Although a particular situation may appear at first to be out of our control, if we are mindful, and by now we surely are, of our long-term goal,

Final Frame

then we can regard the temporary inconvenience as a means to an end. So the formal meeting chaired by someone else in which we can not get a word in edge ways, does not mean to say we have lost control.

It can be that we know we must undertake this function in order to get where we want. We need to be patient. We can not click our fingers and make things happen at once. What we can do is use everything there is that might come in useful to help us achieve our outcome. A meeting where we are listening most of the time is an ideal opportunity to practice perceptual positions. We can learn more about the individuals, about how they interact in the group or within the system. We can use this knowledge in future. We can find out bits of information that we can pack away in our rucksack for use when the need arises.

Although it appears that the chairperson is setting the agenda, that does not mean it eclipses our frame of reference, our agenda or criteria. It means that we should be attentive to the needs of our colleagues. Our frame is likely to be wider and longer term, the 'bigger picture'. That is unless our outcome is part of the meeting frame, in which case we will act differently.

> *'We set the boundaries of the frame; it is our map of the world'*

Personal Frame

The point is that our frame is entirely private. No-one else need ever know what our outcome is. In fact it may be beneficial to keep certain outcomes to our self, until we have achieved them, as people may be intimidated or unsettled by our 'ambitious' target.

Our frame therefore is a description to our self of what we need to do in every Context and within every Context, every situation, to achieve our outcome. We need not write this down for every eventuality.

We will be mindful of a clear definition having completed MindFrames. 'This is where I am, these are the things that will help me, and this is the way I would like to behave… This is what my frame looks like, sounds like, feels like.'

We set the boundaries of the frame; it is our map of the world. So although we may be sat at a table in a room with a dozen other people, that does not mean that is all we are. Our frame can reach beyond those four walls and the chitter-chatter of weekly briefing and out into a frame that is expansive and exhilarating. The walls of the frame can be extended, bent and re-shaped at will, as we enter Storage Patterns to invigorate our approach.

The frame is our map of the world, our model of the world.

As we set our outcome, as we define our expectations and progress along the path to meet and exceed our goals, our frames move to meet our demands.

Visual people can perhaps see a clear vision of their frame, how they look and what the landscape is like. They may see themselves in the picture. They may see family and friends and resources they can use. They may see a luxurious retreat which they can enjoy once the have accomplished one of their outcomes. They may see rolling mountains, or the sprawl of the sea. They may see a chocolate pudding or the face of Buddha.

Auditory people may hear their anthem loud and proud, playing every time they pursue a goal. They may hear the orchestra or the heavy rock band. They may whistle to themselves or hear the chirruping of birds or the squawk of seagulls. They may hear the soft ripple of water on a lake shore or the crashing cascades of a waterfall.

Kinaesthetic people may hold a feeling deep within, at the pit of their stomach that glows with warmth every time they move a step nearer to their goal. They may have a light, airy feeling swirling around their head that flows freely as they move along their journey. They may feel a thrill throughout their body, a flow of energy and exhilaration as their frame envelops them and those around.

'As we set our outcome, as we define our expectations and progress along the path to meet and exceed our goals, our frames move to meet our demands'

Trust

If we do not set the frame, somebody else will do it for us. If we do not control our mind, somebody else will volunteer. Once we have control, once we set the frame, set our course and have control of our mind, we can achieve everything.

If nothing else MindFrames is a tool to inspire the self to higher levels. We have a sense of self-perception that is greater and more powerful than any description or label that has been applied previously. We have moved beyond boundaries and labels, beyond limiting beliefs and inappropriate behaviours. We have gained a powerful insight, one that can be used for extraordinary purposes of self-enhancement and gratification, and will empower those around us to reach for new heights.

Above all we are all remarkable, complex and beautiful creatures. And we are so much more than that. Trust the unconscious.

Trust your self.

Acknowledgements

With thanks:

For support, encouragement and kindly sharing your brilliant minds: Bob King and Lisa MacLean. Tina Pickin for a practical and perfect strategy. Mike Fordham for a comradely master class in perceptual positions. Illuminating coaching and mentoring and a wealth of priceless knowledge: Dr Wyatt Woodsmall and Tom MacKay. Masterful coaching in helping me unearth 'something inspirational'; Paul Jacobs. Candy Day for unconscious insight. Great support, warmth and trust: Chris and Alan Moss and every inspirational client at the Circle of Health. Kieran and Carrie for tremendous work on the draft illustrations. Peter, Judith and clan for Lynch family values and the richest mine of resources. Michael Jacobs for endless creativity and camaraderie. Toni Johnson for endless patience, joyous spirit and love. Finally, John Grinder and Richard Bandler, for it all.

If you liked this book please pass it forward.

Visit: www.myspace.com/makeagoodmindgreat

Find out more about coaching and training with Andrew at: www.tlsassociates.co.uk

www.ingramcontent.com/pod-product-compliance
Lightning Source LLC
Chambersburg PA
CBHW070735160426
43192CB00009B/1454